PENGUIN BOOKS

THE TROTSKYS, FREUDS AND WOODY ALLENS

Ivan Kalmar, Ph.D., is a professor of anthropology at the
University of Toronto and a Director of the McLuhan
Program in Culture and Technology. Born and raised in
the former Czechoslovakia, he has lived in the United
States, Italy, France, and the Netherlands. For many years
his principal field of research was the Inuit of Arctic
Canada. Some three years ago, however, he realized that
his curiosity about foreign cultures was due mainly to his
inability to come to terms with his own. He is now considerably less eji than when he started writing this book.

THE TROTSKYS, FREUDS AND WOODY ALLENS
PORTRAIT OF A CULTURE
IVAN KALMAR

Penguin Books

PENGUIN BOOKS
Published by the Penguin Group
Penguin Books Canada Ltd, 10 Alcorn Avenue, Toronto, Ontario, Canada
M4V 3B2
Penguin Books Ltd, 27 Wrights Lane, London W8 5TZ, England
Penguin Books USA Inc., 375 Hudson Street, New York, New York 10014,
U.S.A.
Penguin Books Australia Ltd, Ringwood, Victoria, Australia
Penguin Books (NZ) Ltd, 182-190 Wairau Road, Auckland 10, New
Zealand

Penguin Books Ltd, Registered Offices:
Harmondsworth, Middlesex, England

First published in Viking by Penguin Books Canada Limited, 1993

Published in Penguin Books, 1994

10 9 8 7 6 5 4 3 2 1

Copyright © Ivan Kalmar, 1993

Manufactured in Canada

Canadian Cataloguing in Publication Data
Kalmar, Ivan, 1948-
   The Trotskys, Freuds and Woody Allens: portrait of a culture

ISBN 0-14-017940-2

1. Jews - Identity. 2. Jews - Psychology. 3. Gifted persons.
I. Title.

DS143.K34 1994   305.892'4   C93-093834-6

Dedicated to the memory of my grandparents
Max and Alžbeta Kalmár,
and the hundreds of other victims of hatred
buried in a mass grave at Kremnička, Slovakia,
under three giant crosses
and nothing to tell the world
that most of them were Jews

ACKNOWLEDGMENTS

The idea for *The Trotskys, Freuds, and Woody Allens* was born more than ten years ago when, during a sabbatical stay in Vienna, I was combing through arcane and archaic material on Jewish intellectuals in one of the ornate old reading rooms of the ÖNB, the National Library. Since then I have travelled to Amsterdam, Budapest, Jerusalem, Los Angeles, New York, Paris, and Prague to collect notes, most of which, needless to say, I have ended up not using. Seeing the project grow over the years has been part pleasure, part trouble, but always worth it. Though writing a book is often compared to giving birth to a baby, when I was finally ready to submit my manuscript to a publisher it resembled less a neonate than a full-grown teenager.

Teenagers need a little polishing before they are ready to go out into the big, wide world, and here I was fortunate to have Cynthia Good, Penguin Canada's editor-in-chief, around to help. A number of what I consider the most interesting ideas in the book originally came from her. I would like to acknowledge them here collectively.

Many others have contributed crucial comments and criticism. Among these were Frances Burton, Dominique Cohen, Michael Lambek, Michael Levin, Karen Levine, Richard Lee, Larry Mintz, Peter Reich, Abraham Rotstein, and Waleed Salameh.

The gentle encouragement of my literary agent, Jan Whitford of the Lucinda Vardey Agency, was invaluable. I appreciated the meticulous professionalism, cranberry cake, and tea offered by the copy editor, Mary Adachi.

Writing *The Trotskys, Freuds, and Woody Allens* was an intensely personal experience. In many intangible ways it affected and was affected by those closest to me. I am thankful for the continuing inspiration of family and friends, of all those whom I love and who have loved me. For their wise counsel, I am indebted to Howard Greenberg and to my brother, George Kalmar. And I apologize to those, too numerous to mention, whom I have not included here for lack of space but not for lack of appreciation.

Many readers of the earlier edition have called or written to tell me what this book has meant to them. Some had penetrating insights on this or that aspect of the text. Others said the book helped them discover new turns to take on their personal journey, as Jews and as human beings. Hearing from you has been my main reward.

My son Ethan has never ceased to inspire me with his precocious insight and wit. Much that I have learned from him has in one way or another found its way into this book. Daniel, the baby, was born after the first edition had been published. When they, each in his own time, are ready to read this book, I hope they find in it, as I have, a means of understanding themselves through the culture and history that is their heritage.

For the book's faults I of course accept full and exclusive responsibility.

CONTENTS

The Trotskys, Freuds and Woody Allens

Portrait of a Culture

Ivan Kalmar

Public postures have the configuration of
private derangement.

— Tom Stoppard
The Real Thing

PART I

THE UNCHOSEN PEOPLE

PROLOGUE

AT THE CASTLE

Bratislava, capital of Slovakia. Known in German as Pressburg, Pozsony in Hungarian. I was fourteen.

Even the goats had abandoned the path. As I struggled uphill, I pushed the thorny scrub out of my face, bruising my hands instead. Here and there I came upon a clearing. On one of them stood a forlorn wooden crucifix. Under the termite-eaten figure, a plate referred the date of construction to the late eighteenth century, when the Empress Maria Theresa used to come to the castle above. I heard it whispered by fellow teenagers that Maria Theresa had built a tunnel under the Danube, from the castle all the way to Vienna, fifty kilometres away. She built it just in case some rebels might force her to run. The tunnel was, I was told by furtive classmates, recently discovered by some adventurers, who used it to escape to the capitalist West.

I smiled at the thought of the lucky getaways in the tunnel, running to freedom while, above, unknowing guards trained their binoculars over the empty landscape of the border area. Looking down, I could see it now: trenches, barbed wire, broken-down, unused roads on this side, the mysterious Germanic forest on the other. But my goal was not Austria. I was attempting an escape to the past. Not my personal past — I was still a young boy — but that of my people, whose very existence was a subject that could be dangerous to mention, yet who, I was slowly discovering, had once lived and prospered in large numbers here.

Finally the strangely Mediterranean scrub ended, and I found myself on the castle mount. The castle had been in ruins since who knows what war. It was built on a square plan, with a tower in each corner. Though the roof was gone, part of the towers still protruded to the sky. The townsfolk had long likened the castle to a table turned upside down. From here the panorama was magnificent. I stood beside a few romantic couples who had come the easy way, by the streets of the old Jewish ghetto on the other side. Below, near the Cathedral where once Hungary's kings were crowned, was a building with a short spire topped by a golden dome: formerly the Great Synagogue. At the sight of the dome, I could feel my major arteries rush like a locomotive. It looked particularly beautiful from up here, glistening in the afternoon sun. To the lovers next to me, though, there was nothing there but an odd building that was now a TV studio.

I was ready. I turned towards the path I had discovered on an earlier visit at the castle, and soon came up to the fence of the old Jewish cemetery. The tombstones, most of them stooping with age and overgrown with weeds and grass, bore the mysterious characters of Hebrew writing.

Some also had German, the language of my grandparents, or Hungarian, the language of my mother, or Slovak, my father's tongue — for this had been a provincial capital in Czechoslovakia, the ill-fated country Hitler, in a contemptuous pun, used to call Mosaic-land.

In the city below, where bullet holes remained part of the gloomy exteriors decades after the genocidal war, I was — my documents proved it — "without confession" (the term used by those who claimed that they did not belong to any religious community). I was trained out of fear of discrimination never to admit to friend or foe that I was a Jew. But up here, history was looking up out of its ruins with a semblance of hope. Here truth was still possible.

I passed the open iron gate and, once behind the tall walls, discovered a small plain building stuccoed in fading yellow. On a bench in front of it sat two women with kerchiefs on their heads, and a fat man wearing a hat, yet clad incongruously in a loose white shirt and black shorts. They were speaking Yiddish, a language I did not understand. I looked at them confused, like a rabbit suddenly discovered in the grass. Finally, the man got up and walked towards me. "What do you want?"

I was unable to utter a word.

"What do you want here?" the man repeated bitterly. "We don't go to Christian cemeteries!" And then, recognizing perhaps some telling feature in my face, he added in a kinder voice, "At any rate, boy, you don't have a skull cap on."

I turned and walked away, descending from the hill on the easy side.

Only now have I finally found the language to say what needed to be said at the cemetery gates more than twenty years ago: to the fat man, that you need not wear a skull cap to be a Jew; to the city, that no one is without confession.

The reason I had been mute before is ingrained in the very nature of the culture I shared, though perhaps in an extreme form, with other people living, not always comfortably, squeezed between the Jewish heritage and the secular Gentile world. I call them the "EJI," an acronym for "Embarrassed Jewish Individual." Pronounce it "edgy," for edginess and embarrassment about being Jewish are among the chief symptoms of the cultural condition I am speaking of.

The culture of the eji has been an important element in the mosaic of modern civilization. I feel particularly called upon to speak about it, having grown up in the ruins of what was once one of its most brilliant homes: Freud, Mahler, and Kafka had been born and had worked nearby.

But, strangely, there is a peculiar handicap to being an eji. You are taught that you ought not to speak much about the Jews, or at least, not to speak of them too loudly. Should you be concerned with what Rosa Luxemburg disparagingly called "special Jewish sorrows," you might lose the eji's most cherished right, to speak for humanity in general. You must conduct yourself as if you had no background at all, as if you were "without confession" indeed. For nothing is as singular about the eji as the denial of being singular at all.

Writing about the eji is my personal farewell to being an eji. And I am saying goodbye when others are also doing so, in droves. The culture of the eji has had its day. Not that it is dead, but its brilliance, its originality is gone, as is that of the age in which it flowered, the age of what we now call "modernity." Freudiana, Wittgensteiniana, Kafkiana, are to be had abundantly in better bookstores everywhere. What once inspired passionate devotion, now brings forth nostalgia. We are becoming "post-modern." Is the modern period over? To some, it ended soon after World War II, or even before. To others, we are still living in it. But it is clear that the greatest days of the "modern" are behind us. So it is with the eji. There are still great eji alive today, and most Jews carry in them at least the vestiges of the eji character. But the eji is a has-been, even if not yet a "was."

What is the eji world, what has it been about? As an ancient Middle Eastern tribe, Jews had helped to shape the spiritual heritage of the West. And it is, I think, fair to say that in modern times the Jews have done it again. However, they have not done it this time through the force of Judaism. The root of our modern creativity was not the focused ecstasy of religious vision. This time we were coming from a position of fear, confusion, decadence — but also great hope — characteristic more of the people at the foot of Mt. Sinai than the prophet on top. The root of the modern Jewish efflorescence is, I argue, a kind of neurosis, an edginess, an embarrassment, about being Jewish in a largely hostile, and often violently hostile, social environment — and the need to cope with it.

The neurosis has sometimes manifested itself in exaggerated pride, and other times in masochistic self-hatred. If we Jews are to be cured of our neurosis — and I think, we have gone a long way already, *baruch hashem*[1] — then we must avoid both extremes. I strongly suspect that we are neither better nor worse than other people. Indeed,

---

[1] There is a glossary of Hebrew and other "Jewish" terms at the end of the book, as well as notes on other parts of the text.

worrying about how good we are is part of the neurosis itself. Let's simply accept ourselves. In looking at our past and how it affects us today, let's try to be objective.

Of course, once we have had a dispassionate look at our past — I am talking about the past of the eji — then, for our own sake, we must ask ourselves what is worth keeping and developing, and what is best left behind.

The future of the Jews in the midst of our secular society is important, to both Jews and others. Even if you are not Jewish, you will (especially, I hope, after reading this book) appreciate how much your ideas have been influenced by Jews, and particularly by the eji. And you will wonder whether in the future, you can expect the Jewish intellectual influence on you to continue. Nothing could, of course, be less certain. It is always a good thing to be cured of a neurosis. But some neuroses are creative, and the neurosis of the eji fits the description better than most.

This book is not really a history, a biography, or an ethnography. It is a cultural portrait. A portrait shows a face fully and truthfully, even though it concentrates on but one of its aspects. What we are focusing on here is the way the eji express the one idea that has always obsessed them: the idea that the Jews are, essentially, not different from everyone else.

The eji could be shown in other poses, but this one, I believe, is the most telling.

1

IDENTITY:
THE DIFFERENCE NOT BEING
DIFFERENT MAKES

The Jews are like everyone else, only more so.
— Attributed to Heinrich Heine

The steam engine whistled, pulled into the station, and came to a stop. In a rush to disembark, a young ruffian opened the window in one of the cars and jumped out onto the platform. He turned around to help his friends, pulling them out of the window by their arms and legs, as though he were freeing them from a trap. Inside, Freud saw his opportunity. He got up, walked over to the open window, sat down, and imbibed the nippy, fresh air. Eyed in enforced calm by a hostile pack of passengers, he savoured the sweetness of victory.

The trouble started when Freud had tried to open another window. The passengers of the cheap, third-class train compartment cursed him; they were cold. Freud gave in, but thought it only fair that he should at least be allowed to open the air vent. The passengers protested. "He's a miserable Jew!" one of them called out. Freud defiantly dared the loudest of the anti-Semites to a fight. The man backed off, and Freud ruled the icy silence that ensued. He would let no one close the window again.

One of his detractors stuck in Freud's mind more than the others. "We Christians have a sense of the common good," the bad-mouth had taunted Freud. "You must gain control over your precious ego!" Little did the nameless jester know what he may have contributed to intellectual history. It was December 16, 1883. In a few years Freud, the father of psychoanalysis, would make society's terrible demands for "gaining control over your ego" the topic of a new century.

True, if brawls with anti-Semites ever had any bearing on Freud's scientific thinking, he was not one to let on. At the time, a number of Jews had their children baptized, lest they suffer from the stigma of their origins. Freud wished the same protection for his brainchild, his psychology. When he named Carl Jung, a Swiss Gentile whom he did not particularly like, to head the Psychoanalytic Movement, he was widely thought to have found himself a *Paradegoy*. (This is what people called a non-Jewish figurehead such as was often employed by Viennese business firms.) His choice would, Freud hoped, mask the fact that almost everybody else in his entourage was a Jew.

Freud's associate Theodor Reik once allowed himself to make a remark to a Swiss pastor that Freud interpreted as sounding too Jewish. Freud admonished Reik, warning that he would not be understood by "those goyim."

Only to a Jewish audience was Freud occasionally prepared to confess quietly how much his Jewishness meant to him. He was, he wrote,

completely estranged from the religion of his fathers — as well as from every other religion — and

[one] who cannot take a share in nationalist ideals, but who has yet never repudiated his people, who feels that he is in his essential nature a Jew and who has no desire to alter that nature. If the question were put to him: "Since you have abandoned all these common characteristics of your people, what is there left about you that is Jewish?" he would reply: "[What is left is] a very great deal; indeed, probably, my very essence."

Such comments were not for "those goyim." The passage appears only in the Hebrew edition of Freud's *Totem and Taboo*, his work on primitive religion. It is missing from the original German edition.

To disguise confessions about one's Jewishness under the cover of a work on other cultures is neither as strange nor as rare as it might seem at first. To me, it recalls my own experience as a graduate student in anthropology, when I lived among the Inuit, studying their language and culture for my doctoral dissertation. Between seal-hunting trips and sessions recording old stories and songs, I amused myself by thinking about the irrelevance of Jewish custom in the Far North. Judaism ordains that the Sabbath candles be lit on Friday at sunset. What time do you light them when the sun does not set at all? And again, animals with cleft hoofs are kosher, and the caribou is one of those. But what rituals do you have to follow in slaughtering and preparing one, to make sure you remain within the dietary laws? When the Temple of Jerusalem was destroyed, the Jewish religious authorities devised ways to carry on with Jewish practice, and these were meant to be applicable wherever Jews would wander to. They were indeed applied from the heartland of Ethiopia to the shores of China. But here in the empty tundra was one land that seems to have escaped the wide scope of the ancient rabbis' foresight.

And still... even here, I knew that my Jewishness was with me, as much as Freud's Jewish essence was with him when he was writing his anthropological book. True, I was genuinely excited about the unique culture of the Inuit, an inventive people who made their home in the coldest climate on Earth. But my interest in human cultural diversity went well beyond a curiosity about the Inuit. I was interested in cultural differences in general. Jewish anthropologists often own up to the fact that it is their Jewish background that has brought them into the discipline. Feeling different as Jews, they develop a natural inquisitiveness about all differences between various peoples. However, they seldom turn their curiosity directly to its source, the difference between Jew and Gentile. And neither did I. It seemed a lot more respectable (and a lot more likely to help me get a university job) to do my field work riding a snowmobile-driven sled than putting on a *tallis* in a synagogue. Yet in a sense, every time I took in the blinding, snow-covered vistas of the boundless North, I was trying to fathom not only the soul of the Arctic people but also my own.

No more such subterfuges now. Let us look directly at the object of our interest: the Jews, and more specifically, the "non-Jewish Jews," the Trotskys, Freuds, and Woody Allens, and the millions of nameless individuals that have made up one of the most fascinating and controversial cultural groups of modern times.

Who is an Eji?

One way we might approach introducing the type of people we are speaking of is by reference to a mental state. And the simplest way to characterize their mental state is that they are embarrassed about being Jewish. It is for this reason I call them eji (recall that this stands for Embarrassed Jewish Individuals). The mental state of "ejiness" normally meshes well with a set of other characteristics. Religiously, the eji may or may not respect tradition, but never feels bound by it unconditionally. Socially, the eji does not "live in a matzah ball," but wants to, and does, build contacts with the non-Jewish world. In fact, many and perhaps even most of the eji have more social links with non-Jews than Jews, though more so at work than at home. And finally, intellectually, the eji favour some "attitudes" over others — essentially, those that in some way (a very subtle way sometimes!) support the message that the Jews are not significantly different from others.

These three characterizations of the eji: the mental embarrassment, the social closeness with Gentiles, and the intellectual preference for views that negate the Jewish "difference," neatly set the eji apart from most of the traditionalist, Orthodox Jews. (They also set the eji apart from the more recent, "post-eji" trends among both religious and secular Jews, but those we will leave to the end of book.) To be sure, the traditionalists can be very edgy about Jewish issues as well. They may, for example, be hypersensitive to any suggestion of anti-Semitism in their environment, or to the irreligion of the "assimilated" Jews. But what they are edgy about is not their own Jewishness. It is how other people relate to Judaism and the Jews. What makes a Jew an eji, on the other hand, is personal embarrassment. Eji may or may not mind being Jews in private. But they have problems with being labelled as Jews in public. The traditionalists, on the other hand, make constant public displays of their Jewishness (of which the men's yarmulkes are normally the most obvious).

The question that bothers the eji is: "Are they thinking of me as a Jew?" In dealing with individual Gentiles, an eji often hopes to avoid any reference not only to his or her Jewishness, but by way of prevention, to anything Jewish at all. A Jew who is afflicted with the more severe symptoms of ejiness trembles with apprehension that his or her Gentile conversation partner might utter the terrible J-word. A new professor at a small but prestigious Canadian university decided to join the Faculty Club, and was being interviewed by the club's secretary, a stately woman of British background. Everything went well, the professor relates, until the officer asked, "And what about the Jews?" "The Jews?!" exclaimed the academic, blushing, embarrassed, ready for battle. "Yes," the secretary continued, "the dues are three hundred and fifty dollars a year."

Woody Allen, playing "Alvy" in *Annie Hall*, showed a similar concern with the way informal English changes the sound sequence "d plus y" to a "j." An acquaintance keeps asking him, " 'Jew eat?' ['d'you eat?']." "Not 'did you eat?' " explains Alvy, seething with anger at what he perceives as a deliberate insult, "but 'Jew eat?' "

Just how does it feel to be "eji" about being labelled a Jew? If you have any doubts, try the following experiment — mentally if you wish, though it would work even better should you be able to do it in "real life."

It is a day like any other. You are on your way to work: walking, driving, taking public transportation, the way you normally do. You arrive and are greeted by fellow workers. Nothing embarrassing so far? But now add a little detail. You are not dressed as usual. You are wearing the costume of the ultra-Orthodox. If you're a woman, you masquerade under an oversized, curly brown wig covering what would be your shaved head. For good measure, you might add a scarf over the wig. And you are wearing an awkward, flower-print dress. To make sure you're not mistaken for an East European peasant, display a Star of David on your neck-lace, on your handbag, or anywhere else that is visible. If you're a man, put on a wide-brimmed, black hat, and wear a dark suit, with the strands of your *tsitisis* dangling at your waist. If you want to be thorough about it, you might paste on some *payis*, a lock of hair curling off your temples on each side.

You arrive at your workplace. You greet your colleagues, and take your place. How do you feel?

If you can honestly say that the exercise would cause you no more discomfort than, say, showing up in a joke costume as Cinderella or Papa Smurf, then you are indeed not an Embarrassed Jewish Individual. You might be a Gentile with little understanding of the Jewish experience. (I hope you will gain more of a feel for the eji's embarrass-ment as you read on.) Alternatively, you might be an authentic, self-assured, self-asserting Jew, a model for the eji rest of us. If so, I would guess that you, though secure in your own Jewishness, have no trouble imagining the trepidation felt by the less poised, the less brave. Perhaps you once felt it yourself.

Many of us are now living in a twilight zone, between the total neurosis of the original eji, and the comfortable self-assurance we need and seek. Take the Star of David necklaces that some Jews wear quite visibly around their neck. Some of the wearers are totally "liberated" Jews. But others are still eji, people dipping their toes but who have not yet taken the plunge. They might be putting on the Star, not as much as an act of Jewish pride as the means to declare unambiguously that they are Jewish, to prevent people from making anti-Semitic remarks. In this way, the semi-brave eji can avoid the need to either ignore an anti-Jewish comment, which is humiliating, or to fight back, which is at best unpleasant and at worst dangerous. Such preventative wearers of the *maagen David* are the people most likely to wear what I call the Distorted Star. The real article is composed of two equilateral triangles superimposed on each other. The Distorted Star fools around with these proportions. The star becomes elongated or fattened, ostensibly to cater to the sensibilities of "contemporary" art. The message of such contortionist Jewish stars is "I am Jewish, but I am also 'contemporary.' " In other words, "I am Jewish, but there is a connection between me and you. I am a citizen of today's society, of which you and I are equally part."

The sentiment is, of course, commendable. For many people, wearing a Distorted Star may in fact be a confident assertion of two positive values: being Jewish and being "universal." In Israel, the Distorted Star (usually blue, after the regularly proportioned blue star on the Israeli flag) is as much the emblem of the secular, "modern" segment of the population as the two golden equilateral triangles are of the Jewish religion. It marks official celebratory posters, stamps, and government letterheads. In fact, having made the star on the flag blue rather than the traditional gold is itself in the spirit of "distortion." True, the blue and white of the flag is meant to recall the blue and white of the *tallis*, the prayer shawl whose appearance is partly governed by Biblical precept. But why make the *star* blue? One rejected proposal for the flag of the new state was blue and white like the current flag, but the star between the two blue stripes was gold, not blue. But the founders of Israel preferred to create a visual contrast: blue for Israel, gold for the Jews, symbolizing a rift, at first overtly encouraged by the Zionists, between the Jewish State and the Jewish Diaspora with its antiquated religious tradition. The early Zionists were overwhelmingly secularist in outlook, dreaming of making Jews like other people by giving them a "normal," modern, secular state with farmers, soldiers, and taxes; in other words, a state just like other states. From that point of view, the Blue Star of Israel could perhaps be seen as a positive affirmation of secular Jewish universalism. On the other hand, one might think of it as a sign that even the founders of the Jewish State — people who generally suffered from no shortage of chutzpah — were a bit shy about appearing to be too Jewish.

Speaking for myself, I did once sport a Distorted (14-karat gold) Star around my neck, and I know that when I wore it I meant to assert my Jewishness, but not too aggressively. My star was very narrow, very long, and not very big.

I console myself with the thought that I am not in bad company. I certainly think the three people in our title would be no more equal to the task of comfortably displaying their Jewishness than I am myself. Trotsky denied at every turn that his Jewish origin had anything to do with his life, as vehemently as Woody Allen disclaims any connection between his films and his personal conduct. As we shall see in Chapter 9, Trotsky declined to head the first

Soviet government, fearing that people would identify the revolution with the Jews (which they did anyway).

Freud admitted being existentially concerned with his Jewishness. In the privacy of his pubescent fantasies, his super-hero had been Hannibal, the Semitic general who so bravely fought against Aryan Rome. However, as we have seen, in public and as an adult, he was considerably less belligerent about his "Semitic race," hardly ever mentioning it to "those goyim." Woody Allen talks about his Jewishness incessantly. More precisely, he talks incessantly about the problems his Jewishness causes him. But when in *Annie Hall* he shows up in the no-ifs-and-buts dark clothes and side-locks of the super-religious, then everyone knows it's only a joke.

Apparently, Bob Dylan did dare to do it once. It may have been one of those fake photos forged by the cheap gossip press, but it seemed real enough to me. The photo showed Dylan at the Western Wall in Jerusalem, praying in Orthodox attire. In the Diaspora, many Jews still call this sacred site the "Wailing Wall," for here generations used to lament the destruction of the Holy Temple. The Wall consists of a few hundred giant slabs of stone generously overgrown with grass, a sort of paved ancient piazza turned upright. The more assertive Israelis renamed it "Western," to mark its position with respect to the former sanctuary. I'd like to think Dylan's attitude was as positive as that of the Israelis; that he came here to affirm his origins without embarrassment, and to wail no more. Dylan was a Jew, whose real name was Zimmerman. He was the sentimental symbol of those tender years when a young generation of affluent urbanites saw themselves as a cross between the jungle revolutionaries of Vietnam and the country folk of

America (though the Vietcong and the Appalachians were almost equally distant, culturally, from Zimmerman and his admirers, many of them Jewish). We are all grateful to Dylan for his songs and words. But we know that Zimmerman was not Dylan. It must have been a relief for him to stop performing. He must have looked at old family pictures or something, gone to Jerusalem, put on the *frommie* clothes, and swayed back and forth in the old-fashioned rhythm of Jewish prayer. Then, I like to imagine, he felt true to his real self at last. I'd like to think that he followed the experience by putting the funny outfit aside, no longer embarrassed, no longer eji, affirming his true self as a Jew, not ultra-Orthodox, not "assimilated," just himself. All right, perhaps that is not what happened. (It is rumoured in fact that Dylan became a "Jesus freak.") But I still would like to think of him as accepting himself at last. An example to all of us who are still eji about being Jews.

The Eji and the Modern Age

There are many subtypes of the eji. The title of this book, *The Trotskys, Freuds, and Woody Allens*, is meant to refer to one possible way of subdividing them. It is not my intention to write a biography of three people, but rather to speak of different types of eji — the social and political activist *à la* Trotsky; the intellectual *à la* Freud; and the creative artist, writer, or performer, *à la* Woody Allen. (In the last group, the comedian is particularly important as the professional whose job is to purvey images of the Jews for the Gentiles.)

Another way to subdivide the eji would be in terms of their public identification with their Jewish origin. On the whole, the Trotskys and the Freuds — the politically engaged and the intellectuals — like to talk as little as possible about the issue. To hear some of them say it, they, although born Jewish, have no particular ethnic or religious attachments whatsoever. They do nothing in word or deed that is immediately and obviously recognized as Jewish. Indeed, they are "like everyone else, only more so"! Yet too often the actions of this type of eji give the lie to their words. They tend to choose their colleagues, friends, and even spouses from among a very distinct group: other Jews who also do not feel very Jewish at all. One major eji scholar, the sociologist Karl Mannheim, described "assimilated" Jews as an example of what he called "free-floating existences." In fact, these free-floaters have seldom been able to drift too far off the shores of their own culture: a culture not Gentile, not Jewish, but "non-Jewish Jewish," that is to say, eji. We might refer to this group as the quietly eji.

Then there are those among the eji who, far from being reticent about their Jewishness, never lose a chance to advertise it. These are the loudly eji. The "Woody Allens" are more likely to be loudly eji than the "Trotskys" or the "Freuds." Many if not most Jewish comics make a living off their ejiness. So do some excellent and important "serious" writers such as Philip Roth and Mordecai Richler.

The different types of eji represent different adaptations to the challenge of being a Jew in a secular society. They differ in style and emphasis, but all fit our characterization of the eji: embarrassed about their Jewishness, concerned about living among non-Jews, and trying to deal with the problem by strategies meant to demonstrate that the Jews are NOT unique. This un-chosen people, the eji, the "non-Jewish Jews," appeared, if one ignores the few early harbingers, only in the nineteenth century. The ghetto walls that shut off the Jews from the rest of the world had also been protecting them from the tensions of cultural ambiguity. Eji history begins with the gradual political and social emancipation of the Jews, which began in the late eighteenth century.

At first nothing but shy imitators of the Gentiles, they, the Japan of the intellectual and cultural world, were soon to become the source of some very brave and influential ideas. The heyday of the eji and the "age of modernity" that it was part of lasted from the closing decades of the nineteenth century into the second half of the twentieth. The cast of characters that make up its story include countless eji personalities whose ideas, books, films, musicals, and business adventures became part of the backbone of modern civilization. Marx, Kafka, Trotsky, Luxemburg, Einstein, Schoenberg — the list goes on and on: these were all eji. The eji seemed to concentrate in themselves the creativity, the passions, the aspirations, and the tragedy of the period. "Modernity" cannot be fully understood without being, to play around a bit with Freudian terminology, "Judeo-analyzed."

Not Speaking of the Eji

Some modern artists understood well how typical the destiny of the eji was for the modern experience. James Joyce chose an eji character, Bloom, as the modern Everyman in his monumental novel, *Ulysses*. Matisse liked to include in his still lifes a book, *Histoires juives,* with the title shown conspicuously. (Had Joyce chosen an Orthodox Jew, incidentally, or Matisse the Hebrew Bible or Talmud, the point they were making about modernity would be lost:

an Orthodox Bloom would be a funny joke.) Andy Warhol reminisced of the greats of modernity in his "Ten Portraits of Jews of the Twentieth Century." (Some of these appear on the cover of this book.) None of them were traditional Jews.

Artists often see more sharply than historians and social scientists. Non-fiction writers have seldom grasped Joyce's point. Precious little has been written about the distinctive lifestyles, the characteristic thought patterns, and the peculiar history of the eji. It's not that the experts are blind. It's just that there is, on this subject, a widely observed taboo, a conspiracy of silence almost. No one wants to speak seriously about the eji: not the eji themselves, not the religious Jews, nor yet the Gentiles.

To the strictest among the traditionalists, an eji is as good (or as bad, one should say) as a goy. But even many practising Jews who hold the most liberal religious views consider a Jew who scoffs at Judaism to be at best incompletely Jewish. The word they use is "marginal." In their mind, the eji live in a twilight zone on the periphery of Jewish destiny, probably condemned to be swallowed up, sooner or later, by the Gentile world.

Only when it comes to the rich and, especially, the famous are the religious quite willing to accept the non-observant as very much Jewish indeed. The Rothschilds may gather every December at St Moritz to celebrate Yuletide with a Christmas tree; Marx may have called religion the opium of the masses; Freud may have accused the Jews of killing Moses — still, someone is sure to find in their behaviour unconscious traces of Biblical wisdom and Prophetic reverie. Above all, religious Jews are as proud as any other Jew of Einstein and all the other Nobel Prize laureates.

But this is all a mistake. Non-Jewish Jews have not been foreign to Jewish history, not even the unrich and the unfamous. An unbiased reading of that history proves that in modern times it is Judaism that has been on the margins. And it is the eji that has been centre stage. The "unaffiliated," the "assimilated," the "secular" have been, if not the majority, certainly the creative element, the motor of Jewish cultural life.

The eji, furthermore, is not a new arrival. North American Jews, whose image of European Jewry is often influenced more by Hollywood and Chagall than by genuine recollections of the "old country," are often surprised to find how un-Orthodox the Jews of the Old World were as long as a hundred or a hundred and fifty years ago.

Beyond a doubt, "assimilation" was more rampant in Western and Central Europe than farther to the East, where the ancestors of most North American Jews come from. Nevertheless it is instructive to know that, according to the *Encyclopaedia Judaica*, less than 10 per cent of the Jews of Frankfurt were traditional as far back as 1842. In France in 1905, only five per cent could be considered as observant. Rates of marriage to Gentiles among French Jews were probably almost as high as now, particularly among professionals and intellectuals.

As for Freud's Vienna, Jewish life there showed some striking similarities to what now goes on in North America. A good example is where in the city Jews chose to live. In 1910 in the Leopoldstadt area, the home of almost all the Orthodox, Jews made up 34 per cent of the population, although in Vienna as a whole they amounted to no more than 8.6 per cent. The First District was the closest thing on earth to the glittery fantasy of Johann Strauss's operettas; except that on stage there were no Jews, while they made up 20 per cent of the real First District, not counting the perennial visitors who were always milling about. (There was always a high number of Jews among the theatre-goers and the sweet-shop patrons.) In neighbouring Alsergrund, the home of Freud and many other professionals and intellectuals, the Jewish contingent was 21 per cent. In short, the more traditional lived in a "Little Israel," the most Jewish area of the city; but disproportionate numbers of Jews lived also in the fashionable downtown districts and in the "intellectual" neighbourhoods. Very few lived elsewhere. Is this any different from what one sees in North American cities today? It is not hard to find a Leopoldstadt in Brooklyn, or a First District and an Alsergrund in Manhattan.

While it is true that east of Frankfurt and Vienna, in the Russian dominions which then included much of Poland, assimilation had made less headway, here, too, the numbers of the eji were large and growing. Among them were the Guenzburg and Polyakov families, both of them members of the nobility (the Guenzburgs were Barons), wealthy entrepreneurs who were the unofficial representatives of Jewish interests at the Tsar's court. It was not Hasidim but such secularized Jews who, along with their foreign partners, financed the Russian railway system. Nor was it Hasidim who, with German and German-Jewish help, developed the great oil fields of Baku. And on the other hand, it was not Hasidim who made up the majority of the turn-of-the-century East European Jewish proletariat, as it was not Hasidim who contributed the enormously important Jewish contingent in the leadership of both the February and the November 1917 revolutions.

Nevertheless, in North America, the pious and penni-
less East European ancestor is a cherished myth. And certainly, like most myths, this one, too, has some basis in fact.
(There's a lot of truth in a half-truth, said Marshall
McLuhan.) Irving Howe's beautiful *The Way We Were* is a
photo-history of thousands of wide-eyed immigrants in the
traditional garb of the East European *shtetl*. The women's
wigs and scarves, the men's side-locks, their wide-brimmed
hats and long garb are all very real. They all express elo-
quently the image North American Jews have of their forebears.

But how typical were these tradition-minded immigrants of the immigration as a whole? It is natural that only
people in "ethnic" clothing should be picked out as Jews in
old photographs. People in Western clothing would be
more difficult to identify as Jews, and could hardly create
as much interest. Most North American Jews, asked to
rummage through the family treasure box of old pho-
tographs, are likely to discover somewhat to their surprise
a grandfather with a gold chain and starched collar, and a
grandmother with an elaborate flowered hat — people, in
other words, wearing the uniform of the early twentieth-
century middle class, rather than that of the traditional
Jewish faithful. (The two styles of dress, it is true, were
much more similar then.)

In his thoroughly enjoyable bestseller, *Chutzpah*, the
well-known attorney Alan Dershowitz describes a family
reunion in honour of his great-grandfather, Reb Zecharia.
Many of Zecharia's descendants who came to the party
were ultra-Orthodox. They made fiery speeches urging all
Jews to follow Orthodoxy, to engage in what one young
family member called "reJewvenation." To support their

argument, the extremely Orthodox referred liberally to Reb Zecharia, painting him in the colours of a traditional wise man, a *tsaddik*. Yet Dershowitz, the lawyer used to taking the evidence seriously, knows that, much as his great-grandfather followed and respected his religion, he was no ultra-Orthodox. "I began to realize," writes Dershowitz, that "we — the more secular branch of the family — were his true spiritual heirs."

No one can dispute that the Russian immigrants professed a somewhat less half-hearted Judaism than their Central and West European cousins; but both were ready to modernize. In America, the "German" Jews were a little more likely to join a Reform congregation; the "Russians" slightly preferred the Conservatives; both deserted Orthodoxy en masse. There is no doubt that today in North America, as in most of the world, Jewry is largely a collection of (in terms of the religious tradition) "marginal" Jews. This is so even though recently more and more secular Jews have discovered Judaism, a development I will be addressing later. Despite much "reJewvenation," not all of which by any means takes the form of a "return" to Orthodox traditions, statistics continue to show that in North America (and elsewhere) identification with Judaism continues to be weak.

Yet it would be a big mistake to assume automatically that a weakening of religious feeling and practice also means a withering away of Jewish identity. A Jew is not less of a Jew for not putting on *tefillin*, any more than an Italian is less of an Italian for not doing her rosary. The "marginal," not particularly observant Jew is the normal Jew. This is the way things are in much of North America and the world today, and, despite the bias of many Jewish historians towards the traditional and the picturesque, the way they have been for quite some time.

One reason even the eji themselves resist talking about these rather obvious facts is that speaking about Jewish matters is, they feel, like waving a red flag at a bull. It is best not to wake up the anti-Semites. In Freud's time this was called *Totschweigentaktik*, or "Dead Silence Tactics." There is, however, a more important reason, to which I alluded when referring to Rosa Luxemburg's disdain for "special Jewish sorrows." The eji wish to speak for everyone, not just for the Jews. If they appear too Jewish, they fear their concerns might be taken as reflecting the narrow interests of a despised people rather than the needs of all human beings: One has to speak carefully to "those goyim."

Those among the eji who dismiss the importance of their Jewish background, to be sure, often find a grateful audience among the Gentiles. It is not necessarily exciting for non-Jewish psychiatrists, physicists, or arbitrageurs to think of their chosen field as "Jewish" because of the large number of eji that participate in it.

A fairly well known anthropologist found it troubling that one of his most famous colleagues, whom he admired unreservedly, should be a Jew. "It's true, isn't it, that Lévi-Strauss is Jewish?" he queried, with some anguish in his face. "But," he added hopefully, "I hear he gave it up." (In fact, if the Jewish religion is what was meant, Lévi-Strauss, one of France's most celebrated intellectuals, had nothing to "give up." Though he was the grandson of the chief rabbi of Versailles, he had always kept aloof from Judaism.) The anthropologist, who had been overheard to make the occasional anti-Semitic remark, was relieved to be able to relegate his idol's Jewishness to an accident of birth. He could now admire Lévi-Strauss without fear of being in the throes of "Jewish" ideas.

But our anthropologist would hardly have thought differently had he been a friend of the Jews. If Lévi-Strauss does not want to be thought of as a Jew, he would have reasoned with fellow-feeling, why remind him of being one?

It is tragic that this tripartite conspiracy of silence, in which the religious Jews, the eji, and most Gentiles have so long collaborated, has left the field open to the worst demagogues. More than anyone, it was the Nazis who liked to speak of Jewish business, Jewish sociology, Jewish physics, Jewish art, Jewish music. Rubbing their Jewish origins in the face of the eji was, to the Nazis, a particularly perverse pleasure. "In their hatred of me," the composer Arnold Schoenberg wrote to Albert Einstein, "the Jews and the Swastika bearers are of the same mind." He detested the Jews and felt that they returned the emotion, and found it infuriating that the Nazis still called him a Jew. It was partly in order to advertise that the eji are, simply, Jews, that the Nazis forced everyone of Jewish background to wear the yellow Star of David. To an individual's surname they loved to add a supposed "original" last name in parentheses, a procedure that was equally popular in Stalin's Russia: "Trotsky (Bronstein)," "Kamenev (Rosenfeld)."

A more recent echo of this practice was provided by graffiti at the University of Bucharest, which referred to the handsome prime minister of Rumania's first post-communist government, Petre Roman, by his "real name," Neulander. Roman's father, Valter Roman, was born Ernst Neulander. He joined the international brigades in the Spanish revolution, and married a Spanish republican who was not Jewish. Petre Roman was only half-Jewish, and far

from having been brought up in Judaism, he received a res-
olutely internationalist, secular education, but that was no
reason for Rumanian anti-Semites not to claim that he
"had the Jews behind him." An internationalist, atheist eji
was to them not less, but more of a Jew than an Orthodox
rabbi.

Even Paranoids Have Real Enemies

All this brings into play a serious question of conscience:
When we call people Jews against their wishes; when we
speak of the eji as the typical modern Jew; worse, when we
speak of the eji as possessing a distinctive "Jewish mind,"
are we not doing as Hitler did? *Is this going to be an anti-
Semitic book?*

The proverbial "man in the street," of course, is little
worried about any moral dilemma that may be present
here. Despite the disclaimers offered by some "assimilated"
Jews, most people have always regarded even "baptized
Jews" as Gentiles. Besides Karl Marx, people like Heinrich
Heine or the composer Felix Mendelssohn had been converted to Christianity, but everyone continued to regard
them as "Jewish." Offenbach, too, had been baptized, but
was caricatured as a typical Jewish composer by Richard
Wagner. In late nineteenth-century Germany, both Jews
and Gentiles spoke of *getaufte Juden* (baptized Jews) and
christliche Semiten (Christian Semites).

Some of the converts themselves openly declared their
contempt for a conversion that they considered to have
been forced on them. Heine made no secret of his continuing attachment not only to the Jews, but in his later years,
even to Judaism. "Converts" moved about freely in Jewish
society, provoking the indignation of some of the religious

leaders, who would have liked to see the apostates quaran-
tined. That would have left them rather lonely, for — the
rabbis did not cease pointing out — the Christians, too,
continued to see the converts as stereotypical Jews, and
often shunned socializing with them.

> Everyone understood — everyone, philo-Semite
> and anti-Semite alike — that even those former Jews
> who had repudiated Judaism by religious conver-
> sion to Christianity, or legal disaffiliation from the
> Jewish community, were still somehow Jews: it
> never occurred to anyone to treat converts like Karl
> Marx or the conservative legal theoretician
> Friedrich Julius Stahl, as non-Jews. Berlin was full
> of Jewish agnostics, Jewish atheists, Jewish
> Catholics, and Jewish Lutherans. Indeed, these
> non-Jewish Jews were, if anything, more conspicu-
> ous than those who held, no matter how tepidly, to
> their ancient label, for they labored under the added
> reproach of cowardice, social climbing, secret
> service in a world-wide conspiracy — in a word: self-
> seeking mimicry.

Such was life in pre-war Berlin, according to the
eminent historian Peter Gay.

In America, things were little different. David Selznick,
the Hollywood movie magnate, was adamant when asked
to co-sponsor a fund-raising dinner for a Zionist organization: "I don't want to have anything to do with your cause
for the simple reason that it's a Jewish political cause. And
I am not interested in Jewish political problems. I am an
American and not a Jew." The Zionist activist did not give

up. He challenged Selznick to name three people he liked.
If only one agreed that Selznick was "an American and not
a Jew," the Zionist promised to lay off. Otherwise Selznick
would agree to his request. It turned out that all three were
Gentiles, and all three insisted that Selznick was a Jew. "For
God's sake," fumed Leland Hayward, then a talent agent,
"what's the matter with David? He's a Jew and he knows
it."

Neither the rabbis nor many an eji may like it, but the
facts of life are that ordinary people, Jewish and Gentile,
i.e. not only the Nazis, have an essentially genetic definition of Jewishness: you're Jewish if your parents were. A
few individuals may escape this classification and genuinely pass for Gentiles. Most do not. That this may not
be a nice thing can hardly change the facts. In a Jewish
anecdote, an individual is asked, "Are you Jewish?" and
replies, "Not necessarily." The answer may have made good
sense to the speaker, but is laughed at by everyone else.

Membership in an ethnic group is a tricky thing to
define. According to some very good anthropologists and
sociologists — most of them, not coincidentally, Jewish —
one can freely choose one's own group. People are Ashanti
if they call themselves Ashanti, French if they call themselves French. Israel's first prime minister, David Ben-
Gurion, irked the religious with his insistence that a Jew
was anyone who wanted to be one. But this principle does
not work for the Jews. It is debatable if anyone could be a
Jew by just saying so: there is a wide gap between Ben-
Gurion's stand (championed by some of the non-religious
Israelis) and the traditional religious law, which states quite
clearly that you can become Jewish only by being born to
a Jewish mother or by undergoing a religious conversion.

It is even less certain that a Jew can become a member of a Gentile people simply by self-declaration. Hundreds of thousands of born Jews who not too long ago proclaimed themselves Germans, Hungarians, Croatians, or the like, were murdered without mercy by the collective representatives of their presumed compatriots.

The traditional Jews, incidentally, have never put much store by the "self-definition" idea of Jewishness. A group of ultra-Orthodox Israeli Jews once dug up and removed the body of a woman from her Jewish burial place because, although she had believed herself Jewish, they found out that her conversion had not corresponded to traditional rules. Though she had been born a Christian, they reburied her among the presumed enemies of the State, in a Moslem cemetery. Of course, such excesses must not be attributed to Orthodox Jews as a whole. But there can be little doubt that in their relaxed moments, and not necessarily with any ill intent, most people, both religious and not, both Jewish and non-Jewish, subscribe to the racial definition of "who is a Jew."

The Importance of Being Eji

"Jew" is an inherited label. Because it is given by others on the basis of an involuntary act — being born — it cannot be shaken off easily. With it comes a singular social experience that, at least in the past, has been next to impossible to escape. This social experience makes sure that most eji will at least to some extent be marked by their ethnic origins, whether they like it or not. This is a plain fact, neither "good" nor "bad" in itself, and one that remains a fact, with or without the febrile fantasies attached to it by the Nazis.

I have said that the portrait I am painting will look at the eji from a singular angle: the eji's effort to show that the Jews are not essentially different from others. I call this eji insistence on comparing Jews to non-Jews "Shylock's Defence," as it recalls the famous words of the despised Merchant of Venice:

"Hath not a Jew eyes? hath not a Jew hands, organs, dimensions, senses, affections, passions? fed with the same food, hurt with the same weapons, subject to the same diseases, healed by the same means, warmed and cooled by the same winter and summer...?" asked Shylock — and the eji continues to ask.

In Part I of the book, I show how this desire not to appear to be "different" shapes two major aspects of eji culture: eji religion and eji intellect — the heart and the brains. In Parts II and III we see that there is a specific content to Shylock's Defence. "We are not different" in eji language always means "we are not greedier than you. We are not 'rich Jews.'" For Shylock's Defence was, like all defences, a response to a charge. And the charge was — I will argue that it always has been — that of unscrupulous greed. The cosmic battle between Good and Evil has in Western thought always been associated with a battle between Good and Gold. In the anti-Semite's version, the Jew is identified with the evil side, with Gold.

Like most mythologies, the myth of Good and Gold, too, has a solid underpinning in the social relations of power. "Jewish money" is bad money, while Gentile money can be all right. Traditionally, much of anti-Semitism is grounded in the idea that the Jews are upstarts, *nouveau riches* vulgarians, who do not have the right to enjoy the economic privileges that the public more or less grudgingly grants to the well born and supposedly well behaved. The result, painful for the Jews, is that those among them who have reached through wealth or education to what should have been a place of honour in society have often found themselves being depicted as usurpers: impostors who came by their money through cheating, and their academic or artistic titles through cliquish connections and the championing of flashy but shallow ideas.

At the end of the book I face the question as to whether anti-Semitism is now on the decline or on the increase. But there can be little doubt that in terms of economic and social discrimination against the Jews by the Gentile élites of the Western world, the situation has improved beyond recognition. (I am, for the moment, leaving aside the emotions of the black ghetto, of "white trash" both in the West and in the marginalized ex-communist countries, or of the Third World.) Much of the improvement is due to the many different ways, some of them far from obvious, in which the eji has decided to battle the anti-Semite's charge. Only some of these defences have been effective, however, while others have helped to pave the road to the decline of eji culture that, I believe, is now taking place in front of our eyes.

In Part IV we take stock of this apparent decline. We evaluate the eji legacy and ask what the future may hold for the non-Orthodox Jew. We consider, among other things, the effects of the defeat of communism and the accompanying improvement in the image of capitalism (or "market economy," to use a more appealing term). When Money in general is getting a better press, is it possible that even "Jewish money" looks better or, in other words, that the public has less need of the false charge of Jewish greed?

And, consequently, the Jews (many of whom, it goes without saying, have trouble paying the rent) can now relax a bit about having to prove that they are not "rich"?

Economics and politics is, however, not all we are going to talk about. Our ancestors believed (as the Orthodox still do) that our task was to be a holy people, that God chose us to be His servants, a Nation of Priests who would represent Him to all humans. As eji we believed the exact opposite: that we were just like everyone else — the Unchosen People. What next? In the closing segments of the book, I will suggest some ways that we Jews may be able to build on the humanitarian foundation laid by the eji, yet at the same time reassert our uniqueness, and look to the future with a renewed confidence.

2

BRIGHT JEWS: OF GENES, THE TALMUD, AND CHESS MASTERS

This race has superior abilities that place it on top of all others. A hundred thousand Israelites reside among 36 million French, and they consistently win first prizes at the lycées; fourteen of them have taken first place at the École normale, and one has had to reduce the number of those who are allowed to compete in public examinations.

— Alfred de Vigny, 1856

If there is one thing in the eji character that ought to give us hope for the future, it is that the eji is, incontrovertibly, very bright. Eji scholars and scientists have dominated many fields of inquiry in the late nineteenth and throughout much of the twentieth century. So prominent has been the eji intellectual achievement that it has earned all of us Jews the reputation of being extraordinarily smart. Even the anti-Semites do not say we are stupid, but are reduced to ruminating about the "destructive" nature of what they, too, regard as our intelligence.

A Little Digression: Fischer vs. Spassky
People consider chess to be the typical brainer's game; so no one is surprised that for quite some time a

thoroughly disproportionate number of Jews have won world championships.

I have always wondered where the money comes from to pay top chess masters millions. Chess is not exactly a spectator sport, and although the moves of the game are reported in the papers, I doubt that most amateur chess players play them through, or even understand them. Though many people play a game here and there, the number of those who know the meaning of terms like "Sicilian Defence" is probably not greater than that of Esperantists or ham-radio operators. Neither could marshal a big-bucks event like the Fischer vs. Spassky game the two ex-champions played during the Bosnian war and in defiance of international sanctions against Yugoslavia (or what remained of it: Serbia and Montenegro), on an island off that country's coast.

The embargo against rump Yugoslavia was wholeheartedly supported by most of the world on the humanitarian grounds of protecting the starving residents of besieged Sarajevo. So the chess players' self-important rule-breaking seemed all the more insolent. It added to their already arrogant image: neither man was the official world champion at the time, yet here they were, parading their skill as if this were the real championship, as if the official contest did not exist. Bobby and Boris took on the role of the World Wrestling Federation versus Olympic "Graeco-Roman" wrestling. Against the tame, namby-pamby, highbrow meets of the official organization, they offered the real thing, a genuine, screw-the-rules, macho event.

The comparison with wrestling does not end there, or in arcane incidents like the one where, according to trustworthy sources, Karpov employed a psychic at several games, in order to "psych out" Kasparov — a feat certainly worthy of any bare-chested wrestler. Both chess and wrestling are ultimate contests. Wrestling is the ultimate contest of bodies without brains; chess is the ultimate contest of brains without bodies. In Czechoslovakia, chess was classified as a sport. Consequently, to play a chess match participants, like all athletes, had to be vaccinated against tetanus. One day our town's chess team was scheduled to play a neighbouring town. My father, a physician, was called in to check each team's vaccination certificates. He became something of a local hero when he declared that the visitors had not had their shots. Our town won by default. The joke was, of course, on the dim-witted bureaucrats, for everyone else knew that chess was a game for the mind, not the body.

The wrestling match and the championship chess game each represent in extreme measure one of the two aspects of human nature: the physical and the spiritual, or, as some would have it, the animal and the divine. Like wrestlers in the ring, the contestants at the chess table use their superior gifts in combat: but where the wrestler uses the "low" weapons of muscle and body fat, the chess player's arm is the human intellect, which, no matter how prosaic and atheistic we may have become, we still feel has in it a spark of the divine. Both the World Wrestling Federation and the World Chess Federation give us battles of giants; but where a wrestling match is a scrabble between human animals, a chess game is a battle of gods. That is what creates the news value of a chess championship, bringing advertising revenues and megaprizes in its wake.

It is entirely in concert with popular mythology that the top wrestlers of the chess board have been so often Jewish

men (while the wrestlers of the ring are, possibly, all
Gentile). We will discuss later what being "brainy" has to
do with the image, not only of the Jew in general but particularly of the Jewish male. Here let us just repeat that not
even the worst anti-Semites have ever said that we were
stupid. The arrogance of a goy can be either mental or
physical, expressed in the three hundred pounds of a
wrestler's flesh. The arrogance of an eji is purely mental; it
is the arrogance of Brainy Smurf.

Fischer is Jewish. So is Kasparov. Spassky and Karpov
are half-Jewish, but in the atmosphere of the ex-Soviet
Union that has been enough for most people to think of
them as Jews. (Indeed, the *Encyclopaedia Judaica* includes
Spassky in its list of Jewish chess players.) Top-level chess
has been at least as Jewish as the solo violin.

But was that always so? Chess is an ancient game, and
it has been known in areas inhabited by Jews for centuries.
The Jews have been quite good at adopting Gentile enter-
tainments, from baroque music to betting at horse races.
There is every reason to think that Jews have been playing
chess about as long as the Gentiles around them. Yet there
is little evidence that Jews were particularly good at chess
until the modern period, the period of the eji.

And today, as the eji period ends, the Jewish supremacy
on the chess board may be coming to its end as well. Young
Dutch or Indian non-Jews are entering chess rooms where
previously mainly Russian and American Jews played.

This may be a coincidence. On the other hand, it might
be proof that Jewish "brains," exemplified in this instance
by chess players, are not, or not exclusively, the product of
our "intelligent" genes, or some equally eternal love of
learning and reasoning. Whatever role such factors may or

may not have played, our intellectual successes were also a product of the specific challenge of a specific period — the modern period, that is — when the eji fought back prejudice by elevating the abstract and belittling the particular. (Chess is, perhaps, the most abstract of board games. We shall soon see the relationship between the love of abstraction and the "Jewish mind.") To put it another way, Sicilian Defence had something in common with Shylock's Defence, too.

That non-Jewish chess players are for the first time in a long while a serious threat to the established champions may also not be a coincidence. It may be just one more example of a possible decline of the Jewish pre-eminence in other fields. Let us go beyond chess. Things today are in flux; all of us can do our own research through observation. Do you see as many young Jews distinguish themselves in "abstract" areas as older ones? For that matter, do you see as many young Jews distinguish themselves in the arts and sciences in general?

I am very proud that my son was recently admitted to our city's academically most exclusive secondary school. It used to be one-third Jewish. Now it is one-third Chinese. Is this only because there are so many more Chinese here now? Or is something happening to the Jews? There could hardly be a more important question; but our portrait of the eji needs to be more complete before we can answer it, and so we must defer the matter until the last part of the book.

Jewish Brains and History

The Jewish preponderance in the arts and sciences has no more been "always there" than Jewish success in chess — nor can it be taken more for granted.

As long as the Jews were kept in the ghetto, no one could have guessed their intellectual potential. But from the eighteenth century on, when they were first let out into the wide world, the Jews' contribution to civilization kept up a long crescendo, which is (and that, too, arguably) only now beginning to fade. The élite preparatory schools of Europe were inundated by talented Jewish students, eager to learn and to get ahead in the Gentile-dominated world. What the French poet Count Alfred de Vigny observed about the prestigious *lycées* in 1856 was in no way exceptional. A generation later, the British political writer Sidney Whitman wrote an even more glowing report about the Jewish participation in the German equivalent of the *lycées*, the *Gymnasien*. "At a recent examination in one of the Prussian Gymnasien," he wrote, "the item of religion fell into abeyance, because all those who came up for examination were Jews." Some of the graduates of the *Gymnasium* in question may have made it quite far. By the time Hitler forced the Jews out of research and education, thirty-six Germans had received the Nobel Prize. Of these, eleven are said to have been Jewish.

Things did not look much different in North America, as more and more Jews migrated here. This is how Mordecai Richler remembers his youth at Fletcher's Field High, a school that was "under the jurisdiction of the Montreal Protestant School Board, but had a student body that was nevertheless almost a hundred per cent Jewish":

Again and again, we led Quebec province in the junior matriculation results. This was galling to the communists among us who held we were the same as everyone else . . .

North American Jewry was ready to ensure the continued blossoming of Jewish scientific talent when Hitler destroyed the intellectually ebullient German community. In 1976 the United States received a record twelve Nobel Prizes, an achievement never before reached by any country. Of the twelve, seven are believed to have been Jewish.

Jewish pride in Jewish achievement, however, goes back to before the Nobel Prize was first given, and well before Einstein and Freud. Disraeli delighted in the power of Jewish bankers, and in the high position of many Jews in the governments of Europe and the then still great Ottoman Empire. Other Jews, of course, revelled in Disraeli's own success as Victoria's preferred prime minister. Jewish commentators in Germany pointed out with pride that the mentors of *Junges Deutschland*, the important early nineteenth-century literary movement, had been Ludwig Börne (alias Baruch) and Heinrich Heine. Jews were thrilled by the popularity of the composers Mendelssohn, Offenbach, Halévy, and Meyerbeer.

This feeling of pride extended even to famous Jews whose political views one did not share. Disraeli was a hero in all Jewish communities, even if they did not partake in his conservativism. The liberal circles around the German-Jewish leader Ludwig Philippson, for example, always referred to Disraeli by his noble title, the Earl of Beaconsfield, and Philippson's newspaper, the *Allgemeine Zeitung des Judenthums*, never found a bad word for him. The same paper took an unequivocal stand against slavery and on the side of the North during the American Civil War. However, it was less than convincing in its mild rebuke to the South's Secretary of War, Judah Philip Benjamin, whom it described with apparent pride as a Jew. The newspaper added that the Cameron Dragon Regiment had many Jews and mostly Jewish officers.

Awe at the magnitude of Jewish achievement has not been limited to Jews. Even anti-Semites were impressed — not positively, of course. The influential nineteenth-century literary critic Wolfgang Menzel (1798–1873) bemoaned the omnipresence of Jewish writers, and of Jewish themes among non-Jewish writers, in Germany in the 1860s. This had been a period when, as he saw it, the Jewish literati robbed the German people of its national vigour: "The Jewish demon fanned it [the people] with its vampire wings, while it gently sucked away its blood." Richard Wagner denied that Jews could compose music worthy of the name, and was echoed by his son-in-law Houston Chamberlain, a "theorist" of racism. But even Wagner had to at least recognize that Jewish composers enjoyed the enthusiasm of the public.

To what was Jewish achievement due? The literature of the social sciences, as well as popular opinion, offer two possible explanations. One holds that the Jews are born with genes for superior intelligence. The other maintains that their successes are the result of the Jewish tradition, and especially its emphasis on the value of learning. There are problems with both "explanations."

Jewish Genes?
The gene idea has received support from some rather respectable people, for example, Sir Keith Joseph, the conservative British economist. Some believe that the Jews have come by their fancy genes through restricting marriage, at least in theory, to within their own group. Good

gene management, these admirers say, and one that has helped to maintain a superior "genetic pool." Others, equally genetically minded, say that Jewish gene farming has been successful precisely because, despite what their religion asks them to do, Jews have so often married non-Jews, bringing in fresh blood.

It is understandable why the thought of innate Jewish intelligence is so popular among both Jews and philo-Semites. Unfortunately, not every Jew seems to possess the good genetic stuff in equal measure. Nothing tells the story better than the old Yiddish saying "When a Jew's stupid he's *really* stupid." One may forgive Jews who are something less than an Einstein if they feel that not only does the blood of famous people flow through their veins, but that some choice DNA swims in it. However, there are a few problems. The "superior genes" theory will only be credible when scientists begin to see how the "smart" genes manage to slip out of the constitution of the less swift-minded Jews. And this discovery will have to be coupled with the greater task of understanding just what kind of genes, Jewish or otherwise, are the kind that help one to get a Nobel Prize.

At any rate, genes could never explain an elementary fact about great Jewish intellectuals and scientists: an utterly striking truth and yet one that neither the ordinary Jew nor Jewish historians seem to have paid any attention to. Marx, Einstein, and Freud, as well as thousands of other, more minor Jewish luminaries, had, despite their many differences, this in common: they did not wear a yarmulke. Some had been baptized, others were atheists, some seemed almost anti-Semitic; yet others had a warm cultural attachment to their Jewish roots, and found solace in a reinterpreted Judaism. But none kept kosher, none was a regular guest at the synagogue, none kept the *shabos*. In what follows, I will use "Jewish scientist" and "eji scientist" as synonyms. This is not to insult the few overtly Orthodox scholars and researchers that have graced the history of "Jewish success." It is only to state the fact that the Orthodox contribution has been far outweighed by those of "secular" and in former times even baptized Jews.

If heredity determined the levels of excellence among Jews, there would have been among the "great Jewish minds" a good proportion of the observant. Since there has not been, it follows that the relative success of Jewish scholars, authors, and scientists (statistically significant when compared to non-Jews on such measures as the number of Nobel Prizes won) is due to their social experience. An experience that was not that of the synagogue, not that of the Talmud, not that of the Sabbath, but of the comings and goings of the secular, "non-Jewish" Jew. Jewish genes, it seems, have been of little value in the quest for scientific and cultural success, unless the bearer of the genes came from the religion-neutral milieu of the eji.

The Love of Arguing, Then and Now
Paradoxically, it takes more chutzpah to argue that Jewish distinction is due not to genes but to the eji's cultural environment. I do not just mean that the religious Jews might be upset by my rejection of Judaism as the foundation of secular Jewish "greatness." Above all, my position might upset the group from whom the "greats" themselves originate, the eji. The eji would rather think of themselves as

great because of their genes than because of some specifically Jewish, even if non-religious Jewish, element in their
background.

A smart Jew whose brightness is due only to his or her
genes is smart in exactly the same way as a smart non-Jew.
If there are social or cultural reasons to Jewish "smartness,"
however, then the eji has a problem. Could it be that some
people are not just plain intelligent, but intelligent in a particularly "Jewish" way? This is often not what either the eji
celebrities or their admirers want. To them, after all, the
Jews are just like everyone else.

Luckily for the eji, there is one possible explanation for
Jewish intellectual successes that is based on culture, and
yet does not offend the eji taboo against Jewish singular-
ity. This is the idea that Jewish achievement is due to the
traditional Jewish love for books and learning. For just like
good genes, studious parents are not limited to the Jews.
An education for learning may be something that on the
average Jewish families provide more than non-Jewish
ones. A cheeky claim, perhaps, but not one that might
really threaten a Gentile — or an eji. The difference that
it makes between the Jewish and the non-Jewish family is
one of degree, not of kind.

The image of the traditional Jew in a badly lit room
cramped with books, ceaselessly poring over oversized
volumes, has a basis in fact. Study of religious texts is
perhaps the chief joy of the devout Jew, especially if he is
a man. (Women are also encouraged to study, but not at the
expense of their traditional duties in the home, which are
considered sacred.) Observant boys as young as five years
old are introduced to the formal study of Talmud. Often,
they are started off with a gift of a tablet of Hebrew letters

covered in honey. This they lick off to make their studies
sweet, much as apples are dipped in honey at the beginning of the Jewish New Year to sweeten the year to come.
(The *heder* was hardly all sweetness, however. Former
pupils also remember receiving a judicious blow or two.)

There have always been traditional Jewish men who
preferred work, or gambling, or the love of women, to religious learning. But to this day the Orthodox Jewish male
spends much of his time studying the compilation of law
and wisdom known as the Talmud, and rabbinical commentaries on the same. The popular Yiddish word for synagogue is *shul*, or "school." Typically, it was in the same
space where they worshipped that Jews studied as well.
Few things were as painful for us, children "without con
fession" in a communist country, than the saying, repeated
without reflection by the teacher, "it's noisy here like in a
Jewish school!" The phrase, widely used throughout
Europe, probably comes from the practice of the worship-
pers chanting prayers at their own pace in the synagogue-
shul. Or it might reflect on the way Talmudic scholars
traditionally discuss the rabbinical commentaries with
their study partners. Since each twosome of scholars
carries on the debate at the same time as the other pairs,
the result is that there are more people vocalizing at the
same time than in a classical opera — though the effect is
far from Mozartian. To Gentiles passing by the *shul*, such
devout prattle no doubt sounds like mere noise.

In traditional Jewish communities, to be known as a
chochem Talmud (lit. "a wise person of the Talmud") was
not only a great honour but had distinct economic advan-
tages. Rich men liked to marry their daughters to learned
if poor religious scholars. This helped to couple their

worldly success with "a portion of the world to come," which was believed to be procurable by those who had studied the Talmud well. (Sometimes the rich paid the *chochem* to recite prayers they did not have time to say, with the same "otherworldly" goal.)

But how much does this universe of devout study have to do with the world of the modern Jewish scholar, writer, or professor? There is little reason to believe that a single Jew achieved renown in the secular world of ideas because of having studied the Talmud. Most famous Jewish intellectuals never read a page of it. What the Jewish intellectual has come to regard as Judaism is, as we shall see, often no more than a sort of rationalistic Christianity without Jesus.

To attribute Talmudic wisdom to a descendant of Talmudists who knows not the Talmud seems at first sight to be simply another version of the genetic explanation. The claim, this time, would be that Talmudic learning can be inherited by a non-learner from a scholarly ancestor. It would be the first proof yet of the long-discredited idea known as Lamarckism, that we can inherit what our ancestors learned during their lifetime. But we know as little of genes for Talmudic lore as we know of genes for winning Nobel Prizes.

And yet, what if parents who studied the Talmud passed on to their offspring not the love of studying the Talmud as such, but the love of learning in general? This, of course, is not literally true in the case of most famous eji. Even the *parents* of people like Marx, Einstein, or Trotsky were not particularly observant, and may be assumed to have known little if anything of the Talmud. (An exception was the sociologist Émile Durkheim, whose

father was a rabbi, albeit a "modern" one, as was the grandfather of Claude Lévi-Strauss, the anthropologist.) But the
chain of transmission might last longer than a generation
or two. Parents who knew the Talmud might not pass on
its contents, but they would, perhaps, transmit the mental
habits required for studying it and for arguing its points.

The habits of argument sanctioned by the Talmudists
are rather idiosyncratic. The tendency of the Jewish intellectual towards abstract argument may be, in part, a
genuine throwback to them. For compared to other traditional styles of learning, Talmud study places less stress on
memorization of "facts" and much more on the skills of
interpretation. The excitement exuded by the Talmudic
commentaries — for that is what they are, the Talmud
having the form of commentaries on Biblical text — comes
from the flight of argument, which often leaves the original text as no more than a little speck far below on the
ground. Knowledge comes from debate, more than from
observation.

A major part of the Talmudic book of *Berakhot*
(Blessings), for example, deals with the interpretation of
the Biblical injunction to Jews to recite the *Shema* twice a
day. The *Shema* is a brief statement that reads as follows:
"Hear O Israel: the Lord our God, the Lord is One." The
Bible commands the faithful to recite it "when thou liest
down and when thou risest up, and when thou walkest by
the way, and when thou sittest in thine house." In an astonishing feat of interpretation, *Berakhot* ends up a lengthy
and complex series of arguments by concluding, from this
one line, that a bridegroom about to marry a virgin is
exempt from reciting the *Shema*, while one wedding a
widow is not.

Reading the record of Talmudic disputations, it is difficult to escape the impression that the parties to the argument love arguing itself far above the reaching of a
reasonable conclusion. In fact, the Talmud in this and
other typical cases gives alternative interpretations as well,
recalling the author of each interpretation, and often withdrawing entirely from judgment.

While Talmudic disputation is an art lost to most Jews
today, the love of argument is not. In a study intriguingly
entitled, "Jewish Argument as Sociability," sociologist of
language Deborah Schiffrin discusses a small network of
lower-middle-class families, regular visitors in each other's
homes. They passionately and vocally disagree on a wide
range of controversial topics from intermarriage (i.e. marriage between Jews and Gentiles) to characteristics of the
broader American society. Yet their verbal parrying does
not in the least threaten their friendship. Indeed, it
cements it. Others might express their friendship in going
out together to dine, to bowl, or to watch a game. These
Jews express it through arguing. One can easily see them
switch sides just for fun: the strict endogamist now arguing
for intermarriage; the "open-minded" suddenly finding
good reasons for keeping marriages within the community.
Among Jews, the family that argues together often stays
together. Where there are two Jews, goes the classic saying,
there are three opinions.

Education and Integration
To round off the picture, however, one should add to an
abstract love of learning and disputation a more mundane
motivation for Jews to pursue intellectual careers. Going
to school was a way to get ahead. Jews were informally

discriminated against by many employers; this was one
reason why so many preferred to run their own businesses.
A career as a professional has been an alternative route to
self-employment for the more studious or the less com-
mercially minded. Jewish doctors had been more or less
freely allowed to practise even in the Middle Ages, when
they were appreciated by popes and princes as healing
magicians. Later, the American Revolution and French
Revolution established a Jew's right to practise any of the
other liberal professions, including, importantly, the law. It
is true that although Napoleon took this right in his
baggage wherever his conquering armies went, the Jews'
licences were often revoked as soon as the Corsican was
gone. But despite periodic reversals, by the end of the nineteenth century a career in the liberal professions was available to Jews practically everywhere in the Western world,
though informal barriers remained in some cases, especially in the teaching professions. And the key to such a
career was education.

The eji seized the opportunity with enthusiasm. Their
eagerness to better themselves, so much an essential part
of the "American dream," was not quite so celebrated a
hundred years ago, when much value still attached to
"keeping one's place." A member of the exclusive
"duelling" fraternities in nineteenth-century Germany
found nothing exciting in the following success story of an
East European Jewish immigrant's son in Berlin:

In the very East of Berlin, there was a Galician
Jewish egg-seller. His son was studying medicine
after graduating from the Gymnasium. Whenever
he came home from school or university, he took

the eggs round to the customers on a handcart,
untroubled by occasional abuse from working-
men's wives. After some semesters, all this was put
behind him and he went to the West as a doctor. It
is clear that people who will bear any personal
humiliation for the sake of a penny . . . cannot
understand our system of duelling, the defense of
our integrity and honor. All they can see is a tool for
scaling the social heights.

The future doctor selling eggs — a wonderful beginning for a Hollywood classic — shocked the anti-Semitic
writer, but the egg-seller himself may have thought that he
was doing something that Germans would approve of.
After all, the system of public education, pioneered by
liberal Germans, was meant to be just exactly a venue for
the lowly to "scale the social heights."
The attitude carried over easily to North America.
Cynthia Good, Publisher of Penguin Books Canada, recalls
that at the age of ten her mother made her sign a note with
the following text: "I swear that I will attend the University
of Toronto, and graduate with cap and gown." "We were
not supposed to memorise baseball batting averages or
dirty limericks," reminisces fellow Canadian Mordecai
Richler about his childhood in Montreal.

We were expected to improve our Word Power with
the *Reader's Digest* and find inspiration in Paul de
Kruif's medical biographies. If we didn't make
doctors, we were supposed to at least squeeze into
dentistry. School marks didn't count as much as
rank. One wintry day I came home, nostrils cling-

ing together and ears burning cold, proud of my report. "I came rank two, Maw."

"And who came rank one, may I ask?"

When the young of an entire people decide to go to school (or their parents make the decision for them), it is likely that intellectual giants who will do honour to the traditional learning of their ancestors will emerge. Two centuries after Napoleon, immigrants from Hong Kong began to astonish their "hosts" by a vivacious effort to educate their children. The Chinese, too, have a tradition of scholarship, one that is even older than ours.

There are many young Chinese in North America today who have followed in the footsteps of the Jewish egg-seller of former days. I doubt that it is because Chinese genes have improved recently. More likely, it is because Chinese parents have found a way to adapt the traditional Chinese respect for learning to their new circumstances as immigrants. Likewise, the Jewish achievement in arts and science has been due to a cultural predisposition to study and abstract disputation.

That, at least, is the safe explanation. There is also a less safe one.

The Selectiveness of the Jewish Achievement

All right. So we can say, "The Jews have succeeded because the love of learning runs in their families. Ergo: your kids will do better if you teach them to love studying." How very true. And how safe from the point of view of those who deny any distinctiveness to the "intelligence" of a Jew. Love of learning and the desire to get ahead are laudable qualities which, we have seen, the Jews have possessed, but which are not specifically "Jewish." You can be Chinese, German — why, even WASP! — and possess them in abundance. To pat ourselves on the back for being studious and ambitious is similar to praising ourselves for our love of the Prophets — both are things the Gentiles appreciate.

Yet in addition to the Prophets, we "also" have the Talmud; and in addition to our love of learning in general, we also have interests that are specifically Jewish, or to be more precise, eji. There is proof. Eji scholars and scientists have excelled in some disciplines more than in others. For example, nuclear physics was, in its heroic age of Niels Bohr and Albert Einstein, very much a Jewish affair. On the other hand, to this day there have been few Jews in zoology or astronomy. Show me a *cohenia* plant or a Goldberg Supernova, and I will believe otherwise. Why should a love of learning and an ambition to succeed channel people into some academic disciplines, like nuclear physics, and not into others, like zoology? If the Jewish interest in learning were not different from that of other people, then the Jews would be equally spread among the disciplines. But that is not the case. Jewish scholars tend to have particular interests.

What do the "Jewish" disciplines have in common that sets them apart from those where eji involvement has been none or minimal?

Among scientists as well as artists, we can distinguish between those whose primary concern is things in their own right, and those who are more interested in the relations between things. All thinking people are, of course, interested in both things and relations. But there is a matter of degree. The zoologist and the geneticist may both be interested in how some trait is passed from generation to generation, say, in a species of *macaca*. But the zoologist will more often be curious about the monkey as such; while the geneticist will want to know what the research on *macaca* can tell us about the "genetic code" in general, in monkeys as well as other animals, including humans.

The work of the geneticist is, in this sense, more *abstract*. The word *abstract* comes from the Latin for "dragged away." The zoologist may be interested in the monkey as an individual, or at least as an individual species. The geneticist "drags away" from the characteristics of the monkey only those features that the monkey has in common with other animals of interest to the geneticist, let us say, all primates. The result is an "abstraction": the genetic make-up of primates, regardless of whether they are *macaca*, chimpanzee, or *homo sapiens*. An abstraction tells us about some group of phenomena by referring to their common qualities. On the other hand, it tells us nothing about the *particular* phenomena in question, about how they differ from each other. Our geneticist will not enlighten us on how humans differ from monkeys and apes.

Returning to the Jews: Shylock was asking his detractors, rhetorically, to perform an experiment. "Tickle me," he was saying, "and you'll see that I'll laugh as you would. Prick me, and I'll bleed like you." He was asking the Gentiles to *abstract* from his Jewishness, to "drag away" from his nature not what they — and no doubt Shakespeare — saw in it as his *particular*, distinctive Jewishness (his unfeeling, usurious greed), but to take instead what made him human, in common with them.

"Jews are just like everyone else" is never to be taken literally. Everyone knows that Jews are not like everyone else, if only because there is a name for them, "Jew," that sets them apart. To say, "Jews are just like everyone else" is really not a statement of fact, as much as it is a demand to think at a higher level of abstraction, one where differences among peoples don't matter, where they have been "abstracted from." To say "Jews are just like everyone else" implies the command "Think abstract!"

Suppose we Jews had some sort of a worldwide public relations agency whose job was to devise some clever way to convince the Gentiles to "think abstract," in order to "soften them up" for thinking that "Jews are just like everyone else." And suppose all of the intellectual types among us managed to cover up our differences, in order to lend a hand to that strategy. We would then end up with scholars, writers, and artists all of whom would be pushing, in their respective fields, the merits of abstraction over the pitfalls of only concentrating on the particular. Everywhere, our intellectuals would be saying, "Things mean nothing in themselves! You can only understand them if you put them in context! Don't think of things in isolation; think of the system they belong to!"

Of course, we don't have a PR headquarters. And yet, these are the things that our eji intellectuals and artists have, I believe, always been saying. It is *as if* the eji believed that any endeavour that demands exclusive attention to particulars is "for the goyim." It is *as if* the collective eji brain had been harnessed to spread the word about the primacy of abstraction. Eji scholars tend to be, overwhelmingly, geneticists rather than zoologists.

A few examples:

✡ **Natural Sciences.** Einstein busied himself with the larger relationships of space and time. His mind was essentially mathematical rather than experimental: he carried out no lab experiments. He made far-reaching deductions about the Universe, but it is not clear how familiar he was with the map of the sky. His vision dealt with time, space, and matter in general, and he had little to say about particular planets or stars. Such preoccupation with abstract generalities rather than concrete particulars is responsible for the fact that there are relatively few Jewish astronomers, zoologists, or botanists, for these disciplines require careful classification of individual items, be they celestial bodies, animal species, or plants. The percentage of Jews in these fields contrasts with that in the more "abstract" areas of physics, chemistry, or biology.

Within the human sciences, we see the same pattern.

✡ **Anthropology.** This is a broad discipline, divided among archaeologists, physical anthropologists (who study human evolution and the physical characteristics of human groups), social-cultural anthropologists, and, sometimes, anthropological linguists. The "bones and stones" that occupy the physical anthropologists and archaeologists have only attracted the rare Jewish specialist, unless they have an obvious *relation* to other things relevant to people outside those disciplines. On the other hand, social-cultural anthropology, which focuses on cultural differences and as such on the relationship of one cultural group to another, has always fascinated the Jewish scholar. Many Jewish anthropologists admit that what brought them to the discipline is their feeling "different." Among the preceding generations of anthropologists one ought to mention such greats as Franz Boas, Edward Sapir, Melville Herskovits, Robert Redfield, Leslie White, and many, many others. I refrain from attempting a list of the many leading

Jewish social anthropologists today, for fear of causing offence by leaving out some.

✡ **Archaeology.** With some exceptions, one finds Jewish archaeologists only in Israel, where their finds have relevance well beyond the discipline itself. Digs in Israel have an emotional hold over the Israelis that cannot be explained only by their scientific value: Jewish artifacts in ancient Israel validate the Jewish title to "the Land" that justifies, in part, the Jewish presence there today. The ultra-orthodox have no use for the digs, which they accuse of disturbing the peace of buried ancestors. But to the secular, who cannot without hypocrisy refer to a Biblical right to Israel, the ancient Jewish title to the Land is purely a matter of ancient Jews living there. To them, Biblical archaeology is more important than the Bible. This is why both professional and amateur Israeli archeologists (Moshe Dayan was one amateur accused by some professionals of damaging sites through less than fine excavations) are passionately devoted to the archaeology of Israel, while showing no particular interest in other areas.

✡ **Physical Anthropology.** This, like archaeology, is a field that often focuses on the careful collection of particular facts, which, like fossil human ancestors, are sometimes concrete objects dug up in a manner similar to that of the archaeologist. One of the few Jewish physical anthropologists is Frances Burton, whose work is heavily concerned with primate behaviour. Primate behaviour is obviously the field that has the most relevance to outside physical anthropology. It may or may not be scientifically the most advisable thing to do, but we cannot but make comparisons between the behaviour of our primate relatives and ourselves. Burton was one of the first to conclude that primate females can have orgasms. An interesting finding about apes and monkeys. But an even more interesting finding about the issue, only recently so controversial, of whether women's orgasm is "natural" or "cultural."

✡ Sociology. If social-cultural anthropology is a rather eji field, sociology is even more so. One must not forget the great Gentile sociologists like Max Weber, but the origins of the discipline would be unthinkable without Karl Marx, Émile Durkheim, or the almost exclusively eji "Frankfurt School." Eji sociologists, like eji historians, have always thought more of *relations* among individuals (i.e. "social structure") than the role of the individuals themselves. To rhapsodize about the Great Man of Genius as a determin ing force of history is a very goyish thing indeed, one that most eji scholars shrink from with disgust and fear. To talk about social conditioning, political systems, and the strug- gle of classes (but not of course of races or peoples), on the other hand, is meeting the eji on their home turf.

✡ Language. The distinction between areas that interest the eji and those that do not is possibly even clearer in the science of language. Language is the subject both of lan- guage departments, which deal with specific languages like French or Russian, and of linguistics departments, where language is studied in the abstract, in general, as the common heritage of humanity. A look at the composition of the academic staff at many major North American uni- versities reveals that the language departments are rela- tively goyish, while linguistics is one of the disciplines that attracts an unusually large number of Jews. Leonard Bloomfield is known as the founder of American linguis- tics; Noam Chomsky, as its more recent "star." Chomsky's work has excited much notice outside linguistics, mainly

because of its focus on so-called "innate language universals." His interest in the study of particular languages is
minimal (see Chapter 13).

✡ **Psychoanalysis.** In the history of psychoanalysis, one
finds a curious contrast. The Jews have clustered around
Freud, Wertheimer (the founder of Gestalt psychology), or
lesser lights like Adler. The Gentiles were more likely to
follow Jung. The situation within the psychoanalytic community in Freud's time resembled the way things often still
are in the North American legal and accounting professions today: there are Jewish firms, and there are Gentile
ones. Freud's was a Jewish firm, Jung's, a Gentile one. I do
not find the comparison a distasteful one. But if you do,
count up Freud's Jewish and Gentile collaborators, and
then do the same for Jung. Then perform some statistics.
We shall speak again if you do not find the relationship statistically significant: Freud was surrounded mainly by Jews;
Jung, mainly by Gentiles.

When Freud laid a patient on his couch, the analysis
focused on such abstractions as the patient's ego, id, and
superego — none of them very tangible things. Jung, on the
other hand, interpreted the unconscious as peopled by specific images that he called archetypes. The great Biblical
images, like the Serpent and the Flood, are according to
Jungians innate "archetypes" that get expressed in the
myths of peoples as well as in our personal dreams and fantasies. These archetypes are not abstractions but specific
images with a particular shape. Freud called the stuff hocus-
pocus. So did most eji, *then*. One of the major signs that the
eji period is coming to its end is that today many Jews are so
much more willing to take seriously the powerful imagery of
Jung. The irrational, it seems, frightens us much less today.

✡ **Visual Arts.** The verbal arts and music, which have little "concrete" manifestation, have had much more input from Jews than painting and sculpture, which, after all, produce individual, concrete objects. Yet there is a respectable number of Jews in the visual arts, not bad for a people of about thirteen or fourteen million. The Impressionist Camille Pissarro (1830–1903), born in the West Indies, was the first major Jewish figure in modern French art; and he was followed by Amedeo Modigliani, Chaim Soutine, and Marc Chagall. Sculptors such as Lipchitz and Epstein have made significant contributions to the plastic arts. But note that all of the artists mentioned were in one way or another non-traditional, even anti-traditional (The new art of photography, too, attracted some great Jewish talents, like those of Alfred Stieglitz and Man Ray.) Very few Jews were known to produce high-quality classical or academic art, which aims in large measure to show, even if in idealized fashion, what the subject "really" looks like. (One classicist Jewish painter was the nineteenth-century Dutch artist Josef Israels.) Modern painting is, compared with the classical, more concerned with the general artistic problems of colour, line, light, and medium, at the expense of the representational aspect of art. Even if not always purely "abstract" in the sense the word has in painting, it is always more abstract than traditional art.

✡ **Verbal Arts.** It is not necessary to give a list of major Jewish writers of books, plays, films, and the print and television media — there have been so many wherever large numbers of Jews have lived: present-day America, Israel, Canada, France, or Russia; or, before the Holocaust, the German-speaking countries or Poland. Acting, also a verbal art, has an even longer tradition among the Jews, of which the great nineteenth-century actresses Sarah Bernhardt and Rachel, were by no means the first representatives. There have not been many great Jewish dancers, on the other hand, the dancer's art being more grounded in the "concrete" world of the body than the abstract world of the Word. Curiously, though, some of the foremost mimes, such as Marcel Marceau, have been Jews. But mime is only partly dance. It is acting, too, and it is a sort of speech: nothing could make us more aware of the role language plays in communication than trying to communicate without it.

✡ Music. In contrast to the visual arts, the Jewish contribution to music has been not only respectable but indeed decisive. Here, too, however, we see a specialization of talent and style. Light music from Offenbach through Gershwin to the Broadway musical has been a Jewish specialty; but — despite the pleasing harmonies of Mendelssohn and the bombastic scenes of Meyerbeer — in the romantic period Jewish composers were no match for the greatest of their Gentile colleagues, the likes of Beethoven or Chopin. Jewish talent was, however, already evident in the ranks of the first-class interpreters. The great nineteenth-century Hungarian-Jewish violin virtuoso, Joseph Joachim, was a friend of Dvořák's. The latter, as well as Brahms, composed important concertos for him. Ever since, Jewish violinists have come close to dominating the concert halls. And there have been almost as many great Jewish pianists as violinists.

Yet it is only in the modern period that great Jewish interpreters of "serious" music were joined by great composers — during the same era that saw the rise of the best in Jewish painting. Jewish composers like Mahler, Schoenberg, and Hindemith broke into the first ranks. Why were the Jewish — eji — composers even more significant in creating modern "serious" music than classical? Once again, the answer seems to lie in the "generalist" nature of the "eji mind." More than classical music, modern music is concerned with theory as opposed to practice: with the structure of music in general as opposed to what a particular piece sounds like.

Though many decades have passed since Schoenberg was first performed, to most audiences his compositions still do not quite sound like music at all. How did a great composer make his mark on musical history by composing what to many of us is non-music? Without a doubt by stressing the challenges of musical structure ("theory") to the detriment of the sound it produces. To Western ears, all music must be composed in the familiar eight-tone *do re mi fa soh la ti do* scale. Schoenberg wanted to know what it would sound like to break the shackles not only of this type of scale but even of all musical patterns found in the musical tradition of any culture whatsoever. He wrote his music in a twelve-tone scale, repeating his themes in rigidly defined artificial patterns. One of his favourite devices was to play the theme backwards, starting with the last note. This and other of his experiments produced music that sprung, even more than classical music, from the brain's understanding of the abstract patterns of music rather than from the intuitions of the ear. (In fact, the human ear is unable to hear the relationship between a theme played forward and backward. We hear them as two entirely different themes.) In a word, Schoenberg was to music what Einstein was to physics.

Einstein was the mathematician of matter; Schoenberg, the mathematician of sound.

Music is a good guide on how Jewish talent in general should be approached. It is conceivable that there are genes for music, and that many Jews have such genes. Music is "in our blood" figuratively speaking — many of our ancestors were popular musicians. Isaac Stern said that the Russian Jews were a nation of fiddlers. Even in the Arab world, some of the greatest musical interpreters have been Sephardic Jews; indeed, some music historians believe that Islamic music reflects heavily the heritage of the synagogue. Nevertheless, it would be ludicrous to say that there are genes for modern rather than romantic music. There is no reason why a nation of fiddlers and chanters should have a particular affinity to atonal music rather than to the more classical forms. The particularly interesting, and challenging, problem is to explain not only Jewish "success" in general, but why the Jews have been more successful in some areas than in others. And the answer is, if I am correct, that we have been particularly successful in areas that stress the abstract over the particular. The abstract, the universal, the general is by definition where similarities are emphasized; the particular, where differences come into focus. Shylock's Defence favours similarities over particularities — it favours abstraction. So it is not surprising that the fields of the arts and sciences in which the eji have excelled are the ones that make, in one way or another, the point "Think abstract! Things mean nothing in themselves!"

Both groups who most challenge the eji, the traditional Jews and the anti-Semites, are strenuously opposed to that message.

The traditionalists oppose it because to them the idea of the Jews as a Chosen People is all-important. The idea of chosenness, which is one of the pillars on which traditional Jewish religion rests, cannot easily be explained in universal terms. To the strictly Orthodox, the People of Israel are a "thing in itself." If we are like everyone else, why should God choose *us*? If *everyone* is like everyone else, why should God choose anyone? Ultimately, the question concerns the nature of God's own self.

The anti-abstraction stance of the traditionalist Jews is mirrored by the Jews' enemies. The worst of the anti-Semites detest abstraction almost as much as they detest the Jews. Sartre pointed out that the French anti-Semite believes that French land can never really be acquired by a Jew, no matter how much he or she pays for it; that a French Jewish intellectual can never really understand French poetry; that the most eloquent of French Jews can never say a sentence that is truly French. What is French is French, what is Jewish is Jewish. East is East and West is West, said Kipling, who was one of the voices (a relatively benevolent one, perhaps) of nineteenth-century racism. To a racist (the anti-Semite is a racist; not quite like other racists, but still a racist), each people is an island. Each race has a unique "character" to it. That "character" cannot be acquired by another race, nor can those who have it give it up. The Aryan is heroic and creative. The Mongoloid is industrious and crafty. The Jew is greedy, devious, and domineering. That's it. This is the way things are, says the racist, and to that judgment there can be no appeal.

This bigoted idea of a distinctive "character" was used, as Alan Dershowitz describes in *Chutzpah*, to keep Jews out of important positions in business and the universities. In this case, the anti-Semites used "character" to mean what they understood as *Gentile* character: some set of mystic concepts of superior behaviour, which no one could define. In fact it was important that they could not be defined, so that there would be no objective way for the Jews to protest that they, indeed, did have "character." We see in this example that the mysticism of exclusive, particularistic "character" was really just a means to find some justification to "keep the Jews out."

So it is out of self-defence that the "abstract" eji (the "rootless cosmopolitans," as anti-Semites both on the left and on the right call them) attack mysterious ideas about "unique qualities that cannot be compared to anything." Self-defense, not only of eji jobs, not only against discrimination based on "character," but ultimately of eji bodies and eji lives. As Sartre has pointed out, the racist, whose beliefs are founded in mystic racial conceptions, cannot convince anyone by rational argument. Racists can and have, however, spread their views by violence. The eji, who live among the Gentiles, are too weak to stand up against that violence by force of arms. The anti-violence of their response takes the form not of bullets but of words. They wish to shoot down not people but arguments. And their fury increases when they find that the anti-Semites, secure in their physical superiority, do not wish to argue; indeed, they despise the Jew's "ill-mannered," "characterless" verbal vehemence. The eji's famous argumentativeness is actually a desperate expression of a need to substitute argument for violence. It conceals, says Sartre, a naive love for a communion in reason with his adversaries, and the still more naive belief that violence is in no way necessary in human relations. Where the anti-Semite, the fascist, etc., starting out with intuitions that are incommunicable and that he wishes to be incommunicable, must use force in order to impose the illuminations he cannot impart, the inauthentic Jew [i.e. the eji] seeks to dissolve by critical analysis all that may separate men and lead them to violence, since it is he who will be the first victim of that violence.

I imagine that at this stage someone will protest that the emphasis on abstraction is characteristic of all modern thinking, and not just that of the eji. True. What I have shown here are the specifically Jewish reasons for "thinking abstract." It is just these specific Jewish reasons that have created the fact I have attempted to explain: that while non-Jews are *proportionally* spread between the more abstract and the more "particularist" disciplines, the Jews are found *overwhelmingly* in the more abstract ones. Yes, Jewish sociologists are as excited about sociology and Jewish painters as enthused about painting as their Gentile peers. Yes, Einstein was truly dedicated to solving the mysteries of the physical universe; yes, Freud was sincerely interested in the psyche; yes, Schoenberg lived for pushing outward the limits of music. And yes, Jewish brains are built like other people's brains. Still, Jewish brains are borne by people with a Jewish experience, who must defend themselves against the implied or actual violence of the anti-Semite's racist particularism. (Of course — need we say it? — it is not some conspiratorial public relations headquarters that ordered that defensive fight but the imperatives of self-defence.) So, whatever other reasons there may also be for the eji's success in so many — but by no means all! — provinces of the world of the intellect, there is this, *too*: that the eji penetrated the outer limits of the arts and sciences to foster an "abstract" world view in order to create a medium in which Shylock's Defence, itself an abstraction, can best be propagated.

3

SPIRITUAL JEWS:
CULT, CULTURE,
COUNTER-CULTURE

I don't have any roots. I'm uprooted. My spirituality was drugs, hitchhiking, Kerouac, John Cage, and certain lyrics of Frank Zappa.

— Ron Mann, film-maker

"Monsieur Stoléru, are you French?" France's Secretary of State for Planning was asked. The insolent questioner was the right-wing extremist Jean-Marie Le Pen, whose political fortunes at the time seemed to be riding high. The moderator, knowing well the entertainment value of a television debate between an anti-Semite and a Jew, decided to pour his own oil on the fire, and rephrased the question: "Monsieur Stoléru, are you Jewish?" For some odd reason, the minister had expected a civilized discussion. "Jewish . . . " he muttered, "I thought that was a religion. It is not a nationality."

Hogwash. While Jewishness is not a matter of nationality, it is, as we have seen, definitely not only a matter of religion.

Stoléru's answer was, it is true, in the best French republican tradition. The orators of the French Revolution wanted the Jews to be treated just like everyone else, but the price they demanded was that the Jews (like the other important religious minority, the Protestants) confine their distinctive identity to private religious practice. It was a French count, an aristocratic ally of the middle-class deputies, who spoke the words that were to determine the direction of Jewish political emancipation throughout Europe for almost two centuries. "Refuse everything to the Jews as a nation, and give all to the Jews as individuals," thundered the Count of Clermont-Tonnerre, Stanislas Marie Adelaide:

> Refuse recognition to their judges; they should have none but ours; refuse to their Jewish Corporation the legal protection to maintain their so-called laws; they must not form within the State neither a body nor an order; they must be citizens as individuals. But, you'll tell me, they don't want to be that. Well, then! If they don't want to, let them say so, and we will banish them. It is repugnant that there should be in a State, a society of non-citizens, and a nation within a nation.

(This may have been the first time the phrase "nation within a nation" was used.)

Most Jews did not like the idea a bit. They fumed and even rebelled against their own emancipation as Napoleon's armies carried it to most of the continent, for they preferred to keep their communal, religious privileges even at the cost of accepting second-class status as citizens.

The mainstream (i.e. not Hassidic) Orthodox movement as we know it today was largely started in my own town of Bratislava. Its founder was Rabbi Moses Sofer

(1762–1839). Sofer was born and educated in the prosperous and largely anti-emancipationist community of Frankfurt, where his teacher Rabbi Phinehas Horowitz headed a vigorous campaign against the incipient Reform movement that stood under the influence of Moses Mendelssohn. Mendelssohn's philosophy and Jewish emancipation were, to Sofer, part and parcel of the same undesirable upheaval in the Jewish community. He regarded the way of life of the traditional eighteenth-century German-speaking Jews as a harmonious blend of piety and prosperity. Some of these (aristo*scratchy* Jews, Heine later called them) did very well out of their association with the old aristocracy — the Rothschilds rose as trustees for the money of a fabulously wealthy German prince who had to flee Napoleon. So Rabbi Sofer had no use for the Emancipation, which he saw as a sign that God wanted the Jews to stay in Exile. He ordered the pious to pray for redemption.

This state of things led to an odd paradox: the religious were loath to accept that Jewishness was "only" a matter of religion with no public, legal expression. On the other hand, the rapidly growing community of the "assimilated" (the sociological home of the eji) were those who, although often atheists, insisted, in concert with their Gentile benefactors, that "Jew" referred only to a religion.

Eventually, the Orthodox came around to support equal rights for Jews. But to this day the truly religious, Orthodox or not, seldom if ever say that their Jewishness is purely religious. The Jews who insist that being Jewish is "only" a matter of religion are normally not very devout at all. "I am not religious, personally," they add. They hope their interlocutor makes the connection: Jewishness is a

matter of religion; this person is not very religious; therefore this person is not very Jewish.

The reason the argument has largely gone out of
fashion is that as history proves, it convinces no one. Half
a century after Hitler, a Le Pen could still accuse a Jewish
minister of France of dual loyalty.

Stoléru himself knew how ineffectual his defence had
been. After the "debate," which ended with a handshake,
the poor politico reflected that having grown up in
Brittany, he should have said that he was "a Breton, like
Monsieur Le Pen himself . . ." But everyone knew that had
he done so, he would hardly have convinced the many
viewers who felt that Le Pen had "won the debate."

A little later, the same Le Pen was on television again,
this time taken on by Bernard Tapi, the controversial entrepreneur and football-club owner. Tapi opened up by declar-
ing that the reason he agreed to confront Le Pen (all major
politicians who were invited declined after the Stoléru performance) was expressly because he, Tapi, was a Jew. The
high point in the discussion came during one of Le Pen's
silly tirades on immigration. "Just because you have a big
mouth," interrupted Tapi, "you think you're right? The
French people detest you!" It was Le Pen's turn to squirm.
Viewer polls gave Tapi the victory by a large majority.

Tapi, not an intellectual — and not an eji — had chutzpah. He knew how to talk back to an anti-Semite. He had
no use for the worn-out slogan "It is only a religion."

The "religion only" defence does not work because it is
false. Not being religious does not make a person any less
typical a Jew — most modern Jews have not been devout.
For what has been the modern Jews' connection to historic
Judaism, to any of the authentic traditions derived from

the rabbis of old? For most of them, for Marx, for Einstein, for Kafka and their more recent intellectual descendants, the answer is simple: "None — or nearly none."

Yet, while the eji are seldom religious — certainly not in the traditional Jewish way — they, like other people, do have spiritual needs. How do they express them? This is the question that we now attempt to answer.

Eji Judaism

While very many eji are convinced atheists, others are not beyond cultivating a religious sentiment. Those who retain some sentimental attachment to the ancient rites often clothe their personal religion in a tailored-to-measure mantle of real or imagined Judaic symbols and practices. The fact that the result has nothing to do with historic Judaism does not prevent the "believer" from presenting it to the public as the real thing.

An occultist magazine published an interview with an elderly Jewish woman who claimed to be capable of communicating with animal spirits. A cancer sufferer, she said she had successfully used a leopard "ally" to fight her disease. Discussing her views of death, she told her interviewer that "Jews believe that God is everything. And death is just another part of life." Asked what happened after death, "according to her faith," she replied, "Well . . . you just end."

"That's it," asked the interviewer, "there's no afterlife, no reincarnation, no nothing?"

"Well, not really. You become one with God."

Anyone remotely familiar with Judaism can recognize how far such views are from the Jewish tradition. Ezekiel's vision of the rising dead and the fundamental Jewish concept of *haolam haba* (the world to come) are both lost sight of as the eji explains — for the benefit of the Gentiles — the merits of her "faith." ("Faith" is a Christian term seldom used by traditional Jews.)

The old woman could be dismissed as crazy, and perhaps she was. But many, perhaps most, perfectly sane eji hold the same view about what Judaism teaches on afterlife as she does. Like her, they present "their" religion in a way that would appeal to the non-Jewish readers of her interview. It is an old ploy, used to turn one's Jewishness from a liability into an asset: Present to the non-Jews ideas that you know they admire. Then say (and believe) that these are historic Jewish ideas. You will instantly be perceived as the holder of ancient wisdom. For you will be seen as a person who has in your very blood the same "truth" discovered by the non-Jew through patient soul-searching. That "nothing happens" after death except for us becoming one with God is an opinion that, however far it is removed from historic Judaism, can win you some like-minded Gentile friends.

The Love of the Prophets

When eji do refer to genuine Jewish teaching, they follow the same logic. Which part of the traditional Jewish religion is most impressive to liberal Gentiles (for the illiberal ones are hardly going to listen, anyway)? Most likely, the humanistic, pacifist, rebellious teachings of the Prophets.

The passion for social justice of a Marx or an Einstein is often attributed to the Prophetic heritage. Without disrespect to the many serious people who have said such things, I cannot help but wonder how something your ancestors studied can enter your own brain if you do not study it yourself. Such a transfer of knowledge is, I am afraid, just as mysterious and unlikely as that of the homework that many of us believed as children would migrate, while we were asleep, from the books under our pillow into our heads. It is, of course, not impossible that Marx, Einstein, and the myriad other eji who have fought for social justice have at times been inspired by some quote from the Prophets or another. But let's face it: since they did not study Judaism they probably found the quote not in a Jewish but a secular, if not a Christian, source.

Had they studied Judaism, they might have found that social justice is a motive not only in the Prophets but in the rest of the Hebrew Bible as well. And they would have found, certainly, that in traditional Judaism the Prophets, although important, play only a relatively minor role compared to the Torah. Yet the love of Torah is seldom found on an eji's lips. One cannot help but note that the eji predilection for the Prophets has to do not so much with Judaism as with Christianity. Christian dogma teaches that the Prophets foretold the coming of Christ, and Jesus himself is often considered a Jewish Prophet. So, in Christian eyes, it will increase your stature if you can speak with the authority of an heir to the Prophets.

In the same vein, many eighteenth-century Jews appealed to the then fashionable Freemasons by posing as experts on "Hebrew" secrets. Not surprisingly, these mysteries turned out to have a striking resemblance to Masonic beliefs.

From Cult to Religion
Since the early nineteenth century, however, it is not the occultists that the eji has mostly tried to impress with a

home-grown brand of Judaism. More often, Judaism is presented as an inspiration to the secular, the rational, the free-thinking — and above all, to the humanist who finds religious and ethnic differences unimportant. It is the Judaism of Shylock's Defence, a Judaism of Unchosenness.

Albert Einstein was typical in combining a distaste for historic Judaism with the rather contradictory conviction that Judaism embodied the most modern, humanistic, and rational values. Glancing disapprovingly at a group of black-garbed Orthodox Jews, he would remark that he could not understand why anyone would choose to live a life entirely devoted to an outmoded past. Yet Einstein also liked to attribute not only his concern with peace and justice but also his perception of a rational harmony in the universe to values inherited from Judaism.

The rationality of Judaism became the cornerstone of the ideology of the Reform movement, born in nineteenth-century Germany and carried to North America by German-Jewish emigrants. Its locus has long been the Hebrew Union College of Cincinnati. The rationalist Jews borrowed heavily from nineteenth-century progressive Protestants, who distinguished between "cult" and "religion." Cult included all the historic practices and "superstitions" of what was popularly regarded as religion, ranging from sacrifices, through religious services, to — some believed — even faith in a personal God. Religion was not such obscurantism but something more abstract. True religion was, according to the "progressive" theologians, something that appealed to the essential spiritual truth behind spiritual observance. The most progressive of the progressive went as far as to teach that this essential spiritual truth was the same in every religion. For example, taking communion in a church and reading the Torah in a synagogue ultimately are only two superficial ways of getting at the same truth: the truth of some spiritual power in the universe, which may or may not have to be called "God." In other words, cult is limited to a particular religious tradition, while religion is universal.

It was logical for the eji, who did not like differences between Jews and Gentiles, to choose this type of "religion." A super-religion that ignored the differences among particular religious traditions is an abstract religion after the eji's own grain: we saw in the last chapter how the eji's artistic and intellectual pursuits are abstract, emphasizing generalization and downplaying the world of concrete, particular distinctions. So it is not surprising that this universalist, "modern" view of religion did in fact have a Jew among its progenitors: the great seventeenth-century Dutch philosopher, a lens maker of Spanish-Jewish provenance, Spinoza.

Spinoza insisted that the deeper essence of religion (the Divine Law) did not depend on the particular religious cults, such as Judaism or Christianity, that expressed it: "Divine Law," he taught, "is universal to all people; nay ... it must be esteemed innate, and, as it were, ingrained in the human mind." Spinoza was saying to the Christians that their religion was not better than that of the Jews. The trouble was, he was also saying the same thing to the Jews: "Your religion is just like the religion of everyone else." He was a true eji, but a premature one. The local rabbinical authorities excommunicated him for his views. Spinoza responded by changing his first name from Baruch to Benedict. Both mean "blessed," and Spinoza wished to show that you could be blessed in any language and, presumably, any "cult."

Eventually, "modern" Jews came to accept Spinoza as a great thinker in the "enlightened" Jewish tradition. In many ways, he was a Reform Jew ahead of his time. Recently, Reform Jews have been very sensitive to tradition. Not so the early reformers. They got rid of all the "odd" customs, of the *yarmulke,* the *tallis,* the *tsitsis,* and at one time even experimented with a Sunday Sabbath. They brought flowers and organ music into their "temple." Indeed, they seemed to have sacrificed almost everything positive that distinguished Judaism from progressive Protestantism. There was one difference left: The Reform Jews did not believe in Jesus Christ. But that, they no doubt felt, was a matter of cult rather than religion.

Especially at the start, the Jewish reformists had a good bit of success convincing both Jew and Gentile of the rational nature of Judaism. Count Saint-Simon, the early nineteenth-century thinker and social activist in search of a rational religion, was quite taken in. He articulated his admiration by taking his disciples, who included a good number of Jews, on a ceremonial march to a synagogue.

Conversely, a church was not foreign territory to a reform Jew. Chajim Steinthal, one of the founders around 1860 of the *Hochschule für Wissenschaft des Judenthums,* a leading Berlin Reform Jewish institution, saw nothing wrong with visiting a Paris church during Passover, in order to hear Easter music. What did upset him, he wrote to his faithful friend Moritz Lazarus, was that the French kept talking and squirming during the performance. Steinthal, the Jew, knew how to behave like a fine German Protestant!

The Eji and Christianity

Of course, though Steinthal enjoyed Easter music, he did not have the slightest desire to become a Christian. On the whole, the eji have almost as little interest in converting to Christianity as do the religious traditionalists. They want to be treated like everyone else, but not by simply abandoning their own identity for the sake of someone else's. The eji want to be empowered by overcoming barriers; not to be humiliated by having to give up their own identity. Of the two values, though, breaking down barriers is the more important one. So during periods when this was necessary, a number of eji did become Christians, though hardly any did so out of religious conviction. Before World War I, many ambitious eji had no choice but to convert. This was the period when most famous Jewish converts to Christianity or their children made their name. Marx's father converted to be able to practise law, Wittgenstein's forebears did so to gain acceptance among the aristocratic partners of their banking firm. Mahler converted in order to become Director of the Vienna Court Opera. But even later, and even in North America, many Jews have converted in order to avoid vocational or social discrimination. In the United States, a significant number joined the Unitarian Church.

The choice is instructive. Of all the Protestant denominations, the Unitarians are probably the most universalist. They ask little more of their members than that they believe in God; and they are fully behind the tenet that God can be reached in different ways, including those provided by different religions. This of course means that to a Unitarian, Judaism is essentially just as valid as Christianity, or, in other words, that the Jews' religion is just like that of everyone else. In Unitarianism, the eji converts were seeking out, not so much a Christian church, as a religion that minimizes differences between religious groups. In other words, even as Christians they remained eji, dedicated to Shylock's Defence and to negating the differences between the Gentiles and themselves.

At one time there were so many Jewish converts to Unitarianism that someone made up a joke, which is still remembered by a Reform rabbi of my acquaintance. The Unitarian minister visits his friend, a rabbi. "Funny," he comments, "your Jews are so much more quiet than mine!"

Not only the Unitarians but liberal Protestants in general have attracted more Jewish converts than the Catholics, and for the same reasons. Liberal Protestants are more tolerant of the possibility that other religions may be equally valid ways to worship God — indeed, we have seen that it was liberal Protestantism that paved the way for "rationalist" Reform Jews. In North America, England, and Northern Germany, where most Christians are Protestant, conversion to Protestantism is the natural choice, and was taken by the great majority of the converts. In Catholic countries, on the other hand, the number of Jews who join the Church of Rome has understandably been very much higher. Yet even there an astonishing number of the Jewish converts have chosen Protestantism, considering how small the Protestant community was. In Vienna before World War I, Jews lived in a heavily Catholic environment. Among those who officially left the Jewish community, 42 per cent turned towards Rome, and 26 per cent declared themselves "without confession" — but a full 29 per cent became Protestant.

In recent years, pressure on us to convert for career

or social reasons has almost disappeared in most "enlight-ened" countries. Accordingly, the stream of Jewish con-verts to Christianity, which was never a very lively one, has slowed down to a mere trickle. The great majority of Jews — and in this the traditional and the "assimilated" are one — have always had an attitude to Christianity (if indeed they ever gave the subject any thought) that can be expressed in one question: Why settle for an imitation when we already have (or have already given up) the original?

Even a man like Benjamin Disraeli, Queen Victoria's controversial prime minister and a convert since his child-hood, was evidently not free of the sentiment. In his novel *Tancred* the hero, a nineteenth-century Englishman carry-ing the symbolic name Tancred, falls in love in the Holy Land with a beautiful Jewess named Eva, and tries, hesi-tantly, to convert her. Her rebuttal is clear:

> In this perplexity it may be wise to remain within the pale of a church older than all of them, the church in which Jesus was born and which he never quitted, for he was born a Jew, lived a Jew, and died a Jew; as became a Prince of the house of David, which you do and must acknowledge him to have been. Your sacred genealogies prove the fact; and if you could not establish it, the whole fabric of your faith falls to the ground.

Behind the argument based on birthright, which for Disraeli, the conservative, was quite understandable, lurks the general point that Judaism is the original, and Christianity, at best a reproduction.

The fact that most Jews have converted only as a matter of expedience has been recognized even by most of the converts themselves. The sarcastic Heinrich Heine said that his conversion had been motivated by a desire to own "a ticket to civilization." That it was not as much a ticket to civilized spiritual values as to civilized salons, he made clear in his odes to Jewishness, his *Confessions*.

To this day few Jews would differ with the Prague German-Jewish philosopher Fritz Mauthner. When asked to comment on the possibility of the Jews converting to Christianity, Mauthner replied, "There may be sincere converts, but I haven't met one yet." Mauthner's contemporary, the British writer Israel Zangwill, put it this way: "No Jew was ever fool enough to turn Christian unless he was a clever man."

From Cult to Culture

If revised Judaism gives spiritual solace to some eji, and Christianity to almost none, there is one substitute for traditional religion that counts most eji among its followers: the cult of Culture.

Strictly speaking, culture is not religion. But let us recall the Passover visit to a Paris church concert by Chajim Steinthal, the nineteenth-century Reform Jewish intellectual. What emotions did the fussy Prussian experience as he immersed himself in the music celebrating the Passion of Christ? His feelings were not Christian, they were not Jewish, but they were religious.

In Catholic countries the churches are open almost all the time, and everyone is welcome to walk in for a mass. To the non-Christian, the mass becomes a free concert. Only the lack of a fee differentiates the eji's encounter with

music in a church from what he or she might find in a
concert hall. That — and the setting. As a teenager, I would
sometimes visit a baroque church in one of Bratislava's old
alleys to listen to the beautiful sounds of the organ and the
choir. At times I bent my head in worship like the parish-
ioners in attendance. But I certainly did not think my feelings were that of a Catholic, and I did not for a second
contemplate becoming one.

· Particularly in the old churches of Europe — more or
less created for the purpose — the light filtering in from
the stained-glass windows high up, the statues and paintings of the saints, the smell of incense, and the candles
burning combine with the music to create a spiritual event
that can be appreciated without any commitment to a particular religious creed. The eji, free of any religious dogma,
is particularly qualified to esteem the experience. For it is
not prayers or rituals that inspire the religion of the eji. Eji
liturgy is "culture": art, cinema, the theatre, music.

The obsessive, and sometimes excessive, attachment of
some of the eji to "culture" is familiar to all. A rather sad
case is described by Julian Barnes, the British author, in his
presumably autobiographical, first novel, *Metroland*. The
book is about the relationship between the narrator — car-
rying the very Gentile name of Chris — and his boyhood
soul mate, Toni, who is Jewish. Their adolescence is spent
in reciting French quotations, visiting the British Museum,
and irritating lesser beings, principally adults. The trouble
starts when Chris goes to Paris and falls in love. To Chris's
enraptured letter reporting the happy news, Toni replies,

Get past the next set of lips and you might stir my
interest. What have you been reading, what have

you seen, and what, not who, have you been doing?

Predictably, the friendship is ruined as Chris gets married, founds a family, and settles in the suburbs. Toni goes on dreaming angrily, and, having lost Chris, fails to ever establish any other lasting and meaningful relationship. Caught in a world of rarefied "culture," he is as hopelessly cut off from mundane reality as any mystic or monk.

But is genuine religious vision really possible within religion-neutral "culture"? It is indeed, and no one has proved it better than Gustav Mahler. The naïve religious power of his *Second Symphony (Resurrection)* is well recognized. The highlight of this monumental work is the final movement, where orchestra and choir accompany a vocal duet:

> You will rise, yes, you will rise again,
> My dust, after a short rest!
> He who called you
> Will give you eternal life.
> You are sown in order to bloom again!
> The Lord goes to harvest
> And garners sheaves
> For us, who died.

A non-Jewish reviewer has described Mahler's version of the original poem by Friedrich Gottlieb Klopstock as "Christian in the broadest sense (although Mahler had not yet converted)." A strange comment, considering that the same reviewer had just noted that Mahler took out all "dogma" from Klopstock's verse. "The broadest sense" can here refer only to the commonality between Christianity and Judaism, and indeed all religions. Jesus is not mentioned in this or any other stanza of Mahler's text ("the Lord," *Herr*, does regularly refer to Jesus in Christian writing, but in Jewish texts it is the normal translation of *adonai*, the commonest Hebrew term for "God"). On the other hand, Mahler alludes powerfully to the Hebrew Bible. His vision of resurrection is fully consonant with even the most Orthodox Jewish version — not all Jewish texts on afterlife mention a heaven (Mahler does not either), but all speak of the resurrection of the dead. The image of the gatherer of sheaves evokes that of the poor Jew of the Bible, who was allowed by religious law to "glean" in the fields when the harvest had been completed.

To speak with one voice to Jew and Christian was, and is, the goal of every eji. In Mahler's case the voice was a deeply religious one. *The Second Symphony*

> is designed to be heard in a large, modern concert-hall: the secularized temple of a liberal bourgeoisie in which attention is focused on the conductor's podium, the equivalent of a high altar. In the closing years of the nineteenth century these tabernacles of music, graced with columns, sprang up everywhere: we have the Musikvereinssaal in Vienna (1870), the new Gewandhaus in Leipzig (1884), the Concertgebouw in Amsterdam (1887), and Carnegie Hall in New York (1891). Only in musical cathedrals such as these could Mahler's expansive symphonic style attain its proper effect. . . .

I once had the chance to visit a superb but monotonous art show in Vienna, which consisted almost entirely of

drawings of nudes by Gustav Klimt. It was a welcome distraction to find, in one corner of the exhibit, a pedestrian
painting by some unfamous Viennese. The picture showed
the interior of the Musikvereinssaal. At the turn of the
twentieth century, as much as today, this was one of the
world's foremost concert halls. In the orchestra and the bal-
conies, the painting showed seated all who were talented,
witty, or wealthy in the Vienna of the time. For the benefit
of the visitor, the exhibitors had attached a sketch, a sort
of a translation of the painting. In the picture, there were
monocles and moustaches; in the sketch, all faces were
blank and bore a number: number 9 Klimt, number 11
Freud, number 2 Schnitzler, number 7 Hofmannsthal . . .
An astonishing number were Jews (even if Klimt himself,
unlike many of the women he painted, was not Jewish).

I imagine that it was such a crowd that listened to
the first performances of Mahler's music. The
Resurrection, played in a religion-free cathedral like the
Musikvereinssaal, was able to raise in them a feeling of
intense religious devotion. And here, finally, Jews and
non-Jews engaged in a common form of worship, avoiding both the isolation of tradition and the humiliation
of conversion.

When I travel I make a point to hear the local symphony
whenever possible. And in places where many Jews live, in
New York, in Paris, in Toronto, I feel I still meet very much
the same crowd that once sat with Freud in the
Musikvereinssaal. Unmistakably Jewish ladies and gentlemen parade in their best suits and dresses during the inter-
mission; but occasionally even some of those who appear
to be goyim can be overheard talking of a trip to Israel or a
bar mitzvah.

There are two kinds of ritual that never fail to bring
tears to my mother's eyes: a synagogue service and a symphony concert. There is a connection between the two.
With some exaggeration, one could say that the ancient
rabbis substituted the synagogue for the Temple's ritual
slaughter grounds; and Mahler and his contemporaries
replaced the synagogue service with the musical ritual of
the symphony. It is true that this move from cult to culture
had something to do with class: the better-off eji, who had
easier access to education, are naturally more at home in a
symphony hall (or art gallery) than the Jewish "masses,"
who are predominantly lower-middle-class. However, even
the lower middle class are much more prone to appreciate
"culture" than non-Jews in a similar socio-economic situation. Compared to the upper middle class and higher, it is
true that the "ordinary" Jews might prefer Broadway to off-
Broadway, and the musical to the opera, yet there is a great
love of culture in all strata of the Jewish community, and
this includes "highbrow" culture as well as "middle-brow."

When our family immigrated to the United States in
the late sixties, our first acquaintance with American Jews
was with two men who lived nearby. They were both single,
they both liked to come over to eat some of our food, they
both spoke with a slight Yiddish accent, they both wore the
same polyester that was then in vogue in our predominantly lower-middle-class Jewish neighbourhood. One
man had a little appliance shop; the other played cello at
the Philadelphia Academy of Music.

My own mother was the daughter of parents who were
both strictly Orthodox and dirt-poor. But living in a
crowded, damp house in Budapest's worst *Ostjude* slum
did not prevent her from developing a deep affection for

classical music. Often she would sneak up to the Academy of Music Building, and, unable to afford a ticket to enter, would listen to the concert on the stairs outside, opening up her soul to the sounds that filtered out.

But . . . am I using the traditional eji cop-out of hiding my own vulnerabilities behind a Jewish Mother Joke? The symphony hall is a pretty tough place for my own tear ducts, not only my mother's.

From Culture to Counter-Culture

The symphony hall was only the first type of temple that helped the eji to substitute "culture" for "cult." From the beat generation on, a new, less European and less high-brow, yet equally spiritual, vision of "culture" began to assert itself. With Allen Ginsberg and then Bob Dylan, "counter-culture" took over from plain old "culture" the job of ministering to young Jews' spiritual needs.

Of course, John Lennon was not Jewish. The "counter-culture" was genuinely non-denominational. I am making no conceited effort to give the Jews credit for its creation, no matter how heavily Jews participated in it. There may have been a disproportionate number of Jews among the hippies, and particularly among some branches or off-shoots of the hippies, ranging from the Yippies to the Hare Krishnas. (My former sister-in-law, born in Israel, became a devotee of an "ashram." The guru, respectfully addressed by everyone as "baba," was an impressive figure: his head shaven, his face decorated with paint, and his large frame always resplendent in his orange robes. He was a Brooklyn Jew, once more prosaically referred to as Michael.) But the Jews never formed a majority in any of the counter-culture groups. As is so often the case, the Jews participated in a movement along with non-Jews, and for many of the same reasons. What matters in our context is that the Jewish youths also had additional reasons of their own. What "culture" did for many of their parents, "counter-culture" was doing for the Jews of the flower generation: it helped them define a spirituality that was not only meaningful but which they could share with the Gentiles.

"My family is Jewish," says Ron Mann, prize-winning documentary film-maker (*Comic Book Confidential* and *Twist*), "but I don't belong to anything. I don't have any roots. I'm uprooted." Mann follows with the statement I used as the motto for this chapter: "My spirituality was drugs, hitchhiking, Kerouac, John Cage, and certain lyrics of Frank Zappa." Of course, Kerouac, Cage, and Zappa are not Jews. The spirituality Mann reminisces of was shared by Jew and non-Jew alike. But it did not make the typical Gentile feel "uprooted." During the hippie period, many Christian hippies asserted their faith in Jesus. It was only for Jews like Mann that "alternative" culture meant a radical abandonment of ethnic and religious roots.

I was not one of these. Rather, I was one of those who found in the "counter-culture" a streak that brought me closer to rather than farther from my Jewish background. There was, certainly, no equivalent of the "Jesus freaks" among the Jews, though a few young rabbis with beards and beads had some success with singing religious songs to the accompaniment of a folk guitar. But there was another way you could assert your Jewishness without losing the respect of your friends: the "kibbutz trip." Israel did not yet have the reputation of The Enemy of the Third World — that came later. But it did have the reputation of having good hashish. On the kibbutz, one met a good number of non-Jewish volunteers, *some* of whom came mainly to enjoy the cannabis. The intoxicant was feared and detested by most kibbutzniks, but it was freely available, and cheap, in the towns. It was quite a boost to the young eji's ego to share a joint indiscriminately with Jewish and non-Jewish friends, but on Jewish soil. You were like everyone else, but you were like everyone else, literally, on your own, Jewish ground. For once, being like everyone else did not mean giving up the way *we* were, and becoming like *them*. We and they met halfway.

For me, halfway was the yet largely undeveloped resort of Eilat, where I travelled after my kibbutz stint. There, we spent our nights sleeping on the beach in tiny shacks made of cardboard boxes. In our party there were, along with Jews from all over the world, several non-Jews: an American ex-Marine, an Irishman, and a Maori from New Zealand with his white, Gentile wife. Supposedly, Israel was in a state of war with Jordan, whose border was only a stone's throw away. But all we saw in the magnificent red dusk of the desert mountains, which rose like rocky icebergs from the deep azure of the sea, was the peace of God, a peace that spoke from the times of Sarah and Abraham to all of us, Jews, Christians, and Moslems alike. At night, the empty desert was illumined by the dark-blue heavens splattered by a million crowding, brilliant stars. Often, the Israeli patrol would come and share our tea. One soldier, originally from Morocco, later invited us to his house. We listened to Judeo-Arabic music, and smoked some "hash."

We read *Steppenwolf* by Hermann Hesse. We listened to rock and folk music. We spent hours sipping coffee at the little beach café near our cardboard abodes, never bothering to find out why the music the owner put on was always Greek. Just about the only identifiably Jewish author or artist we were interested in was Leonard Cohen. But we were as "high" on being Jewish as an eji ever could be. Here for a moment was eji utopia: We remained proudly Jewish, yet were "sitting as brothers" (to use the famous biblical phrase) with our Gentile friends, members of the same counter-culture.

One day, a young Swede, a young American Jew, and I swam to a little rocky island off the beach south of Eilat. Taken in by the intense spirituality of the sun-drenched landscape, we chanted the holy syllable of the Indian masters: "ohhmmm. . . ." Then, under the embarrassed eye of our Swedish friend, we two Jews bent down and kissed the rock, touching our lips to the Holy Land. That was the one time on that visit to Israel that I ever allowed my universalist, abstract eji spirituality to take on a distinctively Jewish colour.

I was there for five months, and never saw the inside of a synagogue.

4

GUILT-RIDDEN JEWS: LIVING WITH THE MYTH OF JUDAS

The Jew is the Anti-human. The Jew is the creation of another God. The Aryan and the Jew . . . if I call the one Human, I must call the other something else. . . . He cannot be Man in the sense of being the image of God. The Jew is the image of the Devil.

— Adolf Hitler

The eji may well wish to dissolve any discussion of differences between Jews and non-Jews in the abstract declaration of faith, that "our differences don't matter as much as our similarities." But the anti-Semite is not interested in abstraction. The anti-Semite has a very specific idea of what the Jew is like. And willy-nilly, the eji, living in a society permeated by anti-Semitism, has to respond. For the anti-Semite's image of the Jew has justified vicious slander, discrimination, and murder. Preferring to limit public discussion to the "high" levels of abstraction, it is at the personal, private, individual level that the eji copes with the specific charges of the anti-Semite. To be an eji means to worry ceaselessly, but mostly privately, about what non-Jews (who always *might* be anti-Semitic) think of you. It can be a frightening experience, fraught with self-doubt, self-hate, and self-destruction.

And so it was that on October 4, 1903, screams of terror assaulted the riders and pedestrians in the quaint Viennese suburb of Döbling, as they passed the house where Beethoven died. Those who stopped to investigate learned that a young man had shot himself in the mouth. The dead man laid out on the floor was Otto Weininger, a Jew and an anti-Semite, celebrated author of *Sex and Character*. This worldwide bestseller was a misogynous "classic" that accused the Jews of effeminate cowardice. The choice of the Beethoven shrine was symbolic. Weininger's death was a sacrifice to a god of Culture, the eji's religion. The disturbed youth wanted to do what he felt he could not achieve in life: to join himself to the giants of Germanic civilization.

It was not this, however, that Weininger wrote in his suicide note. That said simply: "I kill myself so as not to kill another." What, at the level of the intellect, were lofty strivings, took, at the level of raw emotion, the form of uncontrollable fury. The known diaries and correspondence of Weininger, a dark and awkward young man of unathletic stature, reveal no evidence that he was ever loved by a woman. His misogyny was probably in large measure the expression of a youth scorned by the opposite sex. Though his book was a success with many influential Gentiles, there is no evidence that, on the whole, the goyim accepted him much better than women did. The young man who dreamed of being admired as a great German knew that, to the Gentile in the street, he was indistinguishable from the Jews he so despised. Weininger was a very angry man, and he feared that he could no longer contain his rage. If he could no longer repress it, who knows who might become its victim.

Weininger's book had been a great success, fondly referred to by the likes of Sigmund Freud and the great Swedish playwright August Strindberg. Weininger claimed that all individuals have something of the male and something of the female in them, as well as something of the Gentile and something of the Jewish, and buttressed his case with precise mathematical-looking formulas. The male and the Gentile were, to Weininger, the active and the heroic part of every person's character. The female and the Jewish were the passive and the cowardly, seeking to satisfy selfish needs by deceit and guile. In the mock-scientific fashion in vogue at the time, Weininger gave precise formulas about how the male and female (and the Gentile and Jewish) interacted in a person's character. The presence of a Gentile element in every Jew could, presumably, allow a male Jew to develop his Gentile side and so to become a "real" man. It seems, though, that in the end Weininger decided that he was not man enough, and too much of a Jew. I will return in another chapter to this crisis of Jewish masculinity, which, unfortunately, was not limited to Weininger, and which continues among Jewish men of our own day. Here I note only that a young Austrian was so obsessed by what he saw as the tragedy of his Jewishness, that he considered avenging it by "killing another." It was only some last glimmer of a moral compunction that made him turn the weapon on himself; remaining, as a Jew and as a person, in life as in his writing, the ultimate self-hater.

Jews and Suicide

Weininger's suicide seemed to fit into a tragic pattern. In

the family of a fellow-Viennese Ludwig Wittgenstein, there were several suicides. Another victim of what appeared almost as a wave of self-destruction was the brilliant young Italian-Jewish philosopher, Carlo Mittelstaedter, whose brother had killed himself first.

These sad cases of self-inflicted violence were proof, if proof were needed, that the Jewish experience was often a desperate challenge, and one that some found impossible to bear. The need to prove that the Jews were like everyone else was not some sort of purely intellectual urge. It was also an exasperated attempt to prove that things were not what they sometimes seemed and that the Jew among the Gentiles was not condemned eternally to an existence of forced, despised solitude. But the hope that Shylock's Defence would work to free Jews from the predicament of their social existence was not a hope that Weininger shared.

Suicide is an individual tragedy, yet, strangely, it shows group patterns. This was one of the earliest puzzles addressed by modern sociology. The classic work in the field is Émile Durkheim's *Suicide*, written in 1897. Without any explicit reference to his own people, Durkheim stated that "the educated man who kills himself does not kill himself because he is educated but because the religious society of which he is a part has lost its cohesion." Durkheim was undoubtedly thinking of the tragic increase of suicides among the Jews. Statistics such as the ones in the table below, reported by the anthropologist Maurice Fishberg on the basis of the official censuses of Prussia, spoke clearly of the Jews as the "religious society" most affected by the general rise in self-inflicted deaths.

Suicides per 100,000 deaths, by religion, Prussia 1849–1907

	1849–55	1869–72	1907
Jews	46.4	96	356
Catholics	49.6	69	104
Protestants	159.9	186	254

As for the United States, Fishberg estimated that 40 per cent of all suicides in New York were Jewish, while the Jews made up only 20 per cent of the general population.

Not surprisingly, the dismal picture on suicide was matched by disturbing reports about mental illness among the Jews. Most cases would today be described as neuroses. "In London and New York," Fishberg writes, "the clinics of nervous diseases can be seen daily to be overcrowded with Jews, and most physicians have noted that no matter what their Jewish patient complains of, his malady is usually colored by the nervous strain which is predominating over all other symptoms." At the Vienna clinic for nervous diseases in 1901, a disproportionate number of the patients were Jews (17.7 per cent of the men and 15.3 per cent of the women, when the Jewish population of the city was 8.86 per cent).

"Vienna is a veritable Mecca for the sick and afflicted Jews of Austria," Fishberg adds, "and particularly Galicia and the Bukowina, and to a certain extent also from South Russia and Rumania. Many who suffer from some intractable disease or defect go to consult some famous specialist in Vienna; even some who are very poor often beg their way to Vienna in hope to obtain relief." Jews, it seemed, were flocking to see a "nerve doctor," the way the

Hasidim travelled to the court of a famous rabbi.

The "neurotic Jew" became a new anti-Semitic stereotype. The anti-Semites were quick to kick their enemy
when he was down. They exaggerated, exploited, and
derided the fact that there were indeed many "nervous"
Jews. Commenting on the great French-Jewish actress
Sarah Bernhardt, the anti-Semitic author Édouard
Drumont mused about a photograph published in the
yellow press, which purported to show Bernhardt lying in
a coffin: "Sarah Bernhardt, with her macabre imagination,
her white satin coffin in her room, is clearly sick." And,
speaking of the general mental state of the Jews he added,
"This neurosis the Jew has, strangely, ended up communicating to all our generation." Those who had once been
accused of poisoning wells to spread the Black Death, now
were supposed to sow the seeds of the "nervousness" that
seemed to be an affliction of modern times.

On the whole, the medical profession was not very
understanding, either. Wilhelm Erb, a distinguished physician, director of the Medical Clinic and "Protector" of the
University of Heidelberg, was on occasion quoted approvingly by Sigmund Freud. However, Freud omitted referring
to Erb's remarks on the Jews. In an 1893 speech celebrating the birthday of the Grand Duke Frederick of Baden,
Erb attributed neurosis to overstimulating the nerves. Due
to the then common belief that characteristics acquired
during one's lifetime could be passed on to one's offspring,
Erb was able to conclude that neurosis was a racially inherited feature of population groups who have taxed their
nerves too much. Neurasthenia and hysteria, he believed,
occurred preponderantly among,

some races and peoples, e.g. among the Latin peoples, and quite especially among the Semites, which latter's neurotic disposition is presumably founded in their earliest family experiences. Because of their untamable acquisition drive, their centuries-old life style, as well as their inbreeding and marriage to relatives, nervousness is common among them to an astonishing degree.

Has the picture changed in recent decades, particularly as psychiatric diagnoses have undoubtedly experienced an improvement, and ethnic prejudice has hopefully been eliminated from the psychiatrist's judgment? There is a relative lack of good recent data on mental illness among the Jews. The United States has the only Diaspora community today that can be compared in numbers and importance to those of pre-World War II Europe, and the American government does not publish mental illness and suicide statistics by religion. What we know is that in the early 1950s twice as many Jews were treated for neuroses — per capita — as non-Jews in New York. This may have been due to the immediate postwar situation. During this period, mental illness was undoubtedly high among immigrant survivors of the Holocaust. It is possible that the situation has improved since then, but we have no recent statistics, and we cannot be sure.

Certainly, the anti-Semites have not let up on the theme. One of the dark spots of the 1992 American presidential race was David Duke's campaign for the Republican nomination. The year before, Duke had run for governor of Louisiana but lost because of his record as a racist and anti-Semite. Among the comments that had come to haunt him was his remark on "Jewish sicknesses," as supposedly depicted in the novels of Philip Roth. And even "moderate" opinion in North America has no doubts about the Jews being more neurotic than the rest: A ridiculously self-torturing, pathologically analytical person is dubbed "a Woody Allen."

What a gap between the Woody Allen symbol and the confident portrait the journalist Joseph Alsop painted of himself as a member of the "WASP ascendancy." "Above all, if you belonged to the WASP ascendancy," he wrote, "you knew pretty well who you were. I have never to this day understood the phrase 'identity crisis' or, indeed, understood why people had identity crises."

Unfortunately, by far not all WASPs can make the same statement. And, on the other hand, there are a lot of self-assured, easygoing, happy Jews. But statistics don't lie. Being a Jew has been, and no doubt often still is, hard on the nerves. Some crack under the challenge. The high Jewish suicide rate suggests that we take a long look at the Jewish experience, outside the customary realm of light comedy and gushy platitude. Something has been bothering the Jews, very, very much.

When so many people of a certain background decide to end their lives, what are they trying to say? And, more important in this case, what has been said of them, and to them? For in the debate between the eji and the anti-Semites, it is not the Jews who have spoken first. The message of the eji, be it in the form of artistic or scientific work, of a comedian's routine — or of a suicide note — often has a hidden dimension in which it is a reply; a reply, above all, to the anti-Semite. So in order to understand the eji, we must first fully understand what they are responding to. We would not have produced so many "abstract thinkers" if it were not for the concrete accusations of the anti-Semites. Nor would we have produced so many neu-rotics. To understand how this happened, we must first understand the charge brought against the Jew by the anti-Semite.

The Unfathomable Charge

Let us steal some terminology from the philosophers, and observe that for us Jews the *existence* of anti-Semitism is there before its *essence*. We know we are hated before we know why. The first thing I found out about anti-Semitism was that many people hated us. Sometimes classmates would forget I was there and tell an anti-Jewish joke. Others smiled at me contemptuously when they talked of their going to church. Friends' parents would occasionally cut off a conversation when I entered their dining room, but not soon enough for me to miss the word, "Jew."

"Jew" was, I believe, the word I remember one older boy calling me, and then coming up to me to slap me. But I am not sure this really happened. I may have assimilated the event from someone else's story. Or perhaps it was a night-mare I once had.

The one shocking experience that did wake me up to the dark intensity of the hatred against us was seeing pho-tographs of mass graves filled with the bodies of Jews of my parents' generation. After the teacher had showed us these terrible images, I learned to look differently at the only family photo surviving in my father's possession. It showed a contented, well-fed family of six children, surrounding my father's parents. Except for my father and two broth-ers, no one else had survived. I was gripped by anger and fear. Could they do this to *me?* And why would they, why did they do it to anyone?

It is a painful, lifelong process, trying to find out. I do not think we ever quite do.

First of all, a Jew never really knows who is an anti-Semite. Woody Allen reveals this sensation in his film *Annie Hall.* The character portrayed by Woody visits the genteel mid-Western family of his girlfriend, played by a charmingly strait-laced Diane Keaton, who was then Allen's mate in real life. As Woody sits down to eat at the elegantly set table, in the eyes of the WASP grandmother he is transformed into a traditionally dressed and coifed Orthodox Jew. Woody seems to equate this Gentile family with the Nazis, who in one of their famous propaganda films showed modern-looking faces of Jewish men fading out, then fading in with side curls and beards. What if the same sequence is played inside the head of every Gentile, hidden behind the polite front? The fear, however much recognized as absurd by the mind, is a nightmare known only too well by almost every Jew.

That secret anti-Semitism may lie behind the façade of Gentile politeness is not only the opinion of the Jews. Frankly anti-Semitic authors have always claimed that they were only saying out loud what everyone else believed. An 1850 pamphlet *(Das Judenthum in der Musik)* attributed to Richard Wagner, the composer, declares bluntly that its aim was "not to say something new, but to explain the unconscious sensation experienced in the People as an inner aversion against Jewish Being; thereby to give expression to [*auszusprechen,* lit. to speak out] something that truly exists, and by no means to bring to life something unreal through the power of imagination."

The antipathy between Wagner and the Jews has been largely mutual (although many Jews, including, for example, Lévi-Strauss, have spoken admiringly of him). Freud described Wagner's *Parsifal* as "puberty-idealism." A turn-of-the-century Viennese anecdote tells of an anonymous Jew who went to see the same opera. "What good is this? It didn't make me laugh," complained the disappointed spectator *(ich kann nicht lachen)*, painfully. In Israel, a powerful informal prohibition inhibits anything approaching a fair presentation of the Wagner repertoire. For more than forty-three years following the establishment of the State, not a sound of Wagner's music was heard on any professional Israeli stage. (Daniel Barenboim first performed a selection of Wagner with the Tel Aviv Philharmonic Orchestra, on December 27, 1991.)

But why Wagner? Many other great composers were anti-Semitic. Beethoven, for example, refused to perform in a concert hall because it was in a hotel rented by the Rothschilds. It's just that Wagner's anti-Semitism was spoken out loud. It is a relief to be able to hate him; he provides an identifiable target. In the case of the vague, civil, hidden anti-Semitism of the polite, one does not know where to shoot.

Far worse still than not knowing who is accusing you is the feeling that you do not know what you're accused of. "Why did they do it?" asks the Jewish child confronted with the Holocaust. "Why do they hate us?" And worse yet, "What did I do?" It is difficult to believe that you can be hated so, yet be totally innocent. You feel the weight of the guilt, though you are not aware of having committed any crime.

To be indicted by an anonymous accuser who does not bring clear charges, to feel guilty though you've done nothing — this is an experience that has had its poet: Franz Kafka.

"Someone must have libeled Joseph K. because, without having done anything wrong, one morning he was arrested." So begins Kafka's novel *The Trial*. (K. stood for Kafka, obviously.) Bertolt Brecht said that the works of the pallid bank clerk of Prague were "damp, dark, and hard to reach, requiring great skill and expert knowledge to read, as though they were illegal writing, made dark by fear of the police." Yet there were no police looking for Kafka, nor did he do or even write anything that might earn him an arrest warrant.

Kafka lived in a nightmarish world where all appearances were suspect, yet appearances were all that there was:

> For we are like branches in the snow. They seem to be lying flat there, and it looks as if with the smallest effort one could push them aside. But no, one can't do that, because they are firmly attached to the ground. But you see, even that only seems to be so.

The Kafkaesque anti-hero languishes in court waiting rooms, uncertain of what he was charged with and by whom; or he gazes towards a hill where his faceless ruler lives in an impenetrable castle. The master of the castle threatens to deliver a terrible judgment, and the accused seems to realize that he is considered guilty. But of what? All is enigma: what is the crime, who is the judge?

Some Kafka specialists have thought that the accused was universal, sinful humanity, and the judge was no other than God. But if so, it was hardly the God of Israel. God has become irrelevant to Kafka. Even his synagogue goers, who pay attention only to the outward forms of worship, no longer pursue the impossible task of knowing Him. In one of Kafka's short stories, "In Our Synagogue," God appears as an irrelevant, frivolous Beast that inhabits the synagogue:

> ... it is only the women that fear the Beast, the men have become indifferent to it long ago ... Of course, it is neither fear nor curiosity that keeps the women excited. If they devoted themselves some more to praying, they could fully forget the Beast. Indeed, the pious women among them would have forgotten it, if the others, who constituted the great majority, let them. These others, however, wanted to be noticed, and the Beast offered them a welcome excuse to that end.

It is reported that Kafka considered passages like this hilarious. Nihilistic humour was the only solace of a man to whom the whole world was a mask, and under the mask there was nothing that could be known.

The guilt imputed to the Kafkaesque hero has all the trappings of Original Sin, but without Paradise, and without God. There is something here that applies to the world of the eji as a whole, well beyond the boundaries of Kafka's dimly lit interiors. The eji as a psychological type appears to prove that it is possible to feel guilty of crimes one does not believe one has committed, and to fear a God one does not believe exists. In *Broadway Danny Rose* Danny, played by Woody Allen, feels utterly guilty, though he does not know why: "It's important to feel guilty," he says:

> Otherwise you . . . you know . . . you're capable of terrible things . . . you know . . . it's very important

to be guilty. I'm guilty all the time, and I never did anything, you know. My . . . my rabbi, Rabbi Pearlstein, used to say we're all guilty in the eyes of God.

When his girlfriend asks if he believes in God, Danny replies: "No. No, *but I'm guilty over it.*"

Woody betrays his lack of knowledge of Judaism by attributing the doctrine of Original Sin ("we're all guilty in the eyes of God") to a rabbi, for that is a Christian not a Jewish doctrine. According to it, we continue to be guilty as the result of what the first people did in the Garden of Eden. We have not earned this guilt, yet we stand accused of it. We are born marked with it.

In Kafka's odd mythology, as in Woody Allen's tortured humour, the Fall from Eden is absent, but the attribution of guilt stays the same.

Kafka's vision of guilt has profound meaning for both Gentile and Jew. As usual, we deal only with its Jewish aspect: There is something that the Jews in particular are supposed to have done, something they know they have not personally committed, yet something that stays with them from crib to grave. But what is this something? What is the specifically Jewish Original Sin — a sin not committed, yet one that we Jews continue to be charged with?

Possibly, it is not that we do not know the answer, but that we have allowed it to become unconscious (Ernest Gellner, the British-Jewish anthropologist, mused that "The Unconscious is a new version of Original Sin.") As if to explain this puzzle, the father of psychoanalysis developed a fantastic scheme, which some have understood as the fruit of cocaine-induced delirium.

In *Moses and Monotheism*, Freud speculated that the Jews continue to feel culpable of an ancient crime. Tradition holds that when Moses came down from Mount Sinai with the Tablets of the Law, he beheld the Israelites frolicking around the idol of a golden calf. Angry and frustrated, he broke the Tablets. In punishment, he was ordered to die in solitude, and not allowed to reach the Holy Land. It is because he died alone that his grave was never found.

For this scriptural story, Freud substitutes a veritable thriller. He says that the Jews murdered Moses. They buried him in a secret grave, then covered up all traces of the act. What they could not quite totally suppress, however, was the racial memory of the event. Unconsciously, the Jews do remember. Hence their ever-continuing feelings of guilt.

The fantasy of us killing Moses has received, to put it mildly, little support from those who should perhaps know: Biblical scholars, historians, archaeologists. And it is, let's face it, a bit odd that we should be feeling guilty for something that 1) we do not know our ancestors did, and 2) no one except Sigmund Freud has ever accused them of doing (though Salvador Dali was quite taken with the idea, and provided one of the editions of *Moses* with some remarkable illustrations). There is, however, another mythological crime of which we have indeed been widely accused, and for centuries. The way Freud transformed the vision of this other murder into that of Moses is nothing short of astonishing for someone who decoded so much of the protective symbolism of the unconscious. It was not the guilt of murdering Moses that plagued the Jewish soul, but the imputed murder of killing another visionary leader sprung from among the Jews — Jesus Christ.

In fact, Freud was well aware of the possible parallels between his version of Moses' end and the story of Jesus, but he declaimed that "The obvious connection of this with the destiny of the founder of a later religion does not concern us here." Perhaps he should have said "should not concern us here." It is likely that one of Freud's hidden agendas was to deflect the charge of that other murder from the Jews: "look at us as Moses-killers, not as Christ-killers," he was trying to say. This is the meaning of the rather opaque passage on anti-Semitism:

> The poor Jewish people, who with their habitual stubbornness continued to disavow the father's murder, atoned heavily for it in the course of time. They were constantly met with the reproach, "You killed our God!" And this reproach is true, if it is correctly translated. If it is brought into relation with the history of religions, it runs: "You will not admit that you murdered God (the primal picture of God, the primal father, and his later reincarnations)." There should be an addition declaring: "We did the same thing, to be sure, but we have admitted it and since then we have been absolved."

To Freud, *both* Judaism and Christianity have father-figure Gods who get reincarnated in human form. The Jews have Moses, the Christians have Jesus. "Our religion is just like yours!" he, the eji, is saying. Naturally, nothing could be further from Jewish theology. Judaism does not see Moses as divine. To Freud, however, this is just part of the cover-up. In Moses' time, he is saying, the prophet had indeed been regarded as a reincarnation of God; and that he is no longer so regarded is most likely a matter of repressing unpleasant memories. The memory of having killed a human teacher is bad enough, but the memory of having killed God would have been intolerable. We may deny it, Freud is telling us, but both we and the Christians have witnessed a reincarnation of God. And both of us killed Him.

We killed Moses, Freud says, and the Christians killed Jesus. However, the Christians admitted to killing Jesus, and have been absolved. We have not admitted to killing Moses, and have not been absolved, though Freud does not say what *not* being absolved means. But it is likely that what he meant was precisely our diffuse, subconscious feeling of guilt, the stuff of which Kafka's world is woven. For in Freud's teaching, guilt feelings can only be assuaged if we own up to our real or supposed crimes.

When Freud talks about the Christians owning up to their murder of Christ, he is alluding to official Christian dogma. The mainstream Christian position is that all Christians (as humans) are responsible for the death of Christ: it was the universal evil in all humans that killed Jesus. Being Jewish (or Roman) has nothing to do with the crime. What Freud is missing, however, is that those many Christians who do indeed admit their own responsibility for the killing of Christ are not the same ones that blame the *Jews* for the deed. The Christian anti-Semites most definitely do not admit to killing their own God, a crime that they blame without hesitation on the Jews.

It may not matter to sophisticated theologians just who killed Jesus, but it matters all too often to the ordinary worshipper. It matters, I think, even to Freud. For there is something childish about his position. To the anti-Semite who says, "You killed our God," he is replying, like a child taunted by playmates, "No, you did!" And if the anti-Semite should generalize and say, "You're all God-killers," Freud would shout back, "So are you!"

Most Jews are content to point a finger at the Romans. Just as it is important to the anti-Semites that it was specifically the Jews who killed Jesus, it is important to us that it was specifically the Romans. Not the Greeks, not the Swedes, not the Azerbaijanis, but the *Romans.*

In the Europe of my father and the two or three generations before him, all educated people, and certainly all educated boys, grew up on a hard-to-digest diet of Latin grammar drills. The unappetizing concoction was served up by pedantic Latin teachers at the *lycée,* the *gymnasium,* or the *grammar school.* The Latin teacher was practically never Jewish, and often had church connections. Many of the Jewish children were sincerely fascinated by Roman history. But it was nevertheless clear that the hoopla about Latin and ancient Rome was very much a goyish thing. The Latin teacher held out the speeches of Cicero and Marcus Aurelius as the paragon of civilization. So it gave Jewish pupils some satisfaction to know that it was this people, the Romans, so idolized by the goyim, who crucified their own God. It was the ancestors of the popes that killed Jesus! "*We* didn't do it; *you* did!"

The Myth of Judas: Money and Christian Blood
But is this still of any importance today? I admit that I do not often think about who killed Jesus. Neither do, I believe, most Jews or non-Jews today. The issue seems obsolete, medieval, like alchemy and the sword of King Arthur. Modern anti-Semites couldn't care less. Although more vicious by far than their medieval forebears, they

have for the most part not been religious. Since they do not believe in Christ, how could they persecute the Jews for being Christ-killers? And since they do not hate the Jews for killing Christ, the Jews could not — so the argument goes — themselves be much concerned with the charge, either. Should we not forget about the Christ story as a source of anti-Semitism today?

True, Lenny Bruce used to end a comedy routine by declaiming unambiguously, "We killed him." Much more recently, a Jewish comedian at the Los Angeles Improv told a joke that went somewhat like this:

> It was hard growing up a Jew in New Hampshire. I was the only Jew at my school. I played basketball for our team, St Catherine's. Every time I'd step on the court, they blew the whistle on me. "What are you doing that for," I said, "I didn't do anything!" They replied, "You killed Christ!"

But is such humour any evidence that we still worry about the ancient accusation against us? Is this not, after all, just a joke?

As Winston Churchill said, a joke is a serious matter; and as Freud pointed out, jokes have a relation to the unconscious. There is every reason to believe that the comics' jokes are pointers to the fact that the Myth of Judas is still with us, though it now lives mainly in our unconscious. Anti-Semites still feel just as hateful, and the Jews just as singled out by a dark accusation of guilt, as when the Jews were still consciously accused of killing the Son of God. Students of mythology know that myths do not necessarily lose their power as they are transformed, and their origin recedes into the unconscious. Quite often, the very opposite is the case.

The charge of Christ-killing has not disappeared; it has merely been transformed into new versions. The latest is known as "economic anti-Semitism," and accuses the Jew of the apparently more prosaic crime of trying to control the world through supposed Jewish riches. But this newer, "economic" anti-Semitism is itself an outgrowth of the older, "religious" kind. The Rich Jew myth, we will see, is an offspring of the Christ-killer myth. As such, it still shows a definite family resemblance to its predecessor.

Between today's economic anti-Semitism and the anti-Semitism based on the New Testament, there was another, earlier transformation of the Christ-killer libel. It is known as the Blood Libel: the fantastic story that the Jews kill a Christian child as part of their Passover ritual. Apparently rational people believed such nonsense to the extent that as late as 1911, a Jew was accused of ritual murder and tried by a Russian court. The trial was lengthy and difficult, but finally the Jew was acquitted under the weight of expert evidence.

When we look at the Blood Libel in detail, it is clear that its roots are not in any actual Jewish practice but in a per-version of Christian ritual; and in particular, of the Eucharist or the Holy Communion. In the Holy Communion, Christians eat the "host," a wafer dipped in sacramental wine. The wafer is traditionally associated with the body of Christ, and the wine, with his blood. The ritual alludes to the New Testament, when Jesus, predict-ing his death, passed out bread to his disciples, saying, "This is my body." Then he passed around the wine, and added, "This is my blood." The occasion was the Last

Supper, which was, as the New Testament makes clear, a Passover Seder. On the Seder, Jews partake of unleavened bread or matzah, handed out by the leader of the ceremony. They are also commanded to drink four cups of wine.

The Blood Libel reads Christian meanings into the Passover ritual, projecting the ceremony of the holy communion back into the Jewish celebration. In the communion, Christians drink the blood of Christ, and so do, according to the Blood Libel, the Jews during Passover. Only the Christians drink mystically consecrated wine, while the Jews, the anti-Christian vampires, drink the blood of Christ in the form of the blood of a Christian child. As a vampire lives on only by taking the life-force of its victims, so does the Jewish religion go on only by re-enacting the killing of Jesus in real blood. In order to recall Jesus more effectively, the Christian victim of Passover had to be a boy. It is apparently for this reason that, in most cases, the Jews were accused of killing a male rather than a female child.

As the influence of medieval Christianity waned in modern times, "economic anti-Semitism" became a new false charge, replacing the Blood Libel. This Greed Libel accuses the "rich Jew" of all the evil in the world that can be caused by, and committed for, money. The new, economic, anti-Semitism does not, on the face of it, have much to do with religion. But the Greed Libel as much as the Blood Libel has its roots back in the ancient anti-Jewish interpretations of the New Testament. There already, the Jew and money went very much together, as did Jewish money and Christian blood.

The New Testament holds that Jesus was crucified by soldiers acting on the orders of the Roman governor

Pontius Pilate. However, Pilate acted reluctantly, and only after heavy pressure from the official religious authorities of the Jews. These "scribes" charged Jesus with breaking Jewish religious law. The New Testament, consequently, presents the "scribes" as guilty of grave judicial error, religious intolerance, jealousy, and fateful moral judgment. Yet even these scribes are not made to look as despicable as the man who delivered Jesus to his tormentors, the traitor Judas. Judas was one of Jesus' disciples. It was his betrayal of Jesus to the scribes that led to Jesus' arrest and eventual death sentence. Judas did not denounce his master out of misguided religious conviction, personal antagonism, or rivalry. He did it for gold.

The Judas incident is absolutely essential to Christianity. For the life of Jesus is a parable, not only about Good against Evil, but also, specifically, about Good against Gold. Jesus loves the poor, not only because he feels sorry for them, but because he thinks them better than the rich: the meek shall inherit the Earth. He upsets the money changers' tables in the Temple. He declares that a rich man has no more of a chance to enter heaven than a camel to pass through the eye of a needle. Finally, his earthly life is cut down due to the treachery of Judas. The incarnation of God is destroyed by the incarnation of Gold.

Biblical names often convey a message about their carrier. Judas, it is hard not to notice, means "Jew."

Money as the enemy of the Holy — the idea need not always have anti-Jewish overtones. In the Middle Ages, it fired the rhetoric of the Christian rebels against clerical corruption. But in the twelfth century, which witnessed the first stirrings of a money economy in Europe, it lead the Pope to restrict Jewish "usury" and land purchases, and to authorize, directly or indirectly, the institution of expulsions and formal segregation. Later, the rhetoric that equated money with the unholy was picked up by the critics of modern capitalist society. Aristocrats and their friends spoke of how money was corrupting morality, and so did nostalgic nationalists mourning the rural past. More importantly perhaps, so did the socialists.

Not all of these varied critics of capitalism were anti-Jewish; most were not. But, as the Jewish socialists, for example, too often had to learn, the attraction of the Judas symbol was too strong. The Jews came to be hated for capitalism as they had been hated for the death of Jesus, and in both cases because of their role as the living metaphor for Gold.

According to a modern Jewish legend, when Jews were made to take last names (for many of them, this happened only in the nineteenth century), officials often assigned to them names that had to do with the noble metal: Goldstein, Goldfarb, Goldberg. They did this to mark the Jews as evil "Rich Jews," as they did when they gave them names starting with "silver" (Silberman, Silberstein). The story is suspicious on several counts. For one thing, it is hard to see why Russian officials would have given the Jews Yiddish or German-sounding names (most "Jewish" names are words that are identical in Yiddish and German), for not only were Yiddish and German not official languages in Russia, but they were also languages that most Russian officials did not understand. Secondly, Jews also carry entirely acceptable and pleasing names like Rosenthal ("rose valley"), Greenberg (German Grünberg, "green mountain"), Zucker ("sugar"), and Himmelfarb ("heaven-colour"). Most likely, in the early period of modernization

the Jews were not yet eji about their image. They freely
chose names they considered pleasing: names of natural
formations, pleasant colours — and of metals that symbolize wealth. It was only later on that they sensitized
themselves to the rhetoric of modern anti-Semitism, and
the label "rich Jew" became not a status to aspire to but a
badge of shame.

Rich Jews

It is not really strange that Gold should be metaphorically
imagined in the form of a people. In the allegories of fine
art, human vices are often represented as gods, satyrs, or
nymphs. In popular thinking, they may be thought of as
ethnic groups. Exaggerated orderliness and martiality is
represented by the German, self-tormenting introspection
by the Russian, superficial materialism by the American.
To John Donne, frivolity and corruption was epitomized by
the Italian: "Utopian youth, growne old Italian," he complained. In this pantheon of masks, there will always be a
need for the evil usurer, as long as "money makes the world
go 'round," and people do not like the fact. The Christian
anti-Jewish tradition ensures that the part will always be
confined to the Jew. (Even if understudies, such as the
American, are sometimes brought in — the parallels
between anti-Semitism and anti-Americanism beg for a
good study. In places like Malaysia, the Philippines or
Indonesia, it is often the Chinese who play the "Jewish"
role.)

Ethnic stereotypes of human vices help people blame
such vices on others, and so to think of themselves as
unblemished. The stereotype of the greedy Jew helps anti-
Semitic non-Jews to affirm that they themselves are free of

avarice. If the essence of greed is Jewishness, then it follows that Gentiles cannot really be greedy, unless they allow the Jews to contaminate them with the disease. "That Johnson is a Jew!" an anti-Semite might curse about a Gentile acquaintance. This means that Johnson is greedy, that he puts money first, that he does bad things to earn money. If "Johnson is being a Jew," it is that he has allowed his non-acquisitive, Gentile nature to be compromised by Jewishness. Johnson is being false to himself as a Gentile. It is the nature of the Jew to be greedy and dishonest, and it is the nature of the Gentile to be generous and true.

Anti-Semitism is, furthermore, not only a means to whitewash individual greed; it is, and this is crucial, also the means to whitewash rich Gentiles as a group, to make people distinguish between bad, Jewish money, and acceptable, Gentile money. Anti-Semitic "Aryans" put up with the idea that there may be people in society who are richer and more powerful than they. But the thought that a "foreign race" can gain the same privileges "only" through money irks them beyond tolerance. Herein lies, as Hitler well knew, the potential of anti-Semitism to create labour peace and the willingness of the disadvantaged to accept the privileges of their "betters." The rich who fear Jewish competition find something to share here with the poor who hate the humiliation of their social position. For the poor anti-Semite, poverty is an outrage if it must be endured while the "rich Jews" prosper, but it can be accepted if the riches are concentrated in the hands of "our people" who keep it away from the Jews. "Aryan" wealth can be enjoyed vicariously by the "Aryan" poor; it is family wealth, like that of the rich uncle who comes to visit every now and then and hands out presents. (The Nazis and their allies always made generous gifts of Jewish property to the populace.) It diffuses the danger inherent in a generalized revolt against the rich, and deflects it on the personage who is said to own wealth illegitimately: the Rich Jew. The English language has a verb, "to Jew," although it is, mercifully, less in use today than it once was. It means to extract money from someone, dishonestly.

The Jews are fully aware that the noun "Jew" is not exactly a compliment, either. A Jew, and certainly an eji, will not easily say, "I am a Jew," "Mr Hirsch is a Jew." The correct expression is "I am Jewish," "Mr Hirsch is Jewish." "I'm not really a Jew; just Jew-ish, not the whole hog," the British television and stage director Jonathan Miller once said.

"Jewish" is related to other ethnic terms by its suffix, "-ish": Irish, Polish, Turkish, Spanish. The "-ish" labels the Jews just as it does other people, and as such it supports Shylock's Defence; "Jew" on the other hand, singles out a people in its stark, isolated individuality, without the solace of a grammatical lifeline to others. That is why the anti-Semite loves the word as much as the eji hates it. In anti-Semitic diatribes, the Jewish businessman becomes a "Jew businessman," a Jewish doctor a "Jew doctor."

A recent incident demonstrated to me how I am, myself, still not free of the fear of the word "Jew." One morning I was walking down my street as usual, on the way to my office. It was autumn, the days were getting colder and shorter, the type of morning that makes it hard to get out of bed. No one else seemed to have made it out of their houses yet. And I certainly had to rub my eyes at what I saw: little white sports car parked at the curb, bearing a licence plate that declared in bold letters for all to see: IM

GAY. Though I consider myself as liberal as anyone about homosexuality, I admit I was shocked. "What chutzpah!" I thought, full of admiration for the unselfconscious homosexual. And I wondered how the word GAY must have slipped by the sanctimonious censors who have banished not only all four-letter words, but even YES — indeed even GOD — from licence plates. Then I walked to the front of the car, and saw a different plate attached to it, an ordinary plate with a mix of letters and numbers. I suddenly realized that the IM GAY plate was not real. It was a licence-plate look-alike that someone had attached on top of the regular plate. Perhaps it was some homophobic prankster practising his hateful nonsense in the middle of the night. More likely, though, it was the owner of the car, a homosexual himself. And I was thinking: we Jews still have a long way to go before we are quite out of the closet.

What if the licence plate read, IMA JEW? Or just: JEW? What would be *your* reaction if you saw one? If I saw WASP on a car, I'd take it to be a humorous statement of one's identity. If I saw BLACK, I'd consider it an expression of ethnic pride. If I saw ITALIAN, or even DAGO or SPIC, I'd think of it as a mixture of the two: humour and pride. I would probably think the same if the plate said JEWISH; but not if it said JEW. The word JEW spelled out loud and clear, to me, reverberates with vicious anti-Semitism. It is scribbled on walls next to swastikas and Stars of David. It is JUDE, the graffiti that identified businesses to be destroyed in the *Kristallnacht*, and the word written over the star that Hitler forced the Jews to wear.

Now let us continue the thought experiment a little further. Imagine that you see JEW on the licence plates of a rusty old Ford. And then imagine it on a Rolls-Royce. I

am certain that the Rolls would shock you more. WASP or
IRISH could appear on any sort of automobile, without
changing the effect. DAGO on the Rolls-Royce would
make one think of the owner as belonging to the Mafia —
the prime anti-Italian stereotype. JEW would mark the
owner out as the arrogant embodiment of mean, evil greed.

Of course, the rich Jew is not merely a metaphor. This
is a sensitive subject. But let's face it: as a Jewish stand-up
comedian once said, "Some blacks have rhythm. Some
Jews are rich."

The Jews have suffered, and in some cases still do
suffer, from unspeakable poverty; yet on the average, in
most places, and during most periods, they have been less
poor than the great mass of the Gentiles, who suffered
even worse. The dweller of the medieval ghetto was better
off than a peasant, the poor Jewish tailor in the Czar's
realm was often less poor than a Ukrainian hired hand.
Statistics show that today the Jews are among the wealthiest groups in many countries, and the wealthiest religious
group in the United States.

I do not wish to dwell on the well-known and well-taken
argument that the Jews were forced into moneylending
during the Middle Ages and that this is the origin of their
continuing association with money. The argument is, on
the whole, true. So are its twin contentions that a) "not all
Jews are rich," and b) "most of the rich are not Jews." But
why enter a debate that assumes at the start that if the Jews
are wealthy, then their wealth is something to apologize
for? I am Jewish, I am not rich — but, frankly, I could think
of worse things to happen to me than affluence.

I suppose that being rich is, in itself, no more a crime
than having rhythm. It depends on how you got your

riches, and what you do with them. "Rich Jew" would not sound so horrible (compared to "rich Swiss," or even "rich American"), if it were not associated with the demonism of the Judas stereotype. In France, the Protestants are a minority group that is considerably richer than the dominant Catholics, and have been so for centuries. Popular opinion agrees that they owe their wealth to hard work, self-discipline, and a dedication to the task at hand; in other words, the "Protestant work ethic." The rich Jew, on the other hand, is not seen as a dedicated hard worker but as a Judas, a betrayer of morality for the sake of profit.

Protestant money is "good"; Jewish money is "bad." There are economic as well as symbolic aspects to this racist "distinction." I take up the economic ones later, in Chapter 14. In terms of the symbolism of modern anti-Semitism, what we see here is a continuation, albeit in a changed, metaphorical form, of the ancient charge that Jewish money is the money of those who seek to destroy all that is holy, those whose hands are stained with the blood of Christ. It is true that modern anti-Semitism seems to "only" blame Jews for making money by cheating and exploiting honest Christians, but its murderous virulence can only be understood if we recognize that the modern "economic anti-Semite" is still in the grips of the ancient myths of Judas and the Blood Libel. Whenever the anti-Semite blames the Jew for attacking "Christian labour" and "Christian values," there is always a hidden message still calling on the anti-Semite to avenge the Jews' alleged spilling of "Christian blood."

"If there were no Jews, we would have to invent them." Who better than a people whose namesake betrayed the Son of God for money (as Christianity, the West's domi-

nant ideology, would have it) could be made to play the role
of evil, bloody greed on the stage of popular myth, where
each group personifies some human vice? It is because no
one can take their place that the Jews and their money continue to be blamed for problems even in places where there
are hardly any Jews left (like Poland or Austria; or my native
Slovakia with its hardly a few thousand Jews, where a 1991
opinion poll showed that 20 per cent of the people considered the Jews to be a "major problem.") And, though it
would be dangerous to generalize, one occasionally hears
astonishingly anti-Semitic remarks from people who have
perhaps never seen a Jew: Filipinos, West Indians.

Whether we like it or not, we have been singled out, not
in an abstract way, but expressly as agents of an evil power,
Greed. We have been depicted as demons who suck the
lifeblood of nations, even as we draw the gold out of their
pockets.

As Jews, we are forced to fight this demonic image of
ourselves wherever it appears; and that means also within
ourselves. It is difficult not to internalize at least some of
it.

The young Viennese of whom we spoke at the beginning
of the chapter completely assimilated the image of the Jew
as a greedy vampire. He knew also that there is only one
way to stop a vampire — it must be killed. Hitler eventually brought the logic of the Judas myth to its logical conclusion, in Auschwitz. It is a horrible thought, but
Weininger, himself a Jew, must also have realized that his
anti-Semitism could only be fulfilled in murder. When he
wrote, "I kill myself so as not to kill another," who was the
"another" that he had in mind? Was he going to fire his

pistol at a Jew or at a Gentile? It is not unlikely that he meant to kill a Jew, and so to finally redeem himself from the burden of his own Jewishness, like Dracula's mistress (Francis Coppola's version), the heroine who had herself become a vampire but frees herself of the curse by slicing off her lover's head.

If so, then this tortured young man must have had, in his last moments, an astonishing change of heart. Instead of a symbolic Jewish victim, it was himself and his hatred that he chose to destroy. His suicide prevented a possible anti-Semitic murder, this time sensationally performed by a well-known Jew.

Weininger is dead, but the myth that killed him, the myth of the Jew-Judas, not quite yet. It still incites hatred in the anti-Semite; and in the Jew, guilt, neurosis, and self-doubt.

5

MERRY CHRISTMAS
AND HAPPY HANUKKAH

I'm dreaming of a White Christmas . . .
— Irving Berlin

To the terrible accusations of the anti-Semite, the eji wants to reply, "No, I am *not* an evil, vicious, greedy, 'Rich Jew.' " But the eji does not want to be so direct. Confronting the anti-Semite head on may, the eji fears, be too dangerous. So the eji becomes a master of talking about Jewish issues without really talking about Jewish issues. One of the oddest ways to go about accomplishing the task is to talk about Christmas.

One fine summer Sunday I took part in a lecture series on our university campus. It was one of those balmy days, when the old-time grace of university life still comes alive. I walked past two small churches where groups of ladies in pastel-coloured dresses and lace on their hair stood smiling on the steps, flattered by the presence of gentlemen who had allowed themselves, for the day, to adorn their sombre suits with ties of blazing, undisciplined colour. Crossing the large college lawn where young people leisurely threw baseballs, footballs, and Frisbees to each other, I entered a large building that matched perfectly the neo-Gothic style of the two churches. I walked the broad, wood-panelled staircase to the large lecture hall. The dark oak panelling continued inside, topped by a quotation in gold on blue that ran the length of all four walls. It seemed to be from Longfellow or some such, but to read it all would have meant taking a walk along the circumference of the hall, and I suspect that no one has ever taken the trouble. The mood inside was brightened by the tall, arched windows, whose stained glass quaintly recalled the wars and exploits of a period when those who used to gather here were the same as those who went to worship in the nearby churches. Even now, many in the audience wore the same pastel dresses and bright neckties as the people in the congregations whose bells would now and then interrupt our speaker. Rostrum and pulpit, lecture and sermon, like estranged cousins, rediscovered for a fleeting moment the significance of a once-meaningful kinship bond.

A prominent American scholar, whom I know to be Jewish, was delivering an intriguing lecture on Chaucer. He must have caught something of the surviving Christian spirit of the place, for he appeared painfully aware of speaking, as a non-Christian, about a very English tale of a Christian pilgrimage, within a very WASP Sunday atmosphere, and to a largely Christian crowd. To hide his discomfort, he peppered his lecture liberally with mocking allusions to Christianity. He started by claiming that he was going to take thirty-three minutes, "a Christian number," and that he would divide his speech into seven parts, "also a number of mythical significance." The various noises of a campus at rest attempted a peaceful invasion of the lecture hall every now and then: an announcement over the PA system for some festive meeting or demonstration, the sounds of a musical instrument, and the like. Several times these interruptions happened just as the lecturer pronounced the word "God." Each time, he would halt his narrative, and roll his eyes in mock expectation of divine punishment at having taken His name in vain. Reaching for a glass of water, he complained that his lecture was taking place in a "dry state" (in our city, there are certain periods when the bars have to be closed by law) and added, "It's Sunday, I have to be good."

I thought I felt the English specialist's relief as another speaker, also a well-known Jewish academic, came up to the lectern. He was one of America's leading psychologists. This speaker, too, felt obliged to take a rhetorical bow to Christianity, and he used one of the eji's favourite tools to accomplish the end: a cozy reference to Christmas. His topic was relationships between students and their parents. As an example, he referred to a "typical Brooklyn family." To my surprise, this turned out to be not one of the hundreds of thousands of Jewish families who live in Brooklyn but a Catholic family of Italian origin. In loving tones, the psychologist described the experience of a freshman student who returns home for Christmas. The tree smells of the forest, the kitchen smells of festive cooking, everywhere there are decorations, smiles, good cheer. Best of all, the student finds that the rest of the family are "still talking about the same things." So moving was the psychologist's description, one could hardly believe that he himself did not grow up celebrating Noel next to a Christmas tree.

Eji Christmas
The lecturer's reference to Christmas reminded me of the merchant that I visited one December to arrange for a print

to be framed. He had beautified, indeed overdecorated, his store with innumerable wreaths, pine-tree branches, and pendants for Christmas. He expressed his intense disappointment with the fact that it was too late for him to finish my order by the arrival of Yuletide. And he topped up the transaction by wishing a Merry Christmas to me and mine. He appeared quite shaken when I revealed that I did not celebrate Christmas, because I was Jewish. "So am I," the storekeeper replied, dejectedly, and added — "I hate Christmas."

Talking about Christmas is one of the truly favourite devices by which Jewish speakers try to bridge the gap between themselves and the Gentile audience. When the pioneer American-Jewish cineast George Cukor made his first movie, it was a tear-jerker about a poor child at Yuletide. And not everyone remembers that the all-time hit, "White Christmas," is a composition by a Jew, Irving Berlin, who also created "Easter Parade" and "God Bless America." It is in the tradition of these great entertainers that the mainly Jewish army of Hollywood sitcom writers churns out, year in and year out, their obligatory sappy Christmas episodes.

Being nice about the Christmas spirit has a triple objective. First, it may steer attention away from the fact that the speaker is not a Christian. Second, if it does not do so, the speaker will at least have made an appeal to the Christmas spirit of tolerance. And third, the speaker will have demonstrated a positive attitude to the one holiday that makes all Christians and Jews acutely aware of following different ceremonial traditions in the most intimate circle of their family.

I hate Christmas. I hate Christmas, because during the

Christmas season I am put upon, time after time, by well-meaning non-Jews to declare my difference from them. When I am wished a Merry Christmas, what am I to do? If I return the greeting, my Jewish conscience accuses me of not having the chutzpah to say "I do not celebrate it." If I do say so, however, I get into an unwanted discussion, often with someone I do not really wish to chat with; or I might spoil the holiday mood for someone I do care for. I am also not a little upset by the arrogance of people who think it to be a matter of course that *everyone* has Christmas. To hear them talk about it, Christmas is as naturally part of December as snow in Minnesota. I don't care if the Japanese or the Indians have bought the idea and, although not Christians, welcome Santa and erect Christmas trees. We don't have to.

To paraphrase Woody Allen, I feel about Christmas the way he feels about death. I don't mind it; I just don't want to be there when it happens. Whenever I can afford it, I love to spend Christmas far away, preferably in Mexico or one of the Caribbean islands. For one thing, Christmas is celebrated less intensely there — in Mexico it doesn't start in November. More importantly, though people may wish you a Merry Christmas, they are not people you know; and you may even pretend not to understand them. I suspect that others may have similar reasons for going to a largely Jewish resort in the Catskills or in Florida.

However that may be, I certainly do *not* hate Christmas for what it means to Christians. I *like* togetherness, I *like* peace on earth, and I *like* presents (so do the Jewish merchants in shopping malls). I just wish it wasn't rubbed in my face, when I am not part of it. For let's face it, the reason many of us Jews do not like Christmas is that we are jealous.

Worse yet, we fear that our children will be jealous, that the presents their Gentile classmates receive will make them want to become Christians, like the natives who join the church because the missionaries give people bicycles.

So what do we do? The ultra-assimilated put up a Christmas tree. What the heck, they sigh, we do not mean it as a religious thing. My parents did this in Czechoslovakia; it was easy, because the communists encouraged the holiday as a secular event. But many in North America have been doing it, too. The practice was depicted, with perhaps some grotesque exaggeration in the novel and film *Driving Miss Daisy*. Here electrically illuminated reindeer, a fine kitsch Santa, and plenty of other vulgar Christmas decorations welcome Miss Daisy as she reluctantly enters her son and daughter-in-law's Christmas party in prewar Atlanta. Those who do not want to go all the way make slight adjustments to the Christmas tree, turning it into a "Hanukkah bush." This is usually a smallish evergreen, and is often topped by a Star of David or a menorah. Sometimes a real Hanukkah menorah is either next to or under it.

Even the eji who do not put up a Hanukkah bush (for the record it must be said that most don't) have nevertheless made sure that Hanukkah is "our version of Christmas." Hanukkah is probably the least significant of Jewish festivals. Unlike on major holidays, one is permitted to work on Hanukkah. Yet the majority of the eji, who do not even know the dates of such major festivals as Sukkoth or Shavuoth, do not fail to observe Hanukkah. This is profoundly ironic. The events that Hanukkah celebrates are not even in the Bible, but in the Greek-language Book of the Maccabees. The "zealots" of Israel, armed

Pharisee fundamentalists, rose against the Graeco-Syrian rulers of the land, who were amply assisted by "assimilated Jews." One of the things that most shocked the zealots were Jews who ran and exercised naked in Hellenic stadiums in the Holy Land. Hanukkah or Rededication commemorates the zealots' victory. This resulted in their recapture of the Temple, where they relit the "eternal flame." (The little consecrated oil they had for the purpose miraculously lasted eight days — hence the eight days of the festival.) Of course, the eji emphasizes not the religious fundamentalism but the "freedom fighter" aspect of the Hanukkah message. Nevertheless, one would have to be more charitable than necessary not to recognize that the main impetus for elevating Hanukkah to Christmas-like prominence is simply to prove that when it comes to "Yuletide" cheer, we don't play second fiddle to the goyim.

How much Hanukkah has become a Jewish Christmas is demonstrated by office workers who put up "Happy Hanukkah" signs next to "Merry Christmas." Once I was at my office when a non-Jewish employee was posting up a "Happy Hanukkah" sign as part of the "festive season" decorations. I politely reminded her that Hanukkah was already over. Since the holiday is observed according to the lunar Hebrew calendar, it does not always coincide with Christmas, and sometimes comes much earlier. So what sense did it make to celebrate Hanukkah after Hanukkah has ended? My mild protest was not at all well received. It was hushed up almost as an indecent remark, not only by the Gentiles but by the Jews as well.

As far as the kids are concerned, Hanukkah has allowed us not only to match the goyim, but to trump them. Non-Jewish children get presents at Christmas. But many

Jewish children get one every night for the duration of the eight-day festival! True, it used to be traditional on Hanukkah to give a few coins to children, although often these were made of chocolate. But the lavish gift-giving we engage in is very clearly a direct influence from Christmas. Giving gifts for Hanukkah became a custom among the more "assimilated" eji of Europe as far back as the late nineteenth century, along with such curious practices as eating ham, traditional for Easter but thoroughly unkosher, with the Passover matzah. It is, however, in North America that Hanukkah gift-giving has come to be practised by some of the eji with the intensity of a potlatch. Little Josh and Vivian are not going to have reason to be jealous, the parents seem to be determined. The zealots of ancient Israel rebuilt the Temple and banished pagan entertainment and rituals. Today's eji zealots shower Hanukkah gifts on their children, outdoing the Gentiles.

What a farce Hanukkah as a Christmas substitute can be was revealed a few years ago, when a Hassidic group erected a twenty-eight-foot-high Hanukkah menorah in a strip of parkland near the municipal centre of Beverly Hills. Four Jewish residents of the posh and very Jewish Southern California township protested. With the official support of the American Jewish Congress, they went to court to have the menorah removed. The resulting litigation lasted for years. There has never been such trouble in the thousands of places all over the United States where there was, along with the menorah, also a Christmas tree. What the neighbourhood eji were up in arms about was, not the menorah but the lack of a Christmas tree next to it. The Hassidim had the guts to try to recapture Hanukkah as a Jewish holiday rather than as an eji symbol of Shylock's

Defence: Merry Christmas and Happy Hanukkah; we are just like you. You celebrate, we celebrate.

Personally, I hope that the more self-confident, post-eji Jew will abandon the Hanukkah hoopla and abandon the giant candelabras altogether, whether they be next to a Christmas tree or not. I hope they will go back to a simple candle-lighting song, followed by the eating of *latkes*, a game of *dreydlach*, and modest if any gifts. But I doubt it. What children would let their parents stop an eight-night session of gift-giving? Christmas and Hanukkah will stay together, though it will be only for the children's sake. But there is no need for the silly pretence that Hanukkah is the Jewish equivalent of Christmas. As far as I am concerned, "Merry Christmas" posters will do just fine at the office, without "Happy Hanukkah." It would be nice, though, if next fall, when we *really* celebrate a major holiday, someone put up a sign saying "Happy Rosh Hashanah."

6

TALKING LIKE AN EJI: STYLES AND COUNTER-STEREOTYPES

Some one hundred years ago, a historic event took place in Hungary. The legal prohibition against marriages between Jews and Christians was lifted. The first couple to take advantage of this new liberty was a Jewish man — and a woman who was born Jewish but had converted to Christianity.

Eji talk about Christmas — in fact eji talk in general — is like the bride at that peculiar wedding. It is dressed in Christian garb, but has a Jewish core. Aboriginal North Americans call an Indian who behaves white an "apple": red on the outside, white on the inside. This is, of course, hyperbole: few Indians are totally "white" in their behaviour, and even fewer are purely Indian inside. Likewise with the eji: Gentile on the outside, Jewish inside, but always with enough of the Jewish showing through (and enough of the Gentile internalized) to make the picture complicated. Eji talk, too, is singularly Jewish, yet it is couched in terms that make it both familiar and acceptable to the Gentiles.

To sound acceptable, the eji believes, it is important not to sound too loud when talking about the Jews. In the late eighties, I was asked to speak at a conference on

Charlie Chaplin at the Sorbonne. I chose as my topic: "Chaplin: The Great Dictator and the Little Jew." My subject was *The Great Dictator*, Chaplin's first talkie, turned out between 1938 and 1940. In it, he portrayed both an undisguised caricature of Hitler — then in full rage as Germany's *Führer* — and a Jewish barber, the dictator's look-alike. The organizer of the symposium, a distinguished Jewish professor, insisted on changing my title to just *Le Grand Dictateur*, leaving out *le petit Juif*. He said this would make a better fit with the other titles at the session. I am not aware that anyone else's title was modified, but I did not protest. When an eji speaks, I can read between the lines.

The incident reminds one of the fearful antics of Jewish officials under communism. The acting minister of culture of the Byelorussian Soviet Socialist Republic, Davydova, reluctantly gave her permission for a Yiddish theatre to perform — but only if they left the word "Jewish" off their poster!

On the other side of the Iron Curtain, at the Madrid "Conference on Security and Cooperation in Europe" (1980–83), the otherwise uncommonly outspoken U.S. Ambassador, Max M. Kampelman, asked a Baptist colleague to deliver his forthright speech demanding rights for Soviet Jewry. He was apparently afraid that he, a Jew, would not be listened to if he spoke *as a Jew*. When the Baptist turned out to be unavailable to make the speech, Kampelman first considered rewriting it, and then decided that this was a good time to give "quiet diplomacy" a chance.

Jews, even "assimilated" Jews, were not always so shy about the way they talked about themselves. In the nineteenth century it did seem possible to reply to the anti-Semite straight on, and with guts: "I am Jewish, and that does not mean I am evil and greedy. On the contrary, we Jews are as fine a people as ever walked on the face of the Earth." Disraeli, the darling of his Jewish contemporaries, never tired of saying so. His chutzpah was without limit. "Yes, I am a Jew," he would reply to a fellow parliamentarian's taunting, "and when the ancestors of the right honourable gentleman were brutal savages in an unknown island, mine were priests in the temple of Solomon."

As anti-Semitism intensified in the late nineteenth century, however, such "Semitism" convinced no one; it tended only to excite anti-Semitism. The eji became convinced that their only defence was Shylock's Defence. No use trying to persuade people that the Jews were better than, or even as good as, most other "races." The best one could hope was to make people believe that we were just like everyone else (i.e. not *worse*). The basic rule of eji talk has become: Never speak as a Jew, but always as a human. To speak to the Gentiles, even if the topic is the Jews, you dress your message in non-Jewish garb. (You put on a pinstripe suit when you talk to the Mafia.) To talk of the Jews, you must beat around the (Hanukkah) bush.

Eji strategy in presenting Shylock's Defence takes on many forms. I divide the discussion under two headings: "Styles" and "Counter-Stereotypes." Styles are the eji's way of talking about Jewish issues without seeming to be seriously concerned with Jewish issues (if you were too concerned, you might be taken to think that the Jews are not just like everyone else). Counter-stereotypes are images of the Jew fostered by the eji, in the hope that people will prefer them to the anti-Semitic stereotype of the "Rich Jew."

Three Styles of Presenting Shylock's Defence

Example Talk

"Circumcision. It is all I have ever spoken about . . ." writes Jacques Derrida, the celebrated French-Jewish philosopher, and adds, "circumcision, of which I never spoke — or of which I spoke only in passing, as though of an example . . ."

Here Derrida, looking back at his past work, recognizes the central importance to it of his Jewish background. His essay "Circumfessions" is illustrated by biographical photos, showing, among other things, scenes of his childhood in Algiers, and the knife and other tools of the *mohel* or ritual circumciser. Is there a hidden reference here to Heine's *Confessions*? Heine, too, made clear only in his middle age how much Jewishness had meant to him in his work.

Derrida may have had good reason not to speak too loudly of his Jewishness, as I once had an opportunity to see for myself. I was in Paris, having dinner in a Latin Quarter restaurant with a well-respected French professor of American literature. The conversation veered to connections between French and American specialists, and I commented on the fact that Derrida was much more popular in North America than in France. "Of course," replied the man, "Derrida isn't French." "What is he, then?" I asked, completely puzzled. The professor refused to elaborate. At the time I did not know that Derrida was Jewish.

In recognizing at long last that his Jewish condition had always informed his writing, Derrida also points to the verbal technique he had used to conceal the fact: "circumcision, of which I never spoke — or of which I spoke only in passing, as though of an example." This is one of the commonest styles of the eji. It can be summarized by the injunction: "If you must speak of a Jewish matter, speak of it as but an example of something broader. If you must speak of the Jews, mention them along with other groups, so that the Jews are only one example."

The early twentieth-century anthropologist Franz Boas countered anti-Semitic theories by referring to the results of his research on "Slavs," "Italians," and "Eastern European Hebrews." The comedian Lenny Bruce asked, "What colour is God?" and answered, "He's yellow . . . he's Jewish, black, and yellow . . . he's, well, he's part Irish, and Jewish, and black . . ." (Note that "Jewish" never appears first.) That God is not uniquely Jewish (or anything) is a fine message that is undoubtedly shared by people who are yellow, black, or Irish, as well as many "non-coloured" and "non-ethnic" WASPs. But would a yellow, a black, an Irish, or a WASP comedian mumble as Lenny Bruce does in this passage? Hardly. In the pains he takes not to appear to be especially concerned with the Jews, Bruce is being typically Jewish indeed.

A consequence of Example Talk is that, even when they try to help other Jews, the eji feel obliged to stress that they are doing so out of general humanitarian concern, and not because of specifically Jewish concerns. A fund-raiser active among the Hollywood moguls of the forties recalled how:

If you said to [the Hollywood Jews], "It is the ethical goal of Jews to help other Jews," they would have said, "F—k off! Don't give me that shit! Is there a Jew starving? Here's some money. Don't talk to me about Jews having an ethical duty." He might even say, "I'll help anyone who's starving." But what he really meant was, "Yes, I'll help a Jew."

In his heart, in other words, he would help a Jew because he's a Jew, but in public he feels he must say that he is helping him the same way as he would help anyone; a starving Jew is but *one example* of *anyone* who's starving.

Sublimation

Example Talk is related to an even more subtle manner of speaking about the Jews while seeming not to be doing so. This involves projecting from the Jewish experience onto human experience in general, but without acknowledging, even as an "example," the Jewish origin of one's thoughts. I call this "Sublimation," borrowing the term from Freud. To him, the work of the scholar and scientist was infused with the energy of the libido. Sublimation was the process by which this essentially sexual energy was harnessed (and disguised at the same time) to do the work of science. Eji intellectuals transform the message "the Jews are like everyone else" into its equivalent, "everyone else is like the Jews." In this way, they manage to sublimate their Jewish concerns into universal ones. This allows them to generalize the Jewish experience into universal, "purely" scientific themes, whose origin in Jewish concerns is no longer apparent. In Sublimation, the word "Jew" is no longer mentioned at all.

Freud never referred to the Jews by name, even though some of his core theorizing could be seen as derived from Jewish concerns. Whom but the Jews could he have had in mind as the "outsiders" when he claimed that for emotional togetherness people had to have cultural outsiders to hate? Or when he discussed the problem of "host peoples" (*Wirtsvölker*), among whom such outsiders (parasites by implication) live? Yet, literally speaking, he was discussing not at all the Jews as such but outsiders and *Wirtsvölker* in general.

John Murray Cuddihy, in his fascinating book *The Ordeal of Civility*, interpreted Freud's three-part representation of the personality in Jewish terms. The three elements of the personality, the ego, the superego, and the id, occupied Freud's attention particularly in the 1920s. The ego (in German, simply the *Ich*, or "I") was a compromise: it was the conscious self that acted only after balancing the two other elements, the superego and the id. The superego was essentially the values, desires, and restrictions that the personality had assimilated from society. The id, on the other hand, was the untamed individual with his or her uncensored, instinctual desires.

Cuddihy referred to the id as the *id-yid*. And the superego he interpreted as the Gentile culture, into which the eji expected, and was expected, to fit. In a Jewish sense the ego was, to Cuddihy, a sort of a tight-rope walker who balances precariously between the twin weights of an abandoned tradition and of a civilization imposed, more or less, from the outside. Cuddihy's implication was that Freud's scheme of the human personality had been *sublimated* from his specifically Jewish experience.

In some of the work of Émile Durkheim, Sublimation

is even more clear. His father, a rabbi, meant Émile to
follow in his footsteps, and there can be little doubt that
he taught his son a good deal about Judaism. Durkheim's
sociology of religion shows this influence, though the word
"Jew" figures in his work as seldom as in Freud's.

According to Durkheim, the essence of religious feeling
is the separation of the sacred and the profane. The same
distinction is at the very heart of Jewish religious practice.
The myriad of minute ritual practices, which determine
the way the Orthodox Jew dresses, washes, eats, and travels,
have the purpose of "sanctifying" (lekadesh), of marking the
profane environment with the special presence of the
sacred. The Talmud tells a story about King David taking
a bath. David became frightened when he saw his own
naked body: he wore no "precepts"! (The "precepts" one
wears are reminders of the sacred, such as a skull cap or the
tsitsis strands worn by pious men over their shirt.) David
regained his calm, however, when he noticed his circumcision. The circumcision is a permanent reminder of the
sacred on what some consider the most profane part of a
man.

The essence of Jewish religious practice is the marking
apart of the Sabbath as sacred. Every Saturday night, the
observant Jew recites the Havdalah (separation) marking
the end of the Holy Sabbath and the beginning of the
profane week. The ritual culminates in the closing passage,
"Blessed be the Lord, King of the Universe . . . who sepa-
rates the sacred and the profane (ha-mavdil beyn kodesh le-
hol)." One would think the text to be modelled on
Durkheim! But surely, the modelling went the other way
around.

Sublimation is not limited to intellectual discourse.

One favourite sublimation of "ordinary" eji culture is to generalize from the Jewish experience to the minority experience in general.

Here the point is, not quite that we're just like *everyone* else, but, more modestly, that we're just like other "oppressed people." This not only erases important differences between ourselves and other groups, but also helps to establish us as a people wronged rather than a people doing wrong. To be so seen is very important to the eji, who has internalized the charges of the Judas stereotype. If we are oppressed, how can you think of us as the arrogant Rich?

I have seen Jewish human-rights advocates criticize native activists for their political strategies, giving the Jews as an example of how to do things right. Similar advice used to be given to blacks. In public, but more so in private, many Jews, some of them very sympathetic to the blacks' cause, wonder aloud, "Why can't they do it like we did? We too are disliked, we too were oppressed, we too were poor."

Other minority groups have, however, not always been grateful to us for lumping them together with us under the one label of Oppressed Minority. Black anti-Semitism is a detestable, despicable phenomenon about which more will be said later; it has no justification whatsoever. Yet, without excusing black anti-Semitism, let us admit that the Sublimation practised by some of the Jewish liberals has justifiably irritated black activists. The eji liberal wants to fight for both Jewish and black rights by standing up for "oppressed people everywhere." The self-respecting black knows that there are no oppressed people who are not also Jewish, native, women or blacks; and the differences in their oppression are as important as the similarities. A self-respecting Jew knows as much. It just so happens that the eji is sometimes not self-respecting enough.

Funny-Jew Talk

If Example Talk and Sublimation are two major styles of the eji, "Funny-Jew Talk" is a minor one. I mention it here for its curiosity value as the exception to the rule: this is one type of eji discourse that brazenly violates the "commandment" to speak as little of the Jews as possible. In Funny-Jew Talk the eji consciously and exaggeratedly talks about the Jews — but not in earnest. This is the province of comedy. Jewish comedians, both professional and amateur, love to make Jewish jokes. Every country where Jews live has had its share of ebullient Jewish entertainers whose staple fare includes joking references to their own and other people's Jewishness. In a later chapter we will be particularly concerned with the humour of Jewish comediennes, but male comedians like Lenny Bruce have been equally active in getting a laugh out of their Jewishness.

The comic self-deprecation of such professional comedians finds plenty of amateur imitators among the Jews, and the non-Jews love it. The practice has secured us a sterling reputation as a funny people. In one episode of the BBC television series "Alexei Sayle's Stuff," the board of directors of a corporation is meeting to welcome Mr Gold, their new accountant. They are told by the very Aryan-looking new arrival that despite his name, he is not Jewish. Though this happens to be the truth, everyone takes it to be a funny Jewish joke. The distinguished directors break out in inextinguishable guffawing. From then on they greet everything the accountant says with wild laughter. "Jewish humour," the chief executive exclaims, "very funny . . ."

It seems that people can no more imagine an unfunny
Jew than an Italian who hates spaghetti. But why is
humour so important in eji culture? I say "eji" culture deliberately, for the traditionalist, Orthodox Jew is not very
funny at all. A classic group of anecdotes about awkward
shtetl dwellers on the train, and even the well-known folk-
lore about the "wise men of Chelm" (a Jewish hick town
peopled by fools) are today often taken to be the typical
humour of the traditional, rural Jew. But these jokes were
told not for the most part by the old-fashioned Jews of
Eastern Europe but by their more urban, relatively "assimilated" fellow Jews, who were making fun of the tradition-
bound country bumpkins.

Perhaps the major function of Jewish humour is to
enable eji to talk about Jewish issues without appearing to
be serious about them. The eji's jokes about the Jews are
often like the "fatso's" jokes about fat (or the "baldie's"
jokes about hair). The last thing the jovial fat man wants
us to do is to take his belly seriously: he'd like us to laugh
it off. Through humour he wants to disarm us, to prevent
us from disliking him — he tells us fat jokes before we get
a chance to tell them. The eji who engages in Funny-Jew
Talk tells Jew jokes instead.

There are, of course, limits to how much the fatso can
joke about his belly before our amusement turns into irritation. The outrageously "Jewish" comic like Lenny Bruce
or Woody Allen seems to have become acceptable only
after World War II. Previously, Jewish entertainers had to
be more subtle, often limiting their Jewish references to in-
jokes. So it is that Groucho Marx, posturing as a famous
traveller, arrives at an elegant party, and everyone breaks
into a song, with the refrain as follows:

The Guests: "The African Explorer!"
Groucho: "Did I hear: 'A shnorrer'?"

(A *shnorrer*, butt of many pre-war Jewish jokes, is a cunning beggar who lives by misusing Jewish charity.)

An earlier personality who was very fond of surreptitious Jewish references was Jacques Offenbach. In an episode of *The Tales of Hoffmann*, the lover of the Venetian prostitute Antonia is called Schlémiel, the name of a Yiddish folk character and generally the Yiddish word for a hapless person. Schlémiel is not, of course, found at all in the original stories by Ernst Hoffmann. Offenbach also liked to use synagogue melodies to create popular songs for the general public: his song "Rebecca" is one of the best-known examples.

But brazen or low-key, Funny-Jew Talk, as much as its more obvious counterpart — and as much as Example Talk and Sublimation — fulfils the essence of the eji's strategy in presenting Shylock's Defence, which is to blunt the edges of any discourse that might deal directly and without disguise with the serious problems and concerns of the Jews. I summarize the three styles as follows:

Style	Description
Example Talk	Mention the Jews as but one example among many
Sublimation	Generalize from the Jewish experience to that of everyone
Funny-Jew Talk	Talk a lot about the Jews, but only in jest

Example Talk, Sublimation, and Funny-Jew Talk are ways for the eji to escape from being branded as too concerned with Jewish matters. They have little to do with battling anti-Semitism in general; the person using them aims only to prevent being personally suspected of Jewish bias.

In principle, that might be enough for some eji. But the effort to achieve a merely personal exemption from the anti-Semites' wrath can be rather pathetic, as in the case of the Jewish woman of Sartre's acquaintance whose son had to make some business trips to Germany in the early period of the Hitler government. "This son had the typical characteristics of the French Jew," wrote Sartre,"— a hooked nose, protruding ears, etc. — but when we expressed anxiety about what might happen to him during one of his absences, his mother replied, 'Oh, I am not worried; he doesn't look like a Jew at all.'" The incident recalls the old joke about a Jew on a transatlantic voyage, who finds that there is another Jewish passenger on board, a hunchback. "Let me tell you a secret," he tells the hunchback, "I am a Jew." "I'll tell you a secret, too," replies the other. "I am a hunchback."

To the anti-Semite, all Jews "look Jewish," even if not always physically. So even eji with no personal commitment to Jewishness are forced to fight the "Jew" image in general, seeing that it is applied to them as much as to the rest. The eji do this by fostering a number of alternative images of the Jew, or "Counter-Stereotypes." Counter-Stereotypes refocus the attention of the public from supposed negative Jewish characteristics to positive ones: sense of humour, immigrant chumminess, resistance to oppression, etc.

Counter-Stereotypes

I will deal with only two classes of Counter-Stereotypes, each of them important enough to merit a chapter or two below. One I call the Jewish Proletarian Counter-Stereotype, and the other, the Jewish Bad-Woman. For now, I sketch only the most general characteristics of each of these Counter-Stereotypes. And I note that to each corresponds a "practitioner," a type of person who aims to confirm the Counter-Stereotype by his or her life and/or work. The fictional poor Jew of the Jewish Proletarian Counter-Stereotype is matched by the "real" left radical who fights for the rights of the economically disadvantaged. On a more humorous note (but Jewish humour is a very serious matter), the Jewish Bad-Woman is brought to life — at least on the screen and stage — by some of the Jewish comediennes, impersonators of a proverbial Jewish Mother or of a Jewish American Princess.

The Jewish Proletarian

The Jewish Proletarian is, to put it plainly, a poor Jew. The two major subtypes of this counter-image are the following:

✡ **The Fiddler.** Eji lore provides a number of images of the poor but jolly Jewish folk that lived in the realms of the Tsar. These well-loved images are the staple fare of Hebrew School productions as well as of many Broadway musicals. The best-loved example is Tevye, the hero of *Fiddler on the Roof.* Every sentimental Ashkenazi Jew (and we are a very sentimental people) believes he or she had a great-grandfather "just like Tevye." Not only is it nice to have such folksy, yet wise ancestors, but an ancestor *à la* Tevye is proof that we, and the Jews in general, are not inherently "rich." "If I *were* a rich man . . . ," Tevye sings. Would a rich man have to *dream* of being rich?

✡   **The Brooklyn Jew.** The East European *shtetl* dweller often ends up in some poor Jewish neighbourhood of a big city across the Atlantic, having taken a torturous trip, with no money, in the bottom compartment of a rickety immigrant ship. Typically, his or her children are represented as a noisy family living in a crowded apartment. They, too, are certainly not rich. The mother is overwhelmed by looking after the large, unruly household. The father may be employed in any one of a number of low-paying, hard-working occupations, but the most typical example is the cabby. Similarly, the Brooklyn Jew family may be living in a variety of cities, such as the Bronx, Montreal, or Philadelphia. But its (counter-) stereotypical home is in Brooklyn. Much here, as in all counter-stereotypes, is in fact based in truth: many less well-off Jews have taken to taxi driving, and many have lived in Brooklyn. But, as we shall see, there are also parts of the counter-stereotype that are little more than the product of the eji's sentimental imagination.

✡   **The Proletarian Internationalist.** The Fiddler and the Brooklyn Jew, in the sense I have been using the terms, are fictional images (much as the fiction may be rooted in reality). The Proletarian Internationalists are real-life figures, the "Trotskys" as opposed to the "Freuds" (intellectuals) and "Woody Allens" (authors, artists, and entertainers). Though themselves often neither poor nor proletarian, they carry on the fight for those who are. Often they confess that they are inspired by their parents and grandparents, whom they present as counter-stereotypical

"Brooklyn Jews" and "Fiddlers." Apart from a genuine concern with social justice, the Proletarian Internationalists sometimes admit a concern with the Jewish image as a motivating factor in their political work. How can you be accused of taking the side of Gold against Good if you are fighting on the side of the working people?

The Jewish Bad-Woman

The brilliant and funny Hollywood performer Bette Midler, who is married to a German, declared: "My husband and I like to play war. He plays Germany and I play Poland, and he invades me." From a Jewish woman speaking of a German husband, one might expect to hear about the German treatment of the Jews. But mercifully, Midler turns the Jewess into a Pole.

However, everyone knows that Bette Midler, who, like most American Jews, has ancestors who came from Poland, is not *really* Polish, but Jewish. Her joke is in the tradition of the provocative, vulgar character I call "the Jewish Whore," one of the varieties of an important eji Counter-Stereotype, the Jewish Bad-Woman. The Jewish Bad-Woman is a perverted form of eji "defence," in which the anti-Semite is asked to despise, not the Jew in general, but the Jewish female. In their desire to find new stereotypes to replace those held by the anti-Semite, many Jews seem to think that even anti-feminism will do. Some of the variations of the Jewish Bad-Woman counter-stereotype are the following:

✡   **The Jewish Whore**, a raunchy, ribald, and totally materialistic personage played on stage by Jewish comediennes. The heyday of this role lasted from Sophie Tucker to Joan

Rivers. Bette Midler often lapses into the role as well. But she, fortunately, not only can, but mostly does, do much better; mercifully, few younger performers are coming forward to continue the questionable tradition of the Jewish Whore. This may be one of the benefits of the decline of ejidom.

✡   **The Jewish Mother**, butt of untold numbers of tasteless jokes and anecdotes, a common cliché of North American Jewishness as popular as lox and bagels.

✡   **The Jewish Princess**, a silly, spoiled, and expensive daughter who becomes a silly, spoiled, expensive, and frigid wife. In the eighties the popular form of this character, featured in countless jokes, was the "Jewish American Princess," or "JAP."

We will see that all Jewish Bad-Woman characters are merely negative stereotypes of Woman in general; they simply have been given a Jewish form. The supposed faults of the Jewish woman — demanding, silly, blaming, and above all, valuing money over love — are the same faults that woman-haters ascribe to all women, regardless of race and creed. The Jewish Bad-Woman image supports Shylock's Defence: Jewish women are bad but they are bad in the same way as non-Jewish women.

As we will soon see, Jewish men are hardly less misogynous than others (though they may seem to be). So one can understand, though hardly approve of, eji men who tell JAP jokes or Jewish Mother anecdotes. It is harder to see why eji women would tell them as well. Are they saying, "Hate me if you must, but hate me as a woman, not as a Jew"?

Before we take a more detailed look at the two examples of Counter-Stereotypes, let us summarize them in the following table:

Counter-Stereotype	Varieties	Meaning	"Practitioners"
Jewish Proletarian	Fiddler, Brooklyn Jew	Jews are not rich	The Proletarian Internationalist
Jewish Bad-Woman	Jewish Whore, Jewish Mother, Jewish Princess	Jewish women are bad, just as all women are bad. (Jews are like everyone else.)	The Comedienne

PART II

COUNTER-STEREOTYPES

7

The Fiddler

In the days of the Tsar, there lived two Jews who passed their lives in ways that could not be more different from one another. One wore a yarmulke and *tsitsis*. The other wore a broad tie under a starched high collar. One spoke mostly Yiddish and fondly quoted and misquoted Bible and Talmud. The other spoke Russian, and read Gogol, Chekhov, and Gorky. One got his education in the traditional *heder*, the other, in a Russian school. One was a dairy farmer; the other augmented his inheritance and his income as a writer, with profits from the Kiev Stock Exchange.

The first man was a fictional character, Tevye. Best known from the Hollywood classic film *Fiddler on the Roof*, he became to future generations the living voice of the *shtetl*, the Jewish small town of Eastern Europe. The other man was a real flesh-and-blood person, Sholom Rabinovich. He was a Yiddish writer and the creator, under the pseudonym Sholom Aleichem, of the first Tevye.

Sholom was a "modern" Russian Jew. His life bore even less resemblance to Tevye's than the Hollywood Tevye did to the original. Ironically, Jewish nostalgia regards the fictional Tevye as the truest of real characters, while many Jews today are surprised, if not shocked, to find that modernized Jews like the real Sholom Aleichem existed at all in the Tsar's realm.

Tevye is one of the most poignant examples of the Jewish Proletarian Counter-Stereotype, *shtetl* version. A stalwart Jewish peasant, with a native wit and a naïve religiosity, ever sturdy in the face of unending adversity, he is the epitome of Jewish nostalgia. But Tevye never existed. Sholom Aleichem was not like his fellow Yiddishists, who went about the countryside in the manner of the German and Slavic folklorists, asking common folk to talk into the horns of their early gramophone recorders. The voice that spoke to him was not that of a real man, but that of the muse. Like all writers, Sholom Aleichem told the truth through lying. In doing so he helped to invent, along with the image of Tevye and his *shtetl*, Yiddish literature itself.

From the rather provincial confines of Yiddish publishing, the imagery of the *shtetl* passed into the limelight of the secular press, stage, and screen. *Shtetl* bittersweet came to be the obligatory taste in any depiction of "ordinary" Jews, even if they lived in New York and did not sport sideburns or wigs.

Fiddling with the Tevye image may incur me the wrath of the reader, and I hesitate to do so: the Fiddler is so much a part of the way we think of our Jewish background — as much as bagels and lox. But bagels did not form part of the diet of most East European Jews (and are not very well known among their descendants in Israel or Western

Europe). And although smoked fish was popular with Jews everywhere because *kashruth* permits fish to be eaten with both meat and dairy products, it is a safe bet that smoked salmon was not readily available in most inland *shtetlach*. I apologize for any offence, but the Fiddler is hardly much more genuine an image of old-time East European Jewish life than bagels and lox. Like those "typically Jewish" foods, the Fiddler image has some basis in reality, but it is also very much part of a nostalgic reconstruction of our past, an example of what anthropologists call "invention of tradition."

The Jew as Ukrainian
True, the original Fiddler was created by a true Russian, or more precisely, Ukrainian-Jewish writer. But even in old Russia, Jewish authors tried to create stereotypes of the Jews that would identify them with less wealthy groups who were looked at more favourably by the greater society. Sholom Aleichem's Tevye is very much a Ukrainian peasant. To counter the idea of the Jew as a "parasite," Sholom Aleichem presents Tevye as a dairy farmer, who sells not the Gentile peasants' products but his own.

North American Jews have enthusiastically accepted the validity of Sholom Aleichem's Tevye as a metaphor for the Eastern European Jew of old. One critic wrote of Sholom Aleichem that he "was Russian Jewry itself. It is hard to think of him as 'a writer.' He was the common people in utterance." Irving Howe and Eliezer Greenberg are two American authors who did perhaps more than anyone else to popularize Sholom Aleichem's image of the common Jewish folk, the *amcho*. To them, Sholom Aleichem was "the great natural genius of Yiddish literature

. . . one of the very few modern writers who could be said to speak for an entire people." The admiration for Sholom Aleichem felt by Irving Howe, whose stature as an interpreter of the *shtetl* is augmented by his position as a leading American democratic socialist, is easy to understand. Tevye is the antithesis of the "rich Jew" capitalist, and the natural precursor of the great Yiddish socialists of Russian Poland and Lithuania, the Jewish Bund.

Of course, there were in reality Jewish peasants like Tevye, but compared to the Slavs, the percentage of Jews who farmed was minuscule. (It became almost zero in 1882 when Tsar Nicholas II ordered that all Jews must live in towns or townlets, but not villages.) Nevertheless, Sholom Aleichem's counter-stereotype, helped along generously by scores of American authors as well as Norman Jewison's film, has become deeply entrenched as an example of a real, authentic period Jew from pre-Soviet Russia. Most North American Jews know that their grandparents who came from Poland or Russia with "five cents in their pockets" were armed with a mixture of tired Orthodoxy, the Jewish equivalent of the Protestant Work Ethic, and socialistic ideology. However, they are convinced that those who stayed in Eastern Europe were quasi-Hassidic, quasi-Ukrainian peasants *à la* Tevye.

The truth is that when Sholom Aleichem set out to chronicle the life of Kasrilevke, Tevye's fictional home, the traditional *shtetl* was, as the editor's introduction to one of the translations of the Tevye stories puts it, "already passing into the collective memory of his generation." Sholom Aleichem's work fell into the category of nostalgic fiction that celebrated both a lost childhood and a lost world. Childhood stories appeared early in Sholom Aleichem's career, and memories of childhood loomed large in his autobiography. Like Maxim Gorky, who was probably his favourite writer — and like Woody Allen later in *Radio Days* — Sholom Aleichem used the genre of childhood recollection to depict a personally viewed fragment of social history.

That the common people were Sholom Aleichem's inspiration is generally accepted. But it is also generally accepted that writers are influenced by other writers. For, as Northrop Frye said, "Poetry can only be made out of other poems; novels out of other novels."

It could not have been mainly Yiddish literature that inspired the young Sholom, if only because there was not that much Yiddish literature around before him. His literary inspiration was the Russian realists — Gogol, Chekhov, and Gorky above all. Like them, he portrayed the changes going on in Russia through the eyes of the little man. Like them, he critiqued Russia's ancient religious and folk traditions, while worrying about the effects of the new, capitalist society.

Sholom Aleichem spoke more Russian at home than Yiddish. In his youth he served as a tutor to a rich man's daughter, whom he later married secretly. He was hired because of his education at a Russian school, which he attended after he had quit the traditional *heder,* just before his bar mitzvah. His employer was a rich bailiff called Loyev. His pupil, Olga, was thirteen when Sholom arrived at their estate. She was sixteen when he left. Sholom and Olga fell in love. Together they read the Russian classics, and Western literature in Russian translation. Sholom later reminisced about writing "long, heart-rending novels, melodramatic plays, complicated tragedies and comedies" at the time. These first of Sholom Aleichem's literary efforts were made in Russian. (None of this work has survived.)

Sholom and Olga became man and wife. When Olga's father died, she inherited much of his fortune. Olga's mother moved in with Sholom, Olga, and their daughter, who bore the rather un-Yiddish name of Ernestina. The mother was affectionately referred to as "grandma." The term used was the Russian *babushka*, not the Yiddish *bube*.

Sholom Aleichem's interest in Yiddish may have been awakened by the savage pogroms of 1881. It was a time when the Russian-Jewish intelligentsia gaped at their Russian friends' silence in the face of Jewish suffering. Not a few who had wished only to feel fully Russian began in bitter disappointment to search for their Jewish roots. The Yiddish language became an important source of Jewish identity for the many who had little interest in Judaism. These were generally people with left-leaning political beliefs. Some of them were among the founders of the socialist Jewish Bund. Several among the Bundists had to learn Yiddish in order to communicate with the working people they hoped to represent.

Sholom Aleichem's first Yiddish stories appeared in 1883, when he was twenty-four. Soon he was able to raise Yiddish to a high literary standard.

He did so with great originality, but in his criticism of traditional mores he resembled Gorky, and in his detailing of life in the rural home, the major Ukrainian writers like Ivan Nečuj-Levic'kyj, author of *The Kajdas Family*. Tevye's world view is in many ways reminiscent of the folksy wisdom so revered by the Slavs, and which was more recently evident in the public style of the Soviet leader and

Ukrainian ex-shepherd, Nikita Khrushchev. Taking off his shoe to bang it on a table at the United Nations to get attention for justice in the midst of a sophisticated, protocol-ridden, but empty discussion was a gesture worthy of any simple man of heart, a gesture worthy of Tevye.

Only in his religious attitude does Tevye differ significantly from a Ukrainian goy. Tevye likes to argue with God. Would it hurt the divine purpose if Tevye made a little money? How can pogroms please God? Here Tevye goes much farther than the rural heroes of Slavic literature. When in Gorky a quarrelsome Ukrainian great-aunt asks God to punish her daughter-in-law, her shrill tone no doubt resembled that of Sholom Aleichem's real-life mother-in-law, whose curses were the inspiration for one of Sholom Aleichem's first stories. But Tevye argues with God not because of His failure to punish the guilty, but because of His punishment of the innocent.

Reviewers of Sholom Aleichem, as well as of the Jewison film, like to imbue Tevye's religious rebellion with the air of a venerable Jewish tradition. But, although among Jews the theme of accusing God is certainly well established, it is less than ancient. The Hassidic Rabbi Levi Yitzchak of Berdichev is said to have held a trial of God for his injustices to the Jewish people. But despite what the editor of the English translation of the Tevye stories says, the tradition does not go back beyond early modernity (the Hassidic movement originated in the eighteenth century), and certainly not all the way to the Bible. Moses did argue with God, but he did not accuse God of injustice. Job did complain of being treated unfairly, but it turns out that in his case God was being misled by Satan. Job's boils and diseases end up having been but a test, similar to that of

Abraham and Isaac. He heals, and his sheep multiply like never before. The victims of the pogroms, or later of the Holocaust, did not live to receive such rewards. The modern Jew accuses God not of temporary unfairness that is soon to be corrected, but of patently real and lasting punishment that seems to be undeserved.

The difference is illustrated by the shocking claim by a number of the ultra-Orthodox that the Holocaust occurred as a punishment for the Jews not keeping to the ways of the *halakhah*. That claim preserves the image of a God who is always just, though His ways may be inscrutable. The modern Jew (including many of the more modern Orthodox) has given up that perspective. The Holocaust has taught Jews all over the world to ask God some unpleasant questions, but in Russia the pogroms had done so already in Sholom Aleichem's time.

The "God arguer" side of Tevye, billed as typical for a traditional Jew, happens to be one of his genuinely modern Jewish characteristics.

So, where Tevye finally shows unique character, he turns out to be a modern Jew. Where he is being a "typical," folksy, traditional East European Jew, he resembles the romanticized Ukrainian peasant.

The Americanization of Tevye: *Fiddler on the Roof*
Sholom Aleichem may have written much of his work in Geneva or New York, yet he still had a first-hand knowledge of his home country. His fiction could not depart as much from the historical reality as its spectacularly popular American adaptation, *Fiddler on the Roof*. The rich Jews to whom Sholom Aleichem had opposed Tevye are blanked out in the American *Fiddler*: the stage musical by Joseph

Stein and the film by Norman Jewison. Stein is Jewish; Jewison is not. But the Canadian director, bearer of a very English name that sounds Jewish, spoke powerfully to the Jewish heart, as only one other non-Jew, Chaplin, did before him in the *Great Dictator*. Despite what many people said about him, Chaplin was not Jewish.

Just as the *Fiddler* movie has no place for the prosperous, assimilated Jews of Sholom Aleichem's Russia, it largely ignores even the Gentile environment. Sholom Aleichem knew that Russian Jews lived with the Gentiles, who produced much of their food, and for whom they in turn supplied services, primarily as traders and artisans. In *Fiddler on the Roof* one gets the distinct feeling that the Gentiles live in another village. Even at the market, Jew deals with Jew only, and a shot of the Gentile peasants is accompanied by the voice-over comment: "They don't care about us, and we don't care about them." So it is not surprising that the original Tevye is given his expulsion order as the sole resident of a Gentile village, while in *Fiddler* he lives among other Jews, all of whom are evicted *en masse*. (Mass evictions, of course, did take place only too often. The point is that showing Tevye living alone among Gentiles would interfere with the film-maker's image of an independent Jewish peasant community.)

Two Gentiles are nevertheless given important roles in the film. One, the police commissioner, rides in every now and then on a white horse. The other, Fedka, is first seen when he rescues Chava from the harassment of his fellow-Ukrainian peasants, as she leads her cow down a road. Neither of these characters appears to reside in the village. Fedka is the "good goy," who, by his steady love for Chava, Tevye's daughter, proves that Jewish–Gentile coexistence is possible.

The birth of the love between Fedka and Chava is absolutely necessary for the film, which after all was made for primarily Gentile audiences. But it is too much for Tevye, who has already witnessed one daughter choosing a poor man, and another going for an assimilated socialist. Nevertheless, at the end of the film he appears to give Chava and Fedka his blessing, as they leave for Warsaw in protest against anti-Semitism in the local area. "Intermarriage can work!" the film seems to say.

Nothing could be more alien to the original. In Sholom Aleichem, Chava comes home disillusioned after a broken marriage — not an acceptable conclusion for pluralistic Jewish and non-Jewish Americans. Is it any surprise after all this that the "American" Tevye ends up free in the land of opportunity, even though in Sholom Aleichem he takes off, not for America but for a city within Russia itself?

The fiddler, so beautifully pictured at the beginning and end of the film, and who has become a universal symbol for Tevye's *shtetl*, does not even come from Sholom Aleichem. His original is to be found in the paintings of Marc Chagall, who has certainly done no less than Sholom Aleichem for the idealized image of Eastern European Jewry.

My mother once gave a children's book on Chagall to my son. In a comment on a painting showing a fiddler perched on a roof of an old-world cottage, the authors tell the children that Chagall read about the character in the stories of Sholom Aleichem. I had considerable trouble explaining to my son what the word "anachronism" meant.

Our fondness for the Fiddler explains in part the popularity among North American Jews (but others as well) of the much emphasized distinction between the "East

European" and the "German" Jew. The way the story is usually told is as follows: The German Jews were modernized, on the whole, before those living under the Tsar — let us call them "Russian Jews." The German Jews often looked down on the "crude" Russian Jews, whom they called *Ostjuden* or "Eastern Jews." On the other hand, Russian Jews ridiculed German Jews for being pretentious and affected, for in order to gain acceptance by German society, which they praised as tolerant and progressive in much the same way that American Jews now praise America, German Jews emphasized the need for cultured, i.e. German, manners.

The German Jews who immigrated to North America are said to have been wealthy and well educated. They became the élite of North American Jewry. They are said to be cocky and clannish, and to keep out the ordinary American Jew, who is of "Russian" origin.

At least, that is the perception of the "ordinary" (read "Russian") Jew. (Most North American Jews came from the former Russian Empire and adjoining areas of Poland.) In the Chicago Seven trial, the defendants, most of them Jewish, made slights at Judge Hoffman based on the fact that he was a "German Jew." Dershowitz complains throughout *Chutzpah* that anti-Jewish quotas both at universities and in law firms applied particularly against "East European Jews" like himself; that is to say, not against the Germans. Even today, "German Jews" make up the bulk of the aristocratic Jews living off Central Park West in New York, and other such privileged neighbourhoods. Only in the eighties did the "Russian" and "Polish" Jews begin to replace the "German" Jews in the top board-rooms of America, a process chronicled in part in Judith Ramsey Ehrlich and Barry J. Rehfeld's book, *The New Crowd.*

There is much truth in all this, but, as in much other eji lore, also some exaggeration. Neither in Europe nor in America were the German Jews all rich, any more than the Russian Jews were all poor. Robert Brym, a sociologist who has studied the Russian intelligentsia, estimates that as many as half of the Russian intellectuals and professionals before the Bolshevik Revolution were Jewish (Russia included most of Poland then). Wealthy, urban Russian and Polish Jews often knew how to speak German (they and everybody else, until the revival movement of Sholom Aleichem and others, considered Yiddish to be a bastardized German dialect). They dealt with German-Jewish business people, and were influenced by the *haskalah* or Jewish Enlightenment movement, which spread to Russia from Germany. The "Polish" Jews who lived in Austrian Poland (Galicia), and to a much greater extent those who lived in German Poland, often acquired wealth, and once again, they came into the orbit of German culture. So the real "Russian" and "Polish" Jews sometimes behaved and even spoke much like the real "German Jews."

This is not to say that most Russian Jews were not relatively poor, uneducated in a secular sense, and culturally distinct from the wealthy German Jews. They were, but they were not much less culturally distinct from the wealthy Jews of Russia; who, in turn, resembled "German Jews" fairly closely.

It is seldom recognized that the "German" Jews had often been in Germany for only one or two generations before moving on to America. Perhaps the majority of German Jews at the turn of the twentieth century had at least some "Eastern" ancestry, for Germany, just like America, was the destination of great waves of Jewish immigrants from the Russian Empire. Those who did well moved out of the ghetto, and acquired not only money but German culture and manners. Those who did not do so well remained *Ostjuden*. The distinction was a matter of class and culture rather than of origin, strictly speaking. The situation resembled that in Latin America, where an "Indian" is a poor person of Indian culture, rather than simply a person of Indian ancestry; the "assimilated" Indian is regarded as a "*mestizzo*."

The equation of the "German Jew" with the assimilated Rich Jew and of the "Russian" or "Polish" Jew with the poor and more traditional Jew was carried to America, both by the "German Jews" and by the "Russian Jews." Since most North American Jews are in fact the descendants of Russian or Polish immigrants, opposing themselves to the German Jews helps them to define themselves as not Rich Jews (at least not in terms of their descent). I seldom meet a left-wing North American Jew who does not, in a conversation about his or her Jewishness, sooner or later bring up this distinction between German and Russian Jews. But much less radical Jews, even ones with chutzpah, like Dershowitz, are equally fond of their East European origins. You don't have to be a socialist in order to fear the stigma of the Rich Jew. It is to disprove that they are Rich Jews, and to prove that they are just like other people (other "immigrants"), that North American Jews love to think of their ancestors as typical, East European Fiddlers on the Roof.

It also makes them feel more American. For the Fiddler is in fact an American icon. Jolly, optimistic and enterprising even in misery, religious but tolerant, an unshakable believer in an individual relationship with God — is this not the hallowed American stereotype of "our ancestors," Jews, Ukrainians, Italians, Norwegians, Irish, English, who came from the Old Country to make America bloom? Among other things, the Fiddler image is the American Jew's badge of genuine Americanism. (And it works much the same way to make Jews feel at home in Canada.)

8

THE BROOKLYN JEW,
OR THE JEWISH ITALIAN

Negroes are all Jews. Italians are all Jews.

— Lenny Bruce

Tevye is the emblem of the counter-stereotypical East
European Jew: jolly, industrious, poor. In America, the job
of maintaining this sentimental self-image of the non-rich
Jew has been taken on by authors, film-makers, and comedians. At first sight our choice to illustrate this pattern may
be surprising: it is Woody Allen.

Woody Allen's depiction of the Jews bears little immediate resemblance to Sholom Aleichem's. Allen seems
much more to be the self-critical, even self-hating urban-
ite, while Sholom Aleichem focuses on the idyllic, sleepy
towns and villages of the Old World. And yet, the difference is not as great as it seems to be. Sholom Aleichem and
even more so *Fiddler on the Roof*, "the movie," share one
hidden motive with Woody Allen's wry comedy: Shylock's
Defence. The romanticism of *Fiddler on the Roof* and the
sometimes caricatural self-portraits of Woody Allen serve
up very different fare but with the same nutritional value:
lovable or ridiculous, the Jews are shown to have qualities

that folksy Gentiles have, too. And to have just as little money.

Woody Allen's *Radio Days*

There is no better example of the "Brooklyn Jew" or of Allen's treatment of the Jews than *Radio Days*. In this 1980s film, the action takes place sometime in the 1940s. A young boy looking like a little Woody Allen is brought to the rabbi by his parents. They complain that the boy has pocketed the money he had collected for the building of a Jewish homeland in Palestine. The rabbi is very upset. He hits the boy. The father protests; he wants to hit the boy himself. Now the mother insists on her right to strike him. The three end up battering the poor boy, all the while arguing about who really should be doing so.

At first blush, this anecdote from Woody Allen's film does not paint a pretty picture of the Jewish people. As such, it is as typical for Woody Allen as for the self-mocking productions of many other Jewish comedians. Many of Woody's Jewish detractors detested his films for their supposed "Jewish self-hatred," long before they detested him for his questionable erotic preferences. The ultra-nationalists have used the supposed masochism of his films to dismiss Woody's public statements against Israel's Palestinian policies. Such self-haters, they firmly believe, are like the Jewish bleeding hearts who refused to see the approach of the Holocaust.

Yet humorous self-deprecation is something even the most assertive — and the most right-wing — Jews are rather proud of. Many academic as well as TV-room philosophers have considered self-mockery an important part of Jewish humour. Irving Kristol thinks it so, as did a myriad influential authors before him: Sartre, or Freud, or Theodor Reik, who saw Jewish humour as oscillating between mega-lomaniac paranoia, and what Edmund Bergler termed "psychic masochism." Since such masochism can appear brave, it is something the typical Jew, eji or not, is proud of.

Of all the self-deprecating Jewish humour, perhaps the most popular is the kind that puts down the Jewish family.

During the Second World War, a Jewish soldier won a humour contest with a joke that described his in-laws in the Bronx, rather than Hitler, as the most threatening enemy. True enough, this was before the Auschwitz gas chambers were set into operation. With hindsight, never-theless, the joke seems rather sick, and the person who told it, an anti-Semitic, self-hating masochist.

The soldier may have been among the earliest of the Jewish funnies who, since the War, have produced a steady stream of abuse against the Jewish family, for the benefit of the Jewish and non-Jewish public at large. The secret of this genre of humour may be its perversion of what people really think of the Jewish home. Jewish prejudice views family violence as something goyish rather than Jewish. Jewish family agencies regularly complain about the dis-belief with which the community greets their reports on Jewish children in need of help. Even the Gentiles, the anti-Semites included, believe that the Jewish family is exceptionally close-knit. According to Hannah Arendt, the Gentiles' belief in the strength of the Jewish family was responsible for the fantasy of the World Jewish Conspiracy as a secretive tribe headed by the paternalistic Rothschild family.

In the background of the controversy about Woody's

behaviour with his little girl, Dylan, is the shock of the unexpected. The charge of child molesting just does not fit with the image of a "typical" hyper-urban, hyper-intellectual, hyper-sensitive "little New York Jew" that Woody portrays. This disbelief, shared even by the most skeptical, has done much to convince many that the accusations of child abuse were false.

Allen himself confirmed the image of the loving Jewish family when he compared himself, in the wake of the child-abuse charges, to his parents: "I've been a model, model father with these kids. I mean I'm affectionate like my parents were with me, but that's it."

There is a painful irony in the fact that in his private life Woody Allen has been charged with doing what he did in *Radio Days*: turning upside down the public's pro-Jewish prejudice about the Jewish family. For in the film, Jewish parents are shown not as loving nurturers but as child abusers. Now if, on a Jew's own cognizance, there isn't anything special about the Jewish family after all, then that's one big feather off the Jew's hat.

No wonder the eji comic's denigration of his family is so popular. It permits, indeed implores, the non-Jew to accept a view that is critical of the Jews, and without guilt. After all, isn't the story-teller himself a Jew? (It is, of course, absolutely essential that the anecdote be told in the first person, to create the impression that it is autobiographical and, hence, true.) Those who laugh at a true story can hardly be accused of prejudice.

At first sight, such catering to anti-Semitism may seem to be masochistic indeed. But the other side of the coin is more important. Because the Gentiles start out believing that Jewish families are after all close and loving (even though authors like Philip Roth have unearthed for the public the manipulative nature of some of the love and even though a celebrity like Woody Allen has made us all seriously doubt if the love really exists), they are not likely to think the Jewish family colder and more abusive than their own — only just as cold and just as abusive.

A Jew portraying child abuse by Jewish parents to non-Jews is not saying "Look, we're worse than you" but "Look, we're just like you." And that, exactly — Shylock's Defence — is the point. In *Radio Days* Allen presents the Jews not as Jewish but as human.

What's more, he presents them as Italian.

The Jew as Italian

Who has ever heard of a Jewish parent in recent times — unless perhaps a Hassid — taking a child to the rabbi for punishment? It is the stereotypical Catholics who take their sons to the priest. It is something Italians may do, but not Jews.

Modern Jews, both in Europe and in North America, have long had a special "thing" for Italians. The Italian is the best hope for the eji that the Jews are not so different after all. The eji believes that Jews and Italians are very much alike. In the few decades since Lenny Bruce did his famous "shtick" about "Jewish and goyish" ("Fruit salad is Jewish. Lime jello is goyish . . . Negroes are all Jews, Italians are all Jews"), Negroes have become Blacks. And while Negroes may have been Jewish, I think we'll agree that Blacks are definitely not. But that's something we'll deal with in another chapter. What concerns us right now are the Italians. We think of the Italians as in some way just like us, and of ourselves as just like them. Why?

To begin to understand, ask yourself: *which* Italians and *which* Jews are we talking about? Probably not Riccardo Muti and Leonard Bernstein. Probably not Umberto Eco and Susan Sontag. Nor are we talking about an Italian and a Jewish industrialist or banker. What we are talking about are shopkeepers, cabbies, the owners of a corner restaurant or a deli. In other words, we are talking about the lower middle class and the working class. We are talking about the "Brooklyn Jew" and the Brooklyn Italian. We are talking about the *not rich*.

To Northern Europeans, Italians have traditionally represented the "Southern type," a group of people who might not be entirely agreeable in all respects, but who nevertheless appear as vivacious, creative, and essentially harmless. The typical Jew, being "dark" in appearance like the Italian, has no hope of passing for a descendant of the ancient tribes of Yorkshire or the Baltic Coast, but can relatively easily appear as hailing from the shores of Naples. The Jews make much of the fact. I was surprised to witness the following as I watched a comic sketch on "Saturday Night Live": Two women are chatting in a mock TV talk show ("Coffee Talk"). One sighs that her daughter is marrying a "goy." The other replies, "I'll tell ya, my first husband was Italian, but go figure, he looked Jewish." (It was not the reply that surprised me — but that it was given by a character played by Glenn Close, who is certainly not Jewish. I am sure the sketch owed much more to Mike Myers, who played the other "woman.") But the Jewish belief that Jews and Italians look alike is much older than a recent television show. In a mid-nineteenth century comic play by the German author A. Bahn, one of the Jewish characters is made to say, in heavily Yiddishized

German, that Italians "look *nebbich eppes* Jewish." In
Russia, some Jews, afraid to refer to themselves as such
when they might be overheard by Gentiles, replaced the
word "Jew" with "Italian."

Paradoxically, to the Jew the Italians are the prototypi-
cal goyim. In North America, working-class Italians tend to
live in the same neighbourhoods as lower-middle-class
Jews, or right next to them. They end up representing the
non-Jewish world, as the Ukrainians did to the village Jews
of old Russia. Jewish teenagers often have adventures with
Italian neighbours of the opposite sex. To many Jewish
boys — viz. Philip Roth's Portnoy — the Italian girl
becomes their first, and therefore in a way their typical,
shiksa.

The pomp and ceremony of the Catholic church to
which most Italians belong further reinforce the view of
Italians as the arch-Christian people. The visibility of their
Catholic practices is much greater than the rituals of other
Christian denominations. The Pope, furthermore, resides
in Rome, and when not a Pole, is usually an Italian.

The Italian, then, is the most distinctively Christian
group in the neighbourhood, and yet at the same time one
that appears somewhat "Jewish." This makes the Italians
the best choice for those looking for a Gentile group whose
Jewish-like traits prove that the Jews are not unique.

Woody has played up the ambiguity to the fullest. The
"real" Italians parodied in *Broadway Danny Rose* are
resplendent with exaggerated stereotypical and definitely
non-Jewish characteristics: they are superstitiously
Catholic, and given to organized crime and vendettas. But
under that crass veneer, they look and talk just like Jews.
At a party of Italian-American crime bosses, Danny Rose,

the former small-time comic, easily falls into using the same trite routines he had used with a Jewish crowd in the Catskills. There is an immediacy between Danny and Woody's Italians that is far removed from the tension we see in his other movies between himself and the WASPs, or in the desperate anxiety of his jokes about Nazis. Here he is among a related tribe, estranged cousins, long-lost relatives. Danny's shiksa, Tina (played by Mia Farrow), is of course Italian. Their liaison is the fulfilment of what Danny describes as the three principles of his uncle Sidney: acceptance, forgiveness, love. When Danny couples with Tina, the counter-stereotypical Jew embraces the stereotypical goy: they become one. The affair of Danny and Tina is the most innocent and beautiful of all the troubled relationships portrayed by Woody or his surrogates. As if to celebrate this union, the local deli names a sandwich after Danny Rose. The film ends with someone's comment that it must have been a bagel with cream cheese, topped by marinara sauce.

Such a Jewish-Italian sandwich might be a metaphor for the no less pungent, if much less subtle, mix of ethnic stereotypes in *Radio Days*. Here we chance upon a Jewish family who acts like a bunch of Fellini Italians. They talk, eat, and dance wildly, and, like Italians, vacillate between religious obscurantism and Communism. (The fat uncle walks over the yard to the Communist neighbours to complain that they are disturbing the fast of Yom Kippur with their loud music. He comes back mouthing Marxist phrases, and complaining of indigestion after an overindulgent meal of pork.) Typical "Brooklyn Jews," in other words, whether or not they live in Brooklyn; but they could be typical Brooklyn Italians.

As if to counterbalance this Italianization of his Jews, Allen incidentally brings in an Italian Mafia matriarch who talks like a Jewish grandmother. She uses the same Yiddishy voice modulations that Woody put in the mouth of Angelina, the Italian-American fortune teller in *Broadway Danny Rose*. Just a tool to obscure the dividing line between Jew and Gentile by confusing their stereotypes. A similar reversal of ethnic labels takes place in another Hollywood comedy, *Family Business*, where Dustin Hoffman, a Jew in real life, plays a husband of half-Italian, half-Irish (read impeccably working class) origins, who has married into a vivacious Jewish family of the *Radio Days* type.

There are of course important similarities between the real Jews and the real Italians. When, on a shopping trip to one of Rome's open-air markets I explained to the salesperson that I was not Italian, he was incredulous. "Face Italiana!" he exclaimed, adding a gentle slap on my cheek. Quite a few Jews and Italians do look alike. The kids in Philip Roth's *Portnoy's Complaint*, not being able to pass for WASPs, try to pass for Italians. It is the same story with Chico Marx mouthing his famous Italian accent, something that the Marx brothers themselves poked fun at. In *Animal Crackers*, Chico discovers that a man posturing as an industrialist of patrician descent is in fact an immigrant from Czechoslovakia. "How did you get to be Rusco W. Chandler?" Chico asks. "How did you get to be Italian?" replies the would-be Anglo-Saxon, answering, in proverbial Jewish fashion, a question with a question.

Both the Jewish and the Italian family have the image of a strongly cohesive if quarrelsome unit, within which the father has trouble living up to the ideal of the upright patriarch, and the mother lives a life of chronic drudgery, mitigated by the love she feels for her family and they feel for her.

Furthermore, there is now scientific evidence that American Jews tend to talk a lot and talk aggressively, like the stereotypical Italians, if not more so (the linguists Deborah Tannen and Deborah Schiffrin have data to prove it). The lively lack of discipline among Israeli passengers has even reportedly prompted British Airways to show their flight attendants a video on how to deal with a crowd who won't "just sit down and read a book for five hours like other people." Surely, however, there are other people just as unruly, as anyone who has travelled Alitalia — or, for that matter, Yugoslav Airlines — will confirm.

So the Mediterranean temper of the Jews is likely more than just fiction; one suspects it is even a point in favour of their claim to the Holy Land. But that is not the whole story. There are also great differences between the Jew and the Italian, both the typical and the stereotypical ones. What makes Allen's Jews Italian is that the differences are gone in them.

The stereotypical Jew is arrogant; the Italian, like the *Radio Days* Jew, is warm hearted. The Jew is supposed to be cerebral, the Italian physical; the Jewish lawbreaker given to white-collar crime, the Italian to violence. Totie Fields, the Jewish American comedienne, portrayed the crass stereotype of the Italian, and liked to confront it with her own image as a pitiable, insecure Jewess: "I had to smack six Italian men. Not one of them would pinch me, so I pinched them." Joan Rivers, as TV hostess, remembered performing "stand-up comedy for six dollars a night in Mafia strip joints so tough I was afraid to say, 'Stop me if you've heard this one.' "

The contrast between the stereotypical, "cerebral" Jew and the physical "Italian" Jew is in fact nicely illustrated in an incident in *Radio Days* itself. Little Woody is at the zoo with his parents. Another boy, a famous mathematical genius, appears. Little Allen's parents say a few awed words to the arrogant Wunderkind. Then the father violently knocks off little Woody's hat, exclaiming, "Why can't you be a genius?!" Wagner, Goebbels, and Hitler claimed that all Jews were abstract airheads not in touch with reality; but here to prove them wrong is a little Jew who is not an abstract nowhere-man, but a down-to-earth, folksy Jewish Italian.

The most important difference in the stereotypes is that, above all, the Jews are seen as rich and greedy; the Italians, of modest means and working class. The *Radio Days* Jews are, appropriately, working class.

We are talking about stereotypes, not reality. In reality, there are indeed many Jewish members of the working class and of the less well-off ranks of the lower middle class. (Notice, though, that there are many Jewish as well as Italian taxi drivers; however, although Italians are often construction workers, few Jews have joined them in that trade. The taxi driver could be said to be an entrepreneur who works more or less for himself [or herself], and is in direct contact with the public, for the most part without supervision. The taxi driver is the working-class equivalent of a doctor or a lawyer.) However, the anti-Semitic stereotype does not speak of working-class taxi-driving Jews, but of Jews with money and degrees. The function of the "Brooklyn Jew" counter-stereotype is to show that the Jew can be just as working-class as an Italian.

Woody Allen himself likes to joke about the lowly circumstances of his own parents. He claims never to have

seen his parents with a book. When asked about the greatest mistake of his life, he replies, "Besides not having been
born in a good family, probably that I did not choose
another profession when I had the chance." He also says
that his father, like the one in *Radio Days*, drove a taxi, but
naturally, along with doing other jobs.

In reality, it turns out that the "other jobs" were rather
more important than the taxi driving. Woody Allen, whose
real name is Allen Stewart Konigsberg, gave very little co-
operation to his biographer, Gerald McKnight. The film
image of the Allen family shown in *Annie Hall*, living in
miserable circumstances in a tenement house that every
now and then trembled with the shock waves of the nearby
roller-coaster, was too precious to Woody Allen's career to
be dissolved in a report on his real childhood circumstances. But McKnight did discover Allen's parents in
Florida, and he managed to speak with his mother. He con-
cluded that his parents displayed an "unshakable instinct
for survival which only material success, the respectability
of sound education and solid achievement could bring."
Allen's father, Marty Konigsberg, lived in relative prosperity before the Depression as a jewellery engraver. The
Depression, as well as newly developed engraving technology briefly made him superfluous in the early thirties, and
he did resort to taxi driving as a very temporary expedient.
The Brooklyn Jew father, on the other hand, may dream of
becoming a jewellery engraver but never makes it, for in his
wife's words he has "no business sense." Instead, he sticks
to taxi driving, a job he is ashamed of and an activity he
keeps hidden from his children.

The real elder Konigsberg soon found his way back to
engraving. Woody grew up not in Rockaway, the district

depicted in *Radio Days*, but in Midwood, an area "officially described in 1957 as a 'section of upper middle income families . . . comprised of private homes, a few high rental apartment houses . . . the majority falling into [the category of] exclusive private accommodation.' " He went to a prize-winning public school, PS 99, which had one of the best scholastic averages in New York.

Although not particularly wealthy, Woody Allen's parents were no paupers. Why then has it been so important to him to portray them as poor? It is well known that "humble origins" are part of the hero image, and a hero image may or may not be properly ascribed to Allen. But the need to describe his family as poor is also a means to fight the ominous "rich Jew" stereotype of the anti-Semites. It is the same fight that Allen carries on in films like *Radio Days*, where he helps to build the image of the counter-stereotypical "Brooklyn Jew," the North American version of the "Jewish Proletarian."

9

THE PROLETARIAN INTERNATIONALIST: TROTSKY, LUXEMBURG ET AL.

Medem: *"You consider yourself, I suppose, either a Russian or a Jew."*
Trotsky: *"No, you are wrong. I am a Social Democrat and only that."*

The "Fiddler" and the "Brooklyn Jew" counter-stereotypes are in some sense the mild, Americanized offspring of the left radical ideology that motivated earlier Jewish socialists and communists. The credo of the "proletarian internationalists" had been that anti-semitism, like all "national antagonisms," would disappear together with the rule of the capitalists, who used anti-semitism to distract the masses from the class struggle.

One crisp autumn day in St Petersburg, in 1905, the forlorn tricolour flags of Russia still fluttered in the wind, like balloons the day after a child's birthday. Russia was rudely forced to face reality: the Tsar had dispatched his soldiers into a "little war against the Japanese dwarf," and suffered a humiliating defeat. Now angry crowds filled the streets, ripping the blue and white off the flags, and with the remaining red created a sea of "proletarian" banners whose waves overcame all obstacles, drawing in bystanders, pushing aside the helpless police.

A young man in his mid-twenties, with sharp features
and rimless spectacles, forced his way through the agitated
crowd at the University, the goal of the marching, walking,
running masses. He seemed desperate to have his word.
Though not many of the leaders recognized him, he had
little difficulty reaching the speakers' gallery. He took in
the immense crowd. It was the occasion he had been
waiting for for years. His youth belied his skill as a speaker;
he was an orator with a hundred styles. His imagery was
always violent, and so it was now, as he decried the Tsar's
recent offer of limited civil rights:

> Citizens! Now that we have put our foot on the neck
> of the ruling clique, they promise us freedom. It is
> this tireless hangman on the throne whom we have
> compelled to promise us freedom. What a great
> triumph this is! . . . citizens! Our strength is in
> ourselves. With sword in hand we must defend
> freedom. The Tsar's Manifesto . . . is only a scrap of
> paper.

The speaker waved the manifesto in front of the crowd,
and crumpled it in his fist. He was known to some of his
enraptured listeners as Yanovsky. This was a pseudonym
taken from a Colonel Yanovsky, who had sold his southern
Ukrainian estate to the speaker's parents, Jews by the name
of Bronstein. In the South Russian Workers' Union in
Odessa, "Yanovsky" went as Lvov. He signed his articles
written in Siberian exile as Antid Oto. But to posterity his
best-known pseudonym was to be one he took from one of
his prison guards in Odessa — Trotsky.

Trotsky, the founder of the Red Army, did almost as

much to help the Russian Jews as he did to help his Party. But he would never say so.

The Russian Revolution was inextricably involved with the fate of Russian Jewry. The drama began with the failure of the first parliament, the Duma. This assembly was declared by the Tsar as part of the reforms announced in the manifesto, which was rejected by Trotsky with contempt. While radical socialists were excluded from the new institution, it gave the more moderate opposition high hopes about reforming the Tsarist government from within. This moderate opposition, like the radicals, included a good number of Jews.

There were twelve Jewish deputies, the majority of them members of the Constitutional Democratic Party. These were mostly genuine non-Jewish Jews: the Zionist member Shmarya Levin had to explain the customs of the Sabbath to his fellow Jewish deputies, so they could understand a Jewish joke he wished to tell them. Because of increasing anti-Jewish violence in the country, all the Jewish deputies joined in a parliamentary faction that was to vote uniformly on Jewish matters.

The Duma summoned the Minister for Home Affairs, Stolypin, to explain the government's role in the bloody pogroms that then raged more or less unchecked in the Pale of Settlement (the only area, mostly in Ukraine, Belarus, and Lithuania, where the Jews were allowed to reside without a special permit). Stolypin politely promised an answer within a month. But before the month had begun, a savage pogrom had again been perpetrated at Bialystok. The feeling in the Duma was that the government had not only disregarded their concern, but had once again organized, or at best permitted, an atrocity against

Russian citizens. A committee with one Jewish member was sent to investigate. In response to its report, the Jewish deputies Vinaver, Jacubson, and Rodichev made impassioned speeches. With a large majority, the Duma called upon the Tsar to dismiss the government.

The atmosphere during the debate was heavily charged. The deputies knew that they now stood at the parting of the ways. Two days later, when they turned up at the chamber, they found the doors locked and guarded. Outside was posted the manifesto of the Tsar dissolving the Duma. So it was that the Tsar's experiment with parliamentary democracy faltered over a disagreement on a "Jewish issue."

It was also a Jewish matter that split up the radical Social Democratic Party, and created the movement that was to rule Russia for more than seventy years, the Bolsheviks. "Bolshevik" means "member of the majority." The term refers to the fact that at the 1903 congress of the Russian Social Democratic Labour Party, this movement, led by Lenin, gained the majority of votes. But they would not have been the majority if they had not first forced the delegates of the Jewish Bund to quit.

The Jewish Bund wanted autonomy within the Social Democratic Party, paralleling the autonomy they demanded within Russia for the Jewish people. Many of the Jewish as well as Gentile socialists were violently opposed to the idea.

The roots of the conflict went back to the founding conference of the Russian Social Democratic Workers Party in Minsk, in the Pale of Settlement, in 1898. Financial and logistical support was provided by the Jewish Bund. Only nine delegates were present; of these, the Bund had three.

The remaining two-thirds included two representatives of the paper *Rabochaya Gazeta,* and one emissary each from the "Leagues of Struggle for the Liberation of the Working Class" at St Petersburg, Moscow, Kiev, and Yekaterinoslav. Some of these were undoubtedly Jewish as well.

Even more significant than the organizational support given to the Party by the Bund was the superior "consciousness" of the Jewish workers the Bund represented. The 1890s saw the first manifestation of genuine "proletarian activism" in Russia. A set of strikes broke out among Jewish workers in Poland and the Pale, and grew until it reached the mostly non-Jewish work force of central Russia. Jewish workers (overwhelmingly employees of small shops or independent artisans, rather than factory workers) remained foremost among the strikers, however, even as Gentile "proletarians" were joining them steadily. Sure of worker support, the Bundist Arkady Kremer published his famous pamphlet *On Agitation* (1893), which gave the entire Russian social democracy a new strategic foundation. Kremer suggested that socialist intellectuals concentrate on supporting the strikers' immediate demands. In this way they would gain control of the workers' movement. They could then use the strikes as an "elementary school" of revolution, through which the workers would be educated to support the overall goals of the movement.

In the light of the events, it seemed perfectly natural to the delegate of the St Petersburg Workers Organization, Brouckère, to state that "the Jewish proletariat knew its rights better than the Russian proletariat did," and that the Jewish proletariat, as the more conscious one, should come to the aid of the Russian, because "the consciousness of the more advanced proletariat must help to raise the level of consciousness of the more backward one." All delegates to this First Congress agreed that in consideration of its importance in the movement, the Bund would be given autonomy within the new party.

No wonder, then, that the Bundists came to the Second Congress of 1903, which first met in Brussels and then moved to London, with considerable chutzpah. In addition to their historical "rights," they could point to their still remarkably strong position in the workers' movement. A year before, when there was another wave of strikes, Jewish strikers had still been in the majority. In return for the services they had rendered to the movement, the Bundists felt that a formal reconfirmation of their autonomy was not too much to ask.

Most speakers thought otherwise. The consensus appeared to be that the socialist movement had by now taken sufficient hold among the non-Jewish workers, so that special consideration for the Bund was no longer necessary.

To Lenin, the Bundists' demands were a godsend. This was the conference where he wished to foist a policy of tight centralization on the Party. Most of the delegates appeared at best lukewarm to the idea. They wanted a Party based on self-governing, local grass-roots committees. Lenin was no anti-Semite, but he knew that it could not hurt to have a Jewish organization as the most visible opponent of centralization. Most delegates, no matter how much they were against centralization, wanted to show some muscle to those stuck-up Jews of the Bund.

Against the protests of the Bundists, Lenin shrewdly pushed through an agenda on which the Bund's autonomy figured first. In this way, if the Bund were defeated, it would be more difficult for those who wanted a loose party organization to win the day.

Under the less-than-arms-length chairmanship of Mikhail Plekhanov, the discussion was marked by constant acrimony. Emotions flared out of control; accusations of particularism and of dictatorial tendencies were freely exchanged.

The Bund's case was presented for the most part by Max Lieber. Having lost the procedural battle about the place of the Bund item on the agenda, he was now faced with the disagreeable task of presenting a case on whose merits, as he put it, "the majority of the delegates have formed a definite opinion" in advance. He suggested a federation of the Bund and the rest of the Party, and justified it with the following words:

> First and foremost the question arises, why do we need to have an organisation for the Jewish proletariat? It could be justified, in the first place, by those particularly harsh legal conditions under which the Jewish proletariat lives, regardless of the language it speaks; secondly, by the fact that the relation of social forces in the Jewish nation is quite distinctive, in that, for example, there are no nobles, no landowners, and no peasants in it.

What Lieber chose not to stress was that the Jewish socialists were also upset by the treatment they often received from non-Jewish activists. A revolutionary associate of Trotsky's, Lev Deutsch, for example, complained of insensitivity to the pogroms among the exiled socialists whose lot he shared for a time. At the time, in the 1880s, Deutsch was in Switzerland. As a good eji, he was loath to speak out as a Jew himself, so he and his fellow-activist

Pavel Axelrod sought a non-Jewish socialist to write a pamphlet condemning the carnage. No one, including Plekhanov, was willing to find the time to help.

The attitude of the delegates at the congress did nothing to allay the Bundists' fears that the delegates cared little for the Jews. While Lenin allowed no suggestion of contempt to creep into his interventions, provincial delegates betrayed their bias through the very nonchalant manner in which they condemned the Jewish particularism of the Bund. Towards the end of the debate, serious proposals advanced by Lieber met with uncontrolled laughter among many of those in the hall.

It is not known what the many Jews from outside the Bund thought of that. What is certain is that, without exception, they showed themselves hostile. They were incensed by the Bundists' proposal that the Bund represent all Jewish workers in Russia, whether they lived in the Pale of Settlement or not. The Bundists wanted the exclusive right to agitate among Jewish workers throughout the Empire.

This idea seemed perfectly logical to the Bundists. They had adopted the concept of "personal autonomy" championed by Austrian social democrats such as Otto Bauer (who was Jewish as well). This meant giving people "autonomy" on the basis of their ethnic origin, but regardless of where they lived. Such a plan made sense to the Jews, who all lived together with other ethnic groups, as well as to the Bundists, who did not want Jews to be confined to the Pale, and wanted "national" rights for them even if they moved to Moscow or St Petersburg. (Incidentally, Menahem Begin, Israel's prime minister of Lithuanian-Polish ancestry, used this very same Bundist concept of "personal autonomy" in his offers of autonomy for Palestinians in the Israeli-held "West Bank.")

Lenin, who later described Bauer's ideas as "petty bourgeois," was not impressed. But the Jewish socialists outside the Bund were downright angry. The difference of opinion between them and the Bund had everything to do with where each group of socialists lived. Robert J. Brym in his fascinating monograph, *The Jewish Intelligentsia and Russian Marxism*, has shown that for the most part only Jewish revolutionaries in the northern Pale tended to join the Bund, while those outside worked in the "general" movement. The biographies of the leading revolutionaries neatly illustrate the point. Some were first active in the Bund when they lived in the Pale, and then left it upon their move to Moscow or St Petersburg. Conversely, some socialist leaders became Bundists when the authorities forcibly resettled them in the Pale. The explanation for this was simple: in the northern Pale, the Jewish workers approached in number the non-Jewish proletariat, and were better organized and more "conscious" than the latter. The Jewish radicals living there could not ignore this fact. One of the principal reasons for forming a Jewish workers' movement was that the Jews were the most "convenient" group of workers among whom they could agitate. On the other hand, those activists who managed to get out of the Pale lived where few if any of the "proletarians" were Jewish. To stress their Jewishness in these places might have alienated the workers.

For these socialists, the suggestion that the Bundists represent Jewish workers, regardless of where they lived, touched a raw nerve. Would this mean that Trotsky and others, who could be defined as "Jewish workers," would come under the hegemony of the Bund? And what would the non-Jewish workers think of being organized by a Jew, when Gentiles were supposed to leave organizing among Jews to Jews alone?

The opposition to Lieber was lead by Julius O. Martov, arguably the social democrat with the largest grass-roots following in Russia, greater than that of Trotsky or Lenin. Martov, a Russian Jew born in Istanbul, was a radical journalist. He was also the informal leader of the group that was against Lenin's centralization scheme. Perhaps to stress how unconcerned he was with Jewish issues, he walked straight into Lenin's trap, and prepared a resolution rejecting the Bund's autonomy request. It was signed by twelve people — all of them Jews. The debate that followed included a verbal duel between Lieber and Trotsky that was among the most emotional at the congress.

For once presenting himself as a Jew rather than "a Social Democrat and only that," Trotsky described Martov's resolution as a virtual manifesto by the non-Bundist Jewish socialists:

> Trotsky: I think it not without value to add to the resolution moved by Comrade Martov that this resolution is signed by Jewish comrades who, working in the All-Russia Party, have considered and consider themselves also to be representatives of the Jewish proletariat.
> Lieber: Among whom they have never worked.
> Trotsky: I request that both my statement and Comrade Lieber's exclamation be entered in the minutes.
> Lieber: I ask that it be recorded in the minutes that the chairman did not stop Comrade Trotsky

when by his statement he committed a gross piece
of tactlessness.

Chairman (Plekhanov): No special entry in the
minutes is called for, since it will be obvious from
them anyway that I did not stop Comrade Trotsky.

Lieber: I insist on this being entered in the minutes.

Chairman: Then be so good as to submit your statement in writing to the Bureau.

Lieber presented a statement which read as follows: "I
take note that the chairman did not stop Comrade Trotsky
when he mentioned that the persons who introduced the
resolution belonged to the Jewish nationality, thereby committing a gross violation of tact and turning the entire
dispute on this question into a matter of national passions."

The logic of Lieber's intervention qualifies it as a unique
production of the eji mind. How could a Jewish autonomist
feel that referring to people as Jews was a "gross violation of
tact"! Lieber's offence at Trotsky's statement revealed the
peculiarly defensive nature of the Bund's view of Jewishness, at least at this time. The Bundists were as careful as any
other Jewish intellectuals to disassociate themselves from
any particularly Jewish reasoning. They presented the need
for a separate Jewish movement as flowing from the general
principles of social democracy, and not from anything
uniquely Jewish. The resolution of the Bund's Fourth Congress, which brought on the controversy in Brussels and
London, was careful to stress that even in asking for autonomy, the Jews were just like everyone else:

The congress recognises that a state like Russia,
composed of a multitude of heterogeneous nationalities, must in the future become transformed into

a federation of nationalities, with full autonomy for each of them, regardless of the territory they inhabit.

The congress recognises that the concept "nationality" is applicable to the Jewish people as well.

By so appealing to general principles, the Bundists hoped to dispel any suspicion that they wanted special treatment for the Jews as such.

Incidentally, even the left-wing Zionists of the "Poalei Zion" movement justified the need for settling in Palestine by an analysis based on universal socialist rather than particular nationalist grounds. The Poalei Zion ideologist, Ber Borokhov, argued, using Marxian terminology, that before they are ready for socialism, the workers as well as the bourgeoisie must go through a "normal" capitalist phase. But the Jewish workers in Russia were not allowed to go through this development, because they were kept out of the large factories by the non-Jewish employees, and confined to the small-time, old-fashioned, precapitalist workshops. The reason for going to Palestine would be that a Jewish working class would be free to develop there.

If the left-wing Zionists engaged in such intellectual acrobatics to justify themselves as adherents to Shylock's Defence, the Bundists, who were opposed to leaving Russia, were all the more careful not to appear to be particularist. Indeed, their declaration ended with the shy afterthought that a demand for Jewish autonomy, once formulated, ought to be put on the back burner.

Considering, however, that it is premature in the present circumstances to put forward the demand for national autonomy for the Jews, the congress

finds that it is sufficient for the time being to fight
for the abolition of all discriminatory laws against
the Jews, and to record and protest against manifestations of oppression of the Jewish nationality,
while avoiding any fanning of the flames of
national feeling, which could only befog the class
consciousness of the proletariat and lead to
chauvinism.

Lieber was upset that despite such carefully phrased
professions of internationalism, Trotsky encouraged
"national passions" by daring to suggest that it mattered
that the opposition to the Bundists came from people
whose "nationality" was Jewish. This was "the gross violation of tact" supposedly committed by Trotsky.

Trotsky had no comprehension of such odd niceties. All
he was saying was, "You're not the only Jewish social democrats. We are Jews, too. So don't claim to represent all
Jews." He might have thought, too, "Don't force us, through
your personal autonomy idea, to act as Jews. We are Jews but
want to act as Russian, not Jewish, revolutionaries."

The Martov–Trotsky position made sense to most of
those present, and the Bund's request was denied. The five
angry Bund delegates walked out, taking crucial votes from
the camp that opposed Lenin's centralization scheme. As
a result, Lenin won a slight majority. Hence the expression
bolsheviki, or "members of the majority." Lenin was so successful in exploiting his London victory that the term stuck
with his faction, who later became a splinter party.
Although Martov's group had a stronger following among
the workers, it had to contend with the label *mensheviki*,
or "members of the minority."

Trotsky, who continued to have some differences with Lenin, was undoubtedly brought closer to him as a result of their co-operation in marginalizing the Bund. Fourteen years later, the two men triumphantly took stock of the Bolshevik Revolution, which together they wrought.

Trotsky as a Jew

In his autobiography, *My Life,* Trotsky was as loath to ascribe any Jewish character to himself as to the Revolution. He described his father as an almost illiterate "farmer." But the elder Bronstein owned four hundred acres and leased two hundred more, and he employed a number of farm hands. It is perhaps not impossible that he had more familiarity with the three R's than his son would have his readers believe. As a revolutionary, Trotsky naturally preferred the image of a Ukrainian farmer to that of a Jewish land owner and lessee.

When he was a child, his brilliance gained him admission to St Paul's Realschule in Odessa, a German school that had a large number of Jewish pupils, despite its policy of applying an anti-Jewish admissions quota. Here Trotsky received some instruction in Judaism, taught in Russian, although — he assures his readers — the lessons "were never taken seriously by the boys."

The essence of Proletarian Style is to ask people to look at the Jewish revolutionary not as a Jew but as a champion of the working class. When Marx said, "Religion is the opiate of the masses," there is every reason to believe that by religion he meant not only a set of beliefs and practices but also membership in a group defined by religion. Jew or non-Jew, the question of religious origin is a red herring, he and generations of Jewish Marxists were saying. What matters is whose side you're on in the class struggle. Proletarians of all lands, unite! — and forget the nonsense about Gentile and Jew.

So Trotsky was careful to play down any influence of his Jewish background on himself or on his politics. He was not blind to anti-Jewish discrimination, and admitted that this "national inequality probably was one of the underlying causes of my dissatisfaction with the existing order." However, he hastened to add, this concern was "lost among all the other phases of social injustice."

Even so, Trotsky's parents were as proud of him as any good Jewish father and mother. They understood that although their son was "only a Social Democrat," his actions helped the oppressed Jews. Their solidarity with their son was movingly demonstrated during his trial for planning an armed insurrection.

On October 23, 1905, the Soviet under Trotsky's informal leadership planned a mass funeral procession to honour workers who had been shot by police during the preceding strikes. It was learned that extraordinary measures were being planned to repress the procession, and that government forces were secretly planning anti-Jewish pogroms. Trotsky persuaded the Soviet to call off the funeral demonstration. Instead, the Soviet proceeded to form its first armed squads, whose task was to protect the Jews. This anti-pogrom force was the beginning of what was to become, under Trotsky's leadership, the Red Army. It was poorly armed, yet sufficient to prevent the pogroms which, according to evidence gathered by Lopukhin, a police official who conducted an inquiry into the matter, were indeed being planned. Lopukhin wished to testify (but was not allowed to by the magistrates) that the police had printed anti-Jewish pamphlets to be distributed in St Petersburg, and

that the Black Hundreds, armed gangs chiefly responsible
for the recent wave of pogroms, stood under the direct command of General Trepov of the gendarmerie.

When Trotsky took the stand, he did not yet know of
Lopukhin's revelations. He referred instead to the statement of Prince Urusov, who had heard one of the leaders
of the police say, "We can make a pogrom whenever it suits
us, a pogrom of ten people, if we wish, or of ten thousand."

We had no doubt that behind the façade of the
Black Hundreds was the powerful fist of the ruling
clique. Gentlemen the judges! This sinister fist we
see even now in front of us!

The prosecution is asking you to recognize that
the Soviet armed the workers for the direct struggle
against the existing "form of government." . . . I am
asking you: What exactly does the prosecution
mean by "form of government"? . . . if you tell me
that the pogroms, the arson, the violence . . . if you
tell me that all that has happened in Tver, Rostov,
Kursk, Siedlce . . . if you tell me that Kishinev,
Odessa, Bialystok [places where pogroms took
place] represent the form of government of the
Russian Empire, then — yes, then I recognize
together with the prosecution, that in October and
November we were arming ourselves against the
form of government of the Russian Empire.

At the trial, Trotsky's mother wept quietly, while his
father stared at him with pride. Unfortunately, Trotsky's
mother was disappointed in the sentence. She had hoped
that the admiration Trotsky's words earned him in the

audience would have swayed the judge as well. After all, even the prosecutor had complimented him on his courageous speech. Nevertheless, Trotsky and fourteen others were sent to Siberia for life.

Of course, he escaped. The Tsarist officials were furious. Enemies within the Movement later intimated that Trotsky saved himself because his father was rich; Trotsky bribed the guards to let him go.

It was typical of Trotsky that with all the many names he used throughout his early career, he never chose a Jewish-sounding pseudonym. He, like most other Jews of the underground, wished to avoid appearing Jewish to the "masses" of non-Jews, the "proletarians" that he wanted to lead into a new society. He suspected, probably correctly, that the people were still far from ready to give up the opiate of anti-Semitism.

Trotsky's reluctance to have the Revolution appear as Jewish-inspired explains some of the most fateful characteristics of his revolutionary career. When Lenin asked him to be Commissar of Home Affairs, he refused the post, which would have made him responsible for the struggle against "the counter-revolution." Trotsky argued that it would look bad to have a Jew lead the Cheka (the ancestor of the KGB, already quite heavily Jewish in composition). Lenin disagreed, but was swayed by another Jewish communist, Sverdlov, who agreed with Trotsky.

Although Trotsky has not admitted this, it may well be that similar considerations prevented him from taking even more important official positions that had been offered him. There can be no doubt that in the 1905 Revolution he loomed "larger than any of the older leaders." Yet he made sure that it was not he, but the lawyer Khrustalev-

Nosar, who was elected President of the St Petersburg Soviet. In the successful 1917 Bolshevik Revolution, Trotsky's role was even more enormous. Jacques Sadoul, an eyewitness and later a Stalinist, reported that "Trotsky dominates the insurrection, being its soul of steel, while Lenin remains rather its theoretician." To reward Trotsky for leading the uprising, Lenin wanted him to head the first Soviet government. Yet Trotsky refused. In his autobiography, he claims to have refused out of deference to Lenin's seniority. But it is difficult to imagine a man of Trotsky's ambitions, and one whose relationship to Lenin had often been troubled, to have had no other motive than honest respect in giving up the chance to lead the world's first proletarian revolutionary regime. He bowed out, perhaps, out of a desire not to besmirch the Revolution with the stigma of being "Jewish."

It is also possible that Trotsky just wanted to concentrate on his major preoccupation, building the Red Army. He combined sound military judgment with tireless propaganda, continuing to instil in ordinary Russians the enthusiasm that had won the Revolution. It is clear that words as much as anything else gained the Bolsheviks victory in the civil war. Arrayed against them were not only counter-revolutionary troops led by professionally educated officers but invasionary forces from several countries. The enemy had their passions whipped up by religious and nationalist agitation, including a heavy dose of anti-Semitism, which often turned ugly. Yet the discipline and motivation of the Reds enabled them to better their opponents. By 1922, it was clear that the Bolsheviks had won.

Lenin, who never showed any signs of worrying about promoting Jews to high positions, recognized fully that Trotsky had been the chief field commander both in the Revolution and in the civil war. It was hardly surprising that he designated him, in a secret testament, as his successor. At any rate, Trotsky, whom many considered brighter than Lenin, was clearly the number-two man, next in line to chair the party.

Unfortunately, the astute military strategist and seasoned revolutionary plotter showed little dexterity in fighting for the leadership after Lenin had died. Possibly, he was still reluctant to put himself, a Jew, in the job. What is certain is that he allowed himself to be outmanoeuvred by Stalin. At the time of Lenin's death, Trotsky was recovering from an illness at a Black Sea resort. Misled about the date of the funeral, he did not show up for it. Stalin stole the limelight. He was assisted by Trotsky's numerous other enemies. None of the other major leaders, Bukharin or the Jewish communists Kamenev and Zinoviev, were too keen on allowing Trotsky to take over. Despoiled of Lenin's protection, he was eventually forced into exile.

Stalin's Anti-Jewish Counter-Revolution: "Socialism in One Country"

Trotsky himself certainly felt that Stalin let the ugly old prejudice out of the bottle. "Anti-Semitism raised its head with that of anti-Trotskyism," he claimed. This must have been particularly painful for Trotsky who felt that anti-Semites made an exception for him. He once proudly referred to the Cossack who was reported to have come to complain to the anti-Bolshevik White Guards that he was "hurt by someone's taunt that he not only served under, but fought under the command of a Jew — Trotsky." The Cossack "retorted with warm conviction: 'Nothing of the sort. Trotsky is not a Jew. Trotsky is a fighter. He's ours . . . Russian! . . . It is Lenin

who is a communist, a Jew, but Trotsky is ours . . . a fighter . . .
Russian . . . our own!" It is a sad comment on Trotsky's self-
respect as a Jew that he considered such language compli-
mentary. In fact, he interpreted it to be proof of how "the
question of race . . . never had the slightest importance" during the initial stages of the revolution.

With hindsight it seems that the first serious anti-
Semitic campaign within the Communist Party took place
at the Fourteenth Congress, in 1927. Typically, the issue
was internationalism. The Gentile communist leaders,
Stalin and Bukharin, felt it was time to consolidate the
Bolshevik victory. Stalin proposed a policy that he baptized
"socialism in one country." Quietly he began to give a little
more room to Russian national feelings, in order to gain
more popularity for the regime. What happened beyond
Russia's borders, he and Bukharin decided, was a matter
for the future. The Jewish Bolsheviks had no stomach for
this. To them any flirtation with nationalism meant a dangerous distraction from the class struggle.

Kamenev and Zinoviev now joined their former enemy,
Trotsky, to defend the cause of proletarian internationalism in its pure form. They dreamed on about a world in
which the masses break out of the shackles not only of class
but also of nation and religion. Stalin was content to
pervert this ideal as he had many others: His International
was to be a tool, not in the first place for worldwide revolution, but for the extension of Soviet Russian power.

Stalin, of course, was not a Russian but a Georgian from
the remote Caucasus. But this was not to be the first time
that a stranger from the alien provinces stirred the revolution of a people on the road towards National Greatness.
Stalin's Napoleonic pretensions infuriated the three

Jewish Bolsheviks. However, Kamenev and Zinoviev were powerless to prevent Trotsky's expulsion from the USSR in 1929. In 1936, when Trotsky took up residence in Mexico, Kamenev and Zinoviev were manipulated in a show trial to confess to being Trotsky's cronies in a trumped-up plot against Stalin. They were executed, along with Trotsky's rival Bukharin, Stalin's ally on "socialism in one country," but unlike Stalin a moderate on centralizing the government and the economy.

Bukharin's example shows that the Jews were certainly not the only ones to fall victim to Stalin's terror. The largest number were peasants who died as the result of the forced collectivization campaign; either because they were executed as *kulaks* ("rich farmers") or because they starved in the hunger caused by the ill-advised policy. Ukrainian nationalists claim that the deaths of millions in their country during this period were deliberately planned by Stalin, in order to subjugate a nation whose brief independence had been recognized by the 1918 Treaty of Brest-Litovsk, negotiated with the Germans by Trotsky. Still, some Ukrainians (Nikita Khrushchev, for example) fared well under Stalin, as did some Jews. (Lazar Kaganovich, blamed for much of the anti-peasant repression, was one of them.) Although the Jewish role in the government was never to approach even remotely what it had been under Lenin, some Jews remained powerful. The anti-Semitic innuendo of the show trials soon seemed over, and we can well imagine the surviving Jewish communists counting their blessings.

In 1938, Stalin entrusted a fellow Georgian, Lavrenty Pavlovich Beria, with heading the infamous NKVD secret police. It would be hard to defend the record of this shadowy organization, but Jewish NKVD officers did help fellow Jews who survived the Holocaust in the Russian-liberated parts of Europe. (My own father may owe his life to them. After the liberation of Budapest, he was tortured by Hungarian police for serving as an interpreter to Soviet soldiers, who had abandoned him during a spree of pillaging. Only the arrival of two NKVD officers saved him from a possibly much worse fate.)

If the Jewish NKVD officers had any such feelings of solidarity when it came to the Trotsky case, however, they certainly kept them to themselves. It was in 1940, when Stalin still enjoyed his "peace treaty" with Hitler, that Stalin's long arm managed to find Trotsky in far-away Mexico. The architect of the Bolshevik victory was attacked by a Stalinist agent and hacked down by an ax. Never one to give up easily, Trotsky started at his murderer, tore the ax from him, grabbed his finger and bit it. His wife, Natalya, rushed in. Trotsky stumbled into her arms, and quietly collapsed.

Rosa Luxemburg

The tragic death of Trotsky recalled that of Rosa Luxemburg in Berlin twenty-two years earlier. The officer who shot the Polish-born agitator in the head and dumped her body from a bridge into the river may be presumed to have had right-wing sympathies. But the murder took place at a time when Germany was ruled by a Social Democratic government. If proof were needed of the government's reluctance to protect the "foreign Jews" in the radical movement, one sidekick in the murder got two years and two weeks in prison, one got four months, and the others went free. For in some ways, and aside from the not inconsiderable differences, Luxemburg's death was also a betrayal by fellow socialists who had given up internationalism.

The Social Democratic Party had supported

Germany's war effort in World War I. This caused the radical, internationalist faction of Karl Liebknecht, Rosa Luxemburg, and Karl Radek to split off. There were many Jews both in the mainstream party and in the splinter group, which eventually became the core of the new Communist Party of Germany. But the latter was even more closely identified with the Jews in the mind of the public. Two of the trio that led the radicals, Luxemburg and Radek, were Polish Jews. Liebknecht was not Jewish, but he looked like a Jew and was considered one by the anti-Semites. In the following poem, many readers would have equated the three leaders mentioned with "the Jews":

> Many hundred corpses in a row,
> Proletarians,
> Karl, Rosa, Radek and Co.,
> Not one of them is there,
> Proletarians.

Luxemburg's group had attempted a putsch, which had failed. In the bloody fighting during the putsch, many were killed, and the author of the heartless poem was referring to the fact that Liebknecht, Luxemburg, and Radek seem to have escaped with their lives. It was, however, not long before Karl Liebknecht and Rosa joined the rows of victims, as well.

The revenge of the "nationalist" socialists over the internationalist Jews in the movement was to be repeated many times. Just before Stalin died, he was preparing a bloody anti-Jewish purge. He instructed the KGB to "unmask" the so-called "doctors' plot," a supposed attempt by his Jewish doctors to murder him. The dress rehearsal for the repression that was to follow had already taken place in Czechoslovakia. There, practically every Jew was interrogated for supposed connections with the CIA or with the Israeli secret services. Eleven communist leaders were hanged in 1952, after phony confessions had been extracted from them by torturers under Soviet supervision. Of these, nine — including the Party chairman, Rudolf Slánský — were Jews and were so labelled in the show trials. (Artur London, one of the accused who got away with a jail sentence, described the episode in his book *The Confession*, which was later made into a film starring the celebrated Yves Montand and the distinguished French-Jewish actress Simone Signoret.)

Though Stalin died before a similar anti-Semitically tinged purge could take place in the Soviet Union, there was to be considerable anti-Jewish agitation in Communist Poland. In 1969, the Jews were told that they were free to leave, and many were fired from their jobs to make sure that they went. It was a clear victory of the national-minded wing of the Polish Left, which has always been the great majority, over the rival, and largely Jewish, internationalists, once led by Rosa Luxemburg.

Luxemburg had been passionately opposed to the creation of the Polish state in 1918. In her doctoral dissertation, she argued against Polish independence on the grounds that it would slow down the revolution in Russia. Polish independence was, to her, yet another pacifying drug for the masses, "a utopian mirage, a delusion of the workers to detract them from their class struggle." Surely she was of one mind on the issue with the non-Jewish radical, Feliks Dzierzynski. Dzierzynski was a renegade Polish nationalist who later rose to become the head of the first major Soviet secret police organization. Rosa strongly condemned the terrorist policies of her erstwhile friend, but could not disagree when Dzierzynski helped to convince Trotsky's Red Army to make a feeble attempt to conquer Poland — a move that was opposed by Lenin.

Luxemburg and her associates were not necessarily acting out of hostility to Polish interests. They were not against Poland, but against all nation states. Proletarian internationalism was their religion. It never had a more fiery advocate than Rosa Luxemburg. "What other fatherland is there," she asked, "than the improvement of life, the improvement of morality, the improvement of the intellectual strength of the great masses which constitute a people?" Her homeland was not a country, but the "proletariat."

Rosa dreamed of the day when all ethnic-national identities would be submerged in class identity. That day, the Jew–Gentile difference would disappear, not because anyone fought specifically against it, but automatically, as the result of the Revolution. The idea once seemed so attractive that even some rich Jewish bourgeois could not help but support it. The Bolsheviks may never have succeeded without the financial support of the colourful Marxist theoretician turned business tycoon, Israel Helphand alias Parvus. He had his successors. The last of the liberal capitalists with intimate ties to the Soviets, Armand Hammer and Robert Maxwell, almost lived to see the end of the twentieth century.

And yet, in the end proletarian internationalism was not much use. "Cosmopolitanism" cost the lives of Trotsky, Luxemburg, and Slánský, at the hands of, or at least with the connivance of, more national-minded, largely non-Jewish, "left" governments. And the anti-Semitic campaigns only intensified, in the guise of anti-Zionism, in the sclerotic years of communism in Eastern Europe.

The Jews just could not win. By the last years of communism, official anti-Semitism had disgusted most Jews so much that there was hardly a convinced communist left among them. Yet in many countries the "democratic revolutions" went hand in hand with still another wave of anti-Semitism.

Lech Walesa gained the presidency of Poland in a campaign in which he promised to make "clear who was a Jew and who was not." He won hands down against his major opponent, Tadeusz Mazowiecki, scion of a purely Catholic family and the perfect example of a true Polish gentleman. Mazowiecki refused to officially deny the rumours that he was Jewish, considering such a declaration to be beneath his dignity.

In Rumania, the blue-collar hero, the leader of the mine workers, Miron Cozma, equated the communists of yesterday with the *jidan* (kikes) now in the government. He was referring to the Premier, Petre Roman. Cozma was particularly irritated, he said, with the way Roman smiled.

In Hungary, the right-wing nationalist István Csurka publicly alleged that there was a Zionist-inspired international conspiracy against the country, which included the most significant source of foreign money for Hungary and all ex-communist countries: the International Monetary Fund.

... In the meantime, in what was once East Germany, the new leader of the renamed communist party, the noted reformer Gregor Gysi, a Jew, parachute-jumped from airplanes to publicize his new political team. The voters paid him little attention, but he was much noticed by the gossip papers.

Eji proletarian internationlism lived out its last days as a tragic farce.

10

The Mother, the Princess, and the Whore

My own synagogue is the only place in the world where
I . . . am defined exclusively by my being the female child
of my parents. My own synagogue is the only place in the
world where I am not named Jew.

— Cynthia Ozick

An odd thing, but not a rare one: a Jew seeking to be not
Jewish in the company of other Jews. It may even be the
chief motivation for the eji in the Diaspora to attend *shul*.
"Jew," among other things, means "different." The synagogue is one of the few places in the Diaspora where everyone is Jewish: here you are not different, "not named Jew."
In Israel, people would often say, "I don't go to the synagogue. Here, you don't need to." One might understand
them to be saying that in Israel you don't have prove your
Jewishness by going to the synagogue. But that's not it.
The point is rather that, in Israel, you don't have to go to
synagogue to prove, in a sense, that you're *not* Jewish; that
is, that you're *not different*. You can be "just like everyone
else" even out in the street. That, more than anything else,
was the goal of those who, in the smoky cafés of Vienna or
Odessa, first dreamed up the Return to the ancestral home.
   Ozick writes that the comfort she finds at the synagogue as a Jewish "human" compensates for the discrimi-

nation she encounters there as a female. The traditional synagogue docs not by far give women an equal shake.

Is sexism preferable to anti-Semitism? The hard answer to the tough question is — if one judges by what is done by female Jewish writers, cineastes, and performers — yes. Jewish popular culture is utterly sexist, and nowhere is this more obvious than in the sort of fare regularly served up by professional comics to the secular public. As if to counteract the anti-Semites' vicious teasing about the Jewish male's big nose and circumcision, Jewish humour leaves the male untouched. There are jokes about Jewish mothers, grandmothers, and the daughter-wife figure, the Jewish Princess. But the worst that happens to the image of the Jewish male are the comedy routines of male comics who amuse the audience with their neuroses, and particularly their sexual hang-ups. A joke about a Jewish father or a Jewish husband I have never heard.

Some American comediennes have joined in this merrymaking at their own expense. The public has been inundated with the productions of Jewish funny-women who want to be laughed at, not only laughed with. These women have made a subtle choice: they prefer being ridiculed as women to being hated as Jews. To their audience they offer a twisted version of Shylock's Defence: "Are not our women despicable . . . like yours?"

Of all the efforts to represent the Jew "like everyone else," this "Bad-Woman Style" is the most pernicious.

The Jewish Whore
Belle Barth, née Salzman (1911–1971), may have been the first to establish the typical American-Jewish Whore routine. Night after night, the pudgy performer wiggled

and twisted her hips through the thick smoke of the night-
club, where the audience would pause from their drinks to
hear her nasty wisdom on men, love, and sex. "Only two
words you have to learn in the Yiddish language," she would
lecture them: "*gelt* [money] and *shmuck* [penis, used also
to denigrate a foolish or incompetent man]. Because if a
man has no, he is."

The whorish comedienne must treat herself as a body
without a soul, and a body that is for sale. "When Am I
Getting the Mink, Mr Fink?," a song by the early twentieth-century comedienne Sophie Tucker is a classic:

> You made a deal with me
> I kept it faithfully
> I gave you credit for what is always C.O.D.
> You promised to give me the mink in July.
> It's three months overdue and so am I.
>
> A silver fox you're offering me.
> You're such a heel
> Look at the room rent I saved you
> In the back seat of your automobile.
> No, I won't settle for a stole.
> Don't forget, you cheapskate lover,
> The whole of me you've got to cover.
> Now I want my mink, Mr Fink, right now.

The Jewish comedienne is not irresistible. She is a sex
object, but not a first-rate one. Her physical image has been
reduced to a vulgar caricature of the female form. Bette
Midler describes how she once decided to find out how
heavy her breasts were by using a postage scale: "I won't
tell you how much they weigh, but it cost $87.50 to send

'em to Brazil. Third class." In such bawdiness there is much more, or rather much less, than sex appeal. There is in it, in fact, a crass put-down of female beauty.

There is also money, money, money. Men who would cry "Nazi" at the slightest suggestion of a Jewish man's avarice, laugh along with the anti-Semites at these grotesque caricatures of greedy Jewesses, insatiable in their lust, not for sex, but for money. The Jewish comedienne is a symbolic prostitute, a personification of a timeless anti-Semitic male fantasy, the Jewish Whore.

Anti-Semites often like to visit Jewish prostitutes, just like white racists favour black ones. It gives them a chance to feel power both over women and a people they despise. But paradoxically, when a Jewish hooker sells herself to an anti-Semite, she does perform a defence of sorts for the Jews, as a by-product of her service. When she makes the anti-Semitic male desire her as a woman, she forces upon him the recognition of her humanity: a Jewish woman is still a woman.

The Nazis understood the danger that sexual debasement of a Jewess posed for their obsessive desire to show the Jews as not fully human. They limited sexual exploitation of the deportees to concentration camp bordellos staffed by Jewish sex slaves. The inmates, allowed a partial humanity, were thus given a humiliating chance to survive. On the other hand, concentration camp personnel were permitted no sexual interest in the millions of women destined for the gas chambers. The SS men and their henchmen who operated the gas chambers were strictly forbidden to rape their naked victims before forcing them into the "shower rooms." It was essential that those involved in the "special action" should banish all human feelings, even sadistic ones,

towards those to be "processed." *Eine Judin* had to be only
that and totally that, a Jewess. No common ground between
her and other humans was to be tolerated; even if their commonality was limited to the ability to arouse sexual desire in
its most degrading form.

The Jewish Whore, however, has a pedigree as a fantasy
figure that goes back centuries beyond the Nazis. She is,
in fact, a stock character of Western popular mythology.
That she should be so is only logical. The "Jew" and the
Whore are both stereotypes of people who care more for
money than for their soul. The Jewish Whore is a super-
stereotype combining these two creatures of greed.

Part of the New Testament story of Good against Gold
is the tale of Mary Magdalen, the first Jewish Whore. Once
a common prostitute, she changed her ways and came to
be regarded as a saintly woman, in many ways the closest
to Christ. This Holy Harlot is as much a part of traditional
Christian ideology as the reformed (i.e. baptized) Jew. For
Christianity is all about how you can overcome a base
beginning and become a saint.

Mary Magdalen's rise from sin is repeated by one of the
major images of Western fiction before the twentieth
century: *la belle juive,* the Beautiful Jewess. "Their eyes,"
said Balzac of Jewish women, "no doubt retain something
of the infinite that they have contemplated." From
Marlowe's Abigail in *The Jew of Malta* to Walter Scott's
Rebecca in *Ivanhoe* or Maupassant's Rachel in
Mademoiselle Fifi, the beauty and sensuality of the Jewess
is combined with a spirituality evocative of the Holy Land.
Yet most examples of the *belle juive* start, like Mary
Magdalen, as a whore or at best as a mistress. Typically, the
beautiful Jewess falls in love with a wonderful non-Jewish

man who becomes her bridge to Gentile society and, often, to Christian values. Through her uncompromising devotion, she, the ex-whore, becomes even more "moral" than her man, who normally gives in to social pressures and dumps her for a more genteel mate.

Once abandoned, the *belle juive* does not revert to either prostitution or to living in the ghetto. If she does not kill herself, she ends up in a convent or at least, like Scott's Rebecca, retires to a life of charity. For the Beautiful Jewess has traversed the ideal path of Christendom: from Judaism and carnal sin, through enlightenment by a powerful male protector, to chastity and charity.

However, the Jewess's Christian chastity is not always celebrated without equivocation. Balzac was never sure that the conversion of a Jewish Harlot was worth it. In his *A Harlot High and Low*, Esther becomes a devoted and faithful mistress to one man, Lucien, but her new-found devotion makes her admirers less than happy:

> The Torpedo is the one common whore with the makings of a true hetaira. . . . We should have bestowed on our time one of those magnificent Aspian figures without which no age can be great. . . . du Tillet would have bought her a town house, Lousteau a coach, Rastignac lackeys, des Lupeaulx a cook, Finot providing hats, Vernou would have advertised her, Bixious would have supplied her witticisms! Ah, what a loss! she would have embraced a whole century, and is in love with a commonplace young man!

Deep inside, what the nineteenth-century male romantics wanted of the *belle juive* was for her to be a temple prostitute: someone whose body you could use and feel holy

about it. The story of the tragic Jewess always retains a
sadistic kernel, no matter how much it is clad in the vest-
ments of the Church. Of this, the friar in Marlowe's *The
Jew of Malta* provides a franker illustration than most nineteenth-century variations on the theme. Abigail is slowly
dying in her convent, after she and the other nuns have
eaten rice poisoned by her evil "rich Jew" father. With her
last breath, she pleads her new faith to the monk: "Convert
my father that he may be saved, / And witness that I die a
Christian." The priest, however, has other things on mind,
as he retorts, "Ay, and a virgin too; that grieves me most."

Such brutal lechery is ultimately what the female
comedian plays up to when she presents herself as a Jewish
Whore, a crass caricature unprotected by either Christian
symbolism or Jewish self-respect. Jewish feminists are
understandably impatient with the typical ribald Jewish
comedienne. Yet the demand for the Jewish Whore character is so strong that few producers or entertainers can
resist it.

It seems difficult for a Jewish actress to stay out of the
role. For sympathetic Jewish roles, film-makers typically
use non-Jewish women. Vanessa Redgrave (the passionate
"anti-Zionist") and Meryl Streep are among the performers
who have distinguished themselves in such roles. It is true
that in the Israeli film *The Dreamers*, a story about the early
Jewish settlers in Israel, the lead role is played by an Israeli
Jewish actress, but she is — a blonde!

Barbra Streisand is one performer who has refused to
be limited entirely to the usual "funny Jewess" roles. Her
feminist credentials are hardly beyond reproach, and her
positive portrayal of a rather passive mistress in *Prince of
Tides* aroused considerable criticism. Yet in *Yentl* she

charmingly combined a feminist agenda with Jewish pride, and a dose of good old Hollywood shmaltz. This is the film version of I.B. Singer's story of a girl in old Poland who poses as a boy, in order to be allowed to devote herself fully to the study of Talmud.

To make the film, Streisand had to be her own producer. She no doubt realized some savings by shooting in then communist Czechoslovakia. In Prague, she gave the remaining Jewish population, who had been totally "assimilated," an unusual opportunity to act Jewish, as well as to earn some pocket money. Practically the whole "community" was hired as extras. (My uncle, a non-observant lawyer and economist, appeared with a false beard as a Hassidic Jew.)

Yet such pride and generosity is not likely to gain a Jewish woman friends. I have heard a student state, apprehensively and I am afraid correctly, that Streisand aroused more anti-Semitism than the "self-hating" comediennes of the Joan Rivers type. For when Streisand plays a Jewess, she is first of all a Jew. Joan Rivers is first of all a Bad-Woman.

The Jewish Mother

The comedienne who does a Jewish Whore routine is inviting men to laugh at Woman as a sex partner. There are other female roles that get hit by the Bad-Woman Style. Mother is one.

It is not clear how and when the Jewish Mother stereotype originated, though it is a thoroughly untraditional one. In Philip Roth's 1967 bestseller, *Portnoy's Complaint*, the hero is beset by parents who are "the outstanding producers and packagers of guilt in our time! They render it from me like fat from a chicken." It is above all the mother who pesters Alex Portnoy, ostensibly for not being in touch with her and his dad. "Alex," she moans, "to pick up the phone is such a simple thing — how much longer will we be around to bother you anyway?" For this she becomes the subject of the Complaint, which at one point Portnoy summarizes succinctly in an exclamation, presented in capital letters: "BECAUSE WE CAN'T TAKE ANY MORE! BECAUSE YOU FUCKING JEWISH MOTHERS ARE JUST TOO FUCKING MUCH TO BEAR!"

Portnoy perceives his situation as "living in the middle of a Jewish joke." He probably means a joke about Jewish mothers. In fact, he tells a Jewish mother joke right in the body of the novel:

Milty the G.I. telephones from Japan. "Momma," he says, "it's Milton, I have good news! I found a wonderful Japanese girl and we were married today. As soon as I get my discharge I want to bring her home, Momma, for you to meet each other." "So," says the mother, "bring her, of course." "Oh, wonderful, Momma," says Milty, "wonderful — only I was wondering, in your little apartment, where will me and Ming Toy sleep?" "Where?" says the mother. "Why, in the bed? Where else should you sleep with your bride?" "But then where will you sleep, if we sleep in the bed? Momma, are you sure there's room?" "Milty darling, please," says the mother, "everything is fine, don't you worry, there'll be all the room you want: as soon as I hang up, I'm killing myself."

Unless Roth made up this anecdote himself, it would seem to push the origins of the Jewish Mother joke back to at least the time of World War II. But it was Roth's book that popularized the image of the guilt-mongering Jewish mother, particularly among non-Jewish readers. And the book gained much exposure when it was made into a successful motion picture.

The Jewish Mother stereotype stands the traditional image of the Jewish mom on its head. Having a Jewish mother was once considered one of the few aspects of being Jewish that could be described as sheer luck. The Jewish mother supplied the loving support necessary to balance the paternalistic authoritarianism of the Jewish father, whose influence on the children, especially the boys, was much stronger. (Something of that family atmosphere has lingered on in Europe long after it has disappeared in North America. C'est toi qui m'a fait, "You're the One Who Made Me," rhapsodized François Feldman lovingly, in a chanson from his 1989 French hit album.)

As a matter of fact, the mother gets rather little attention in the autobiographical writing of the great male European-Jewish intellectuals. They often confess the strength of the relationship between them and their fathers. Marx loved his father well. Kafka feared his. Wittgenstein probably experienced a mixture of both emotions.

Heinrich Heine was an exception. He seemed to have as little to say about his father, a "confidante" of the House of Rothschild, as do today's North American-Jewish writers. But he reminisced just as extensively about his mother. Heine's mother had all the characteristics that American-Jewish comedians love to make funny grimaces

at: "She played the main role in my personal development.
She made a schedule of all the things I was to study; her
educational plans began even before I was born." She sold
her jewellery to support his education, when the business
of the elder Heine faltered. But, although Heine admits
that her plans were not always in concert with his character, he neither blames her for being overbearing, nor laughs
at her as a neurotic unfulfilled by her own life. The closest
he ever comes to mocking his mother is to poke gentle fun
at her obsession with serving him his favourite meals. He
summarizes his relationship to his aged mother with great
tenderness: "She is now a matron of eighty-seven, but her
spirit has not suffered from aging. She never claimed to be
the master of my true way of thinking, and has been for me
always Love and Care itself."

Heine is here merely restating the classic Jewish rever-
ence for Mother, as evidenced in such staples as *"Mayn
Yiddishe Mama,"* the well-known song whose power to put
Jewish tear ducts into action is surpassed only by the *"Kol
Nidrei"* (particularly if the latter is performed in a movie,
rather than in the synagogue).

Portnoy's complaint was, in part (and this is lost on a
non-Jewish audience), not that his mother kept to the role
of the typical Jewish mother of tradition, but that she had
perverted it. Yet, paradoxically, it is this inquisitive, over-
protective tyrant of a female progenitor that has become
the new North American image of the "Jewish mother."

The complaint that mothering can be smothering is, of
course, universal, and hardly confined to the Jews. "You're
such a Jewish Mother," a Gentile son or daughter might
complain to Mom. True, many a Jew will nowadays recognize his or her mother as fitting the role perfectly. But is

this because she is different from non-Jewish mothers, or because, thanks to the availability of the stereotype, her "Jewish mother" characteristics are more recognizable?

At any rate, in Gentile company all a Jew — a male Jew especially — has to do is to refer mockingly to his Jewish mother, and hilarity is instantaneous. No other Jewish comedy routine is as popular. The non-Jew is allowed to laugh at the Jew's family with impunity, relaxing any feelings of unease towards the Jews. And the Jew feels better that what the non-Jew laughs about is something that absolutely all human beings share: a mother.

The Jewish American Princess
Where the mother is a Jewish Mother, the daughter is a Jewish American Princess, a JAP. This, too, is a character alien to the image European Jews once had of themselves. The Jewish Princess is essentially a girl who refuses to grow up. Even as a wife, she acts like a spoiled brat. She may even despair of her man's ability to cater to her, and cry out — or whine out, rather — for her father: "How many JAPs does it take to change a light bulb? Two: one to pour the Diet Pepsi and one to yell for Daddy." The Diet Pepsi part illustrates the JAP's concern with her appearance: "What's a JAP's idea of natural childbirth? Going into the delivery room without make-up." Above all she loves expensive clothes, so that the way to tickle a JAP is "Gucci, Gucci, goo." However, her interest in looking good has nothing to do with sexual desire: "What's a JAP's idea of perfect sex? Simultaneous headaches." Nor does she, having reluctantly left her father for a husband, fulfil the other chore expected of a wife: she does not like to cook. "How does a Jewish American Princess call her family to dinner? Get in the car, kids." To her wifely

duties she much prefers the pleasures of material possession: "What is a JAP's ideal house? Six thousand square feet
with no kitchen or bedroom."

The JAP, like the Jewish Whore, wants money. She is
rich, selfish, and materialistic, yet complains of being mal-
treated. This is a mix that makes a heady potion for the
anti-Semite. For what the JAP is accused of are exactly the
traits the modern Jew-hater ascribes to all Jews. For this
reason, of all genuinely Jewish humour, JAP jokes undoubtedly appeal the most to anti-Semites, and give the most
concern to Jews who worry about Jewish self-hatred. But
the JAP joke does, like all Jewish humour, divert anti-
Semitism into more "acceptable" channels. The essence of
the JAP's materialism does not have to do with "Jewish
money" as much as with a modern crisis in the family, a
crisis that has nothing particularly Jewish about it at all.

The JAP joke was a phenomenon of the 1980s. It lived
and died with the smug, acquisitive, and superficial
"yuppie," a character that was to be crushed along with the
brilliant Jewish speculators à la Boesky and Milken.

Yuppies were not necessarily or overwhelmingly Jewish.
However, within the professional class that made up most of
yuppiedom, the Jews were disproportionately represented.
More likely than not, the JAP joke originated with Jewish
yuppie and would-be-yuppie husbands. They were frustrated with a life of searching for, and often achieving, material success, but at the cost of a strenuous lifestyle that
took its toll in marital unhappiness and breakdown.

The JAP joke takes its aim, as is so often the case in
humour, at a group of people whose social usefulness is
perceived to be on the wane. The JAP lives with a striving,
go-getter yuppie man, but she does not have a career of her

own, not even as a housewife. The traditional view of the housewife is that of a woman who nurtures and emotionally supports her man, in return for love and financial security. The perfect housewife is the object of sincere, if too often paternalistic, admiration. The JAP, on the other hand, is a housewife who has failed to deliver her side of the bargain. She neither loves nor cooks well, and she neglects the children. On the other hand, she also plays no useful role in society outside the home. In short, she is interested only in spending her husband's money.

And, of course, a JAP does not only cost much to keep, she is also dear to quit. "Why are Jewish divorces so expensive?" asks a greeting card. "Because they're worth it."

In JAP jokes, the last of the husbands who can still afford to keep their wives in the home turn against them in disappointment. Perhaps they are upset that their wives no longer enjoy being confined to the kitchen and the bedroom. Or perhaps they wish they had married a career woman more occupationally compatible with themselves. But in either case, their beef, like yuppiedom itself, is in no way specifically Jewish.

The daughter who refuses to grow up and become a wife is no more exclusively Jewish than the insatiable shopper married to a yuppie male. As a WASP university student mused to a magazine writer, "Anyone can be a JAP." The JAP was nothing but the latest addition to the cast of universal Bad-Women clad in Jewish garb: the Jewish Whore, the Jewish Mother. The Jewish puppeteers who stick up these grotesque marionettes to the gaze of the bemused audience hope that the goyim who laugh will recognize, in the shape of the ridiculous Jewess, something not so funny about themselves.

Part III

Four Important Whys

11

SAY IT AIN'T SO, WOODY; OR WHY DID WOODY DO IT?

The sexual insecurities of the characters Allen plays are quintessentially Jewish. Even the sperm in the funniest scene of Everything You Wanted To Know About Sex *turns out to be Jewish . . .*

— David Biale, *Eros and the Jews*

Why did he do it? What *exactly* happened, we'll probably never know for sure. What is certain is this: Woody Allen, hero of all baby boomers, the soul of serious humour for twenty years and more, the quintessential New York eji male, failed us all. In the late summer of 1992, two awful things became public knowledge. First, Woody had ditched his long-time mate, Mia Farrow, for her adopted daughter. Soon-Yi, born in Korea, was twenty-one according to Woody, and nineteen according to Mia. (At the time, Woody was fifty-six.) The second, and even worse, piece of news was that Woody stood accused (by Mia) of molesting their seven-year-old daughter, Dylan.

According to information generously leaked by Mia Farrow's circle, Woody one day crawled with Dylan into a play space off Mia's bedroom closet affectionately referred to as "the attic." According to *Vanity Fair*, the little girl later told the story of what happened in the "attic" as follows. Daddy asked her to stay still. He promised to take her to

Paris and to put her in his movie. Then he touched what
Dylan described as her "private part." Shocked and outraged, Mia took the advice of her lawyer, and took Dylan
to a pediatrician, who found the girl "intact." He asked
Dylan where her "private part" was. She pointed to her
shoulder. "A few minutes later," however, Dylan told Mia
that she had been too embarrassed to tell the truth. They
went back to the doctor the next day, and this time Dylan
told the story as she was to retell it again and again subsequently, with Woody allegedly touching her genitals.

I do not wish to debate the courts' verdict in the case.
What matters here is that even the actions Woody himself
admits have severely contradicted everything one expects
of Jewish men. Whether or not he is a child molester or
merely an irresponsible lover of his mate's young daughter,
he has caused deep disappointment. Jewish men are not
supposed to abuse women. Not even the anti-Semites deny
the Jewish male's image as a responsible husband and
father. My father says that in prewar Czechoslovakia,
parents whose daughter fell in love with a Jew consoled
themselves with the cliché that Jews made good husbands.
It was said that Jewish men didn't drink or beat their wives.
(A colleague confirmed that he heard the same thing said
quite recently in Poland.) Woody was described in exactly
the same terms by the journalist at *Newsweek* commenting
on the first news of the Woody-Mia imbroglio:

> He didn't get drunk or hit women, and if his char-
> acter chased around now and then, at least he had
> the decency to feel guilty over it.

It's clear, however, that Woody had long felt at least

some discomfort with such a non-drinking, non-violent "good boy" image. In *Play It Again, Sam*, Allan Felix, played by Woody, is attempting to learn how to seduce a woman from his fantasy mentor, Humphrey Bogart. As for drinking and hitting women, Bogart's advice is unambiguous. "Whatever you do," counsels Bogart on alcohol consumption, "don't tell her you don't drink. She'll think you're a Boy Scout." Bogie was also fond of administering to his women a supposedly therapeutic slap or two in the face. In his fantasies, Felix-Woody imitates his mentor: "Sorry I had to slap you around, sweetheart, but you got hysterical when I said no more."

Woody did not hit anyone, nor did he take to drink. Nevertheless, his actions seemed to show a determination to use his real life to shake off the good-guy image he had already parodied in his celluloid fantasies. There is no doubt that his involvement with young Soon-Yi was well rehearsed in his films. There are just too many examples, as we shall soon see, of his preoccupation with both a poor sexual self-evaluation and with potential sex with young women, to dismiss them as cavalierly as Woody himself has done. "Movies are fiction," he insisted. "The plots of my movies don't have any relationship to my life." Only someone who has never seen a Woody Allen film could fall for that.

So do we now dismiss Woody's films, the films we once adored, because in his life Woody has failed us, failed the image of the Jewish man, and failed, as I am about to argue, even his own standards? This is the issue I would like to deal with in this chapter, embedded as it is in greater questions: what does it mean to be a man, what does it mean to be a Jewish man, and what can Jewish men do about the problem?

There *is* a Jewish male problem. And it *is* reflected in Woody's actions. Not in the sense that Jews are more likely than Gentiles to abuse the confidence or the bodies of young women — far from it. Rather, the problem comes from the fact that Jewish men are, more than other men, *not* supposed to do such things. It is precisely because of our image as "nice" males, *that is, as un-macho males,* that we find ourselves under pressure to prove that we are "masculine" enough. In a particularly odious twist on Shylock's Defence, eji men feel pushed to be just like other men: not less macho, not more "nice." The results can be, as in Woody's case, not particularly healthy ones.

The Jewish Nerd

The issue gained some focus for me recently when I was seated on a flight to the West Coast, and picked up the airline's official magazine. What I was reading was an article on American women's fantasies. It confirmed to me the way people, including the half that is female, view the Jewish man. The author, a female psychologist, opined that white, Gentile women distinguished two types of desirable men, and identified each with an ethnic group. The wild, unrestrained giver of animal sexual pleasure was a black. The caring, considerate — and rich — mate was a Jew. Women wavered between the twin fantasies of being wildly fulfilled by the love of a black man and the comfortable security of being pampered by a Jew. Their heart was forever torn between these two extremes.

Male talk reflects this black-Jewish distinction in the imagery of the black versus the Jewish penis. Black men are said to have particularly big members; the Jew, on the other hand, is associated with the circumcision (in spite of the fact that in the English-speaking world Gentiles, including blacks, are also frequently circumcised). Popular humour associates circumcision with a diminishment of the penis. A novelty card from the fifties referred to a circumcision ceremony with the caption, "Abe's first 15% cut." A Hungarian-Jewish joke tells of a young man who agrees to convert to Judaism, and goes to hospital insisting that he be given a "castration." After the operation, the baffled doctor asks the patient if he had not meant "circumcision." "Oh, yes," replies the convert, "that is the correct expression . . ." The joke reveals that in the unconscious symbolism of popular humour, circumcision and castration are not the same thing, but they are close. The subconscious message is that the Jewish male is something less than a man.

The image of the Jewish man as a considerate mate is little compensation for this "castrated" reputation. Being caring and supportive are considered, still, to be essentially feminine qualities (and not the least by some of the most outspoken feminists). The "real" man, the macho savage, is too fiercely independent to be preoccupied with the feelings of other people. His attitude to women is one of domination and self-gratification, above all.

It is an old cliché among scholars who analyze popular female literature that to be available as a constant mate to a woman, a male first has to be feminized. The plot of "cheap" romantic novels is usually a battle between an apparently submissive and long-suffering woman and a "wild," irresponsible male. At the end, the female "wins." She gets to "have" the man for herself, and her reward is that he "settles down" with her.

The stereotypical "nice Jewish boy" is already feminized. He is already settled down. With him, the woman can skip to the end of the novel, but the excitement of the struggle is missing. Is it fun to settle down with someone who did not need to be tamed?

I make no claim that the stereotypes of the black and Jewish man are true. But only a hypocrite could deny that they are widely held. Consequently, every black man has to come to terms with being potentially thought of as a wild, sexually unrestrained savage. And every Jewish man has to come to terms with being potentially thought of as an unmasculine, sexually placid *shlemiel*, or, to use a very rough yet in this context appropriate translation, a nerd.

The nerdiness of the male Jew was once said by anti-Semites to be demonstrated by their unwillingness to fight. And it is true enough that in the past Jewish men were not particularly attracted to war. "Stop shooting, there are people here!" a Jewish soldier in World War I is said to have admonished the enemy, sticking his head out of his trench. Another classic joke, dating back to the Austro-Hungarian monarchy, has a Jew meet a stolid Gentile patrician on the train. "Von Bredow, reserve lieutenant," declaims the Gentile proudly, offering his hand. The Jew shakes it and introduces himself in turn: "Lilienthal, permanently draft-exempt." Woody's film roles confirm the stereotype, as in the following dialogue, from *Love and Death*, where Sonia convinces Boris to get involved in a political assassination:

> Sonia (Diane Keaton): What, you're suggesting passive resistance?
> Boris (Woody Allen): No, I'm suggesting active fleeing.

Laudable pacifism perhaps. But as proud as we Jewish

men may be of our pacific reputation, it is a burden on our self-image as men.

Luckily for us, in recent times our internalized stereo-type of the cowardly Jew has been challenged by the com peting image of the brave Jew of Israel. The classic Zionist movement was in one of its aspects a male self-assertion movement aimed to create a new kind of Jewish man, one whose physical strength and courage were to be a match for his mind. The Zionists approved of learning, but emphasized that it must not be divorced from such down-to-earth physical (and primarily male) activities as fighting the enemy and working the land. The Zionist effort to demonstrate Jewish bravery was the organized culmination of a struggle that had entered the personal histories of many Jewish men from the late nineteenth century on. Freud's fight with the loudmouth on his train, which we followed at the beginning of the book, is an example. During the Dreyfus affair, many Jews (like their non-Jewish friends) challenged anti-Semites to a duel, in part to prove the courage of the Jewish male. A petty French officer named Klein actually lost his life battling a physically supe-rior opponent. Later Franz Boas, the anthropologist, bore a large facial scar said to be due to a sword fight with an anti-Semite. The infamous author of *Sex and Character*, Otto Weininger (see Chapter 4), once challenged a man bigger than himself, but managed to survive unwounded. He won the duel, shooting his enemy through the temples.

The effort to change the image of the Jewish man moved from the personal realm into the collective with the establishment, mostly in the early twentieth century, of Jewish athletic clubs. This was the beginning of the "Maccabi" federation of teams, still very much alive and kicking today. It was also the time of the great Jewish boxers in America, young men some of whom, or some of whose fathers, learned to fight the hard way resisting pogroms in what was then Russia. These included the early Bolshevik militias organized by Trotsky to fight the pogroms.

Most of the organized efforts to build a more manly Jew went hand in hand with, and was often an organized part of, the Zionist movement. In practical terms, the Maccabi sports camps between the wars functioned as a training ground for potential members of the Jewish army in Palestine. But the psychological aspect was just as important. Here, menfolk once thought of as outmoded, pallid bookworms were trained to be "real men." Being a "real man" meant being capable of doing two things: work their own land with their own hands, and defend it against the enemy. That is exactly what the founders of Israel's earliest kibbutzim had in mind to do, and they did it, too.

To the credit of the Zionist idealists, women were involved in the building of agricultural settlements and the Jewish army in Palestine, and to an extent practically unheard of elsewhere. Women were trained to fight and to do the same jobs on the kibbutz as the men. Although in practice most women did not enter combat and took second place to the men on the kibbutz executive, it remains true that the males in the mainstream of Zionism did not strive to acquire, along with a more masculine image, an increased dose of misogyny; on the contrary, especially at the start, equality of the genders was part of their program. (It must also be said that among all the human rights violations that Israeli soldiers have unfortunately been accused of, one seldom if ever hears the charge of rape.) Nevertheless, it was clear from everything they said and did that the Zionist men's goal was to get rid of the unmasculine, "cowardly" image of the Diaspora Jew. So embarrassing was the stereotype to the Israelis, that until relatively recently they largely neglected the study of Holocaust history, ashamed of the supposed ease with which their Diaspora relatives allowed themselves to be slaughtered. What Israelis did tell their children about these tragic events stressed the role of the Jewish resistance.

The best example of how the Israeli male views itself is the term *sabra*, used to refer to a native-born Israeli. The *sabra* is an edible cactus (prickly pear) that grows in the arid regions of the country. It is rough and prickly on the outside, but soft and sweet inside: a symbol neither Gary Cooper nor John Wayne would have been ashamed of. Both men and women are referred to as a sabra. But when Israelis talk of the contrast between the outside and the inside, they are talking mainly of the character traits they associate with the Israeli male. The Israeli woman is allowed a lot more of the soft and sweet — on the outside as well.

The establishment of the State of Israel and its survival of numerous attacks by its enemies has done immeasurable good for the self-esteem of Jewish men everywhere. It proved that we can stand up for ourselves and fight. Still, in the Diaspora we remain for the most part an urban, upper- and lower-middle-class group, concentrated in the un-macho world of business, commerce, the liberal professions, arts, publishing, and academics. There are probably even fewer farmers and soldiers among us than a hundred years ago. Few of us volunteer to serve in the army. And, although many Jews are quite athletic, it is still true that, as a sports agent once remarked, bar mitzvah is the age when a Jewish boy finds out that he can look forward more confidently to owning a major league team than to playing on one. Much as the image of the Israeli male may have helped the image of the Diaspora Jewish man, we men outside Israel are still thought of and think of ourselves, to a large extent, as non-physical and un-macho. We think of ourselves as "Woody Allens."

Woody the Nerd

Woody Allen has, like many great comics before him — Charlie Chaplin, W.C. Fields, the Marx Brothers, Mae West — created a stock character of the cinema. Such characters have a continuity from film to film, regardless of the fact that in each film they play an ostensibly new role with a new name. From the buffoons of his earlier, "funny" films to the more philosophical *shlemiels* of his more mature period, Woody comes back as the same Jewish nerd, his laughable yet somehow serious dilemmas already familiar to us from the films before.

One of the most typical incarnations of the "funny" Woody character was Allan Felix in *Play It Again, Sam.* Allan Felix was an extreme case of a nerdy Diaspora Jew. Woody has Felix suffer not only from a bad male self-image but from a bad *Jewish* self-image, a sentiment that is subtly expressed in a scene where Allan fantasizes about his ex-wife. He sees her riding a motorcycle behind a man she calls "strong," a blond man with blue eyes. "We're divorced two weeks and she's dating a Nazi!" Allen sighs.

There are plenty of scenes in Woody's films where he depicts himself as an awful lover. In *Manhattan,* the Woody character falls in love with a woman played by Diane Keaton. After sex with her, he comments, "For two minutes I thought you were faking it." In the same film, Woody is left by his wife, as he is in several other films, but this time for "another (sic) woman." One of the things that continues to irritate the Woody character, Isaac, about his ex is that she has taken to writing her memoirs, where she says things about him that he does not like. An example: "Making love to this deeper more masterful female [her new lesbian lover] made me realize what an empty experience, what a bizarre charade sex with my husband was."

Woody-Isaac, too, is writing a book at the same time, but his description of himself is quite different: "He was as tough and romantic as the city he loved. Behind his black-rimmed glasses was the coiled sexual power of a jungle cat."

Let us not speculate too much on the "jungle" (Africa? Black men?). But let us be clear that here we are dealing with fantasy. The Woody Allen character's reality is that of a man who does wear black-rimmed glasses, but is decidedly *not* a jungle cat.

History of the Jewish Nerd
The Jewish nerd played by Woody in his films is not a new role. The troubles of the Woody character are hardly comparable in degree with those of young Otto Weininger, whose suicide in early twentieth century Vienna we spoke of earlier. But they are, perhaps, comparable in kind. In *Sex and Character*, Weininger equated the character of the Jew (cowardice and a related lack of the heroic imagination) with that of Woman. He thought that every man had something both of the Jew and of the Woman in him. The proper way for a Jewish man was to live a life dedicated to overcoming this double handicap: the handicap of not being a "normal" human (i.e. a Gentile), and the handicap of not being a real man. This double struggle of self-denial

unfortunately has remained that of many an eji male, including, in a sense, that of Woody Allen.

It is significant that Weininger was a Viennese. One of the most powerful cultural sources of early modern misogyny is Vienna, and particularly Jewish Vienna. This is not only the city where Weininger wrote his infamous classic. It is also where the celebrated playwright Arthur Schnitzler kept a meticulous diary of his tortured attempts to balance exploitative relationships with several women at the same time. In Prague, then a provincial capital northwest of Vienna, Kafka was making entries in his diary about his and his friends' visits to the brothel, and commented, "I passed by the brothel as by the house of a beloved." The quintessential Viennese Jewish man, however, was the journalist Karl Kraus, widely admired for his wit and political skepticism by the city's intellectuals. One of Kraus's most famous sayings captures the misogyny of the time and place better than any: "I have never met a woman who has not been understood, though I have met women who have not been grasped."

Why Vienna (or Prague)? The Austro-Hungarian monarchy was the one state in Europe where, more than in any other, the traditional populations of the "East" mixed with genuinely established eji of the "Western" Jewish type. Within the boundaries of a single realm lived the traditional Yiddish-speaking Jews of Galicia and Bukowina, who in most respects resembled their cousins across the border in the *shtetlach* of Russian Poland, as well as the prosperous, modern, German-speaking eji of Vienna, Prague, or Budapest (the Budapest Jews also spoke Hungarian). Earlier, these populations were relatively separated, but in the late nineteenth century, migration by

Jews and others to the big cities was so heavy that Vienna and Budapest (and to a lesser extent Prague) became over-whelmed by country people, among whom the *Ostjuden* in their distinctive garb were a veritable visible minority. They were a great embarrassment to their *eji* compatriots, who were themselves descended from parents or grand-parents of a similar appearance. They felt particularly put upon to prove to themselves and to the Gentiles that they were genuinely modern people, rather than some disguised cousins of these awkward migrants. In Austria-Hungary, unlike in Germany, France, or America, these migrants came from the same realm, and could not even be ridiculed as "foreign" Jews. The embarrassment they caused to the *eji* was correspondingly greater here, and especially so in the major cultural centres, and particularly Vienna. Among the main criticisms of the *Ostjude* voiced by the "assimilated" Jews was that their men were pale, dirty, and unathletic — the opposite of Germanic masculine virtue. If ever the *eji* felt the pressure not to display the suppos-edly negative characteristics of Jewish manhood, it was here.

This was Freud's home. Feminist scholars are more or less agreed that much of Freud's thinking was sexist. But few if any have related his misogyny to his ways of coping with his Jewishness. Yet his misogyny is the most telling where he is at his most Jewish: in his famous book on humour, *Jokes and Their Relationship to the Unconscious* — fondly quoted by Woody Allen, among others. A very great number of the jokes Freud cites are *shadchen* jokes. The *shadchen* was a traditional Jewish, *Ostjude* match-maker. In the jokes, the *shadchen* tries to pass onto a prospective bridegroom's family an unattractive female by pretending she is all the young man could dream of. Example: The *shadchen* presents an unattractive woman to the disappointed bridegroom and his parents. The young man whispers, so as not to offend the would-be bride: "But she's ugly, old, and squints!" The *shadchen's* face lights up with an optimistic smile as he replies: "You need not lower your voice. She's deaf as well!" Almost invariably, the poor lady's defects are described in physical terms. Freud lists several jokes where she is lame (need not worry about hurting her legs when she falls, she has hurt them already), or hump-backed (yes, she has a hump, but what a hump it is!). The prospective bride is the ultimate reject as sex object.

Freud used these ugly stereotypes of the Jewish woman much as later comics have used JAP jokes: He presents her as universal woman in Jewish guise, and so aims to refocus the anti-Semite's wrath from the Jews to women (including their own women). His book presents to the public an early example of the Bad-Woman counter-stereotype.

In both *shadchen* jokes and JAP jokes, the male character is usually left out of sight. But what *of* the JAP's husband? What *of* the boy who forms the *shadchen's* target? A "real" man would never marry a JAP, or if he did, would "teach her" as Petruchio did with Katharina in Shakespeare's *Taming of the Shrew*. A "real" man would not be the object of a *shadchen's* schemes, because a "real" man would choose his own wife.

Shadchen jokes were about traditional Jews, but they were not primarily told by traditional Jews. They belong to the humour of the "assimilated" eji of Freud's time. Freud's friends laughed about the customs of the traditional Jews, the *shadchen* included, for they wished to prove to them-

selves that they, to use a favourite phrase of the anthropologist Franz Boas, had broken the "shackles of tradition."
Yet, when the eji laugh about the traditionalist Jews, they
know they are laughing about something that is still there
in themselves. When Freud laughs about the hapless
Jewish man passively watching as an unattractive Jewish
woman is foisted upon him, Freud is laughing nervously
about himself, the Jewish male, the wimp who is less than
a man.

One way out of the embarrassment was to propose that
the discomfiture of living with a hidden wimp in one's soul
is not exclusive to the eji man; that it is, instead, typical of
all men. Indeed, Freud developed his personal experience
as an eji of turn-of-the-century Vienna into a theory of psy-
chosexual behaviour in general. David Biale, in his fascinating book, *Eros and the Jews,* speculates that behind
Woody Allen's portrayal of the sexually hapless, "castrated"
Jewish man, there is a hidden agenda: "to identify America
with Jewish culture by generalizing Jewish sexuality and
creating a safe, unthreatening space for the shlemiel
[hapless person] as an American antihero." If so, Woody
had an ancestor in Freud. Freud was hoping that the
Gentiles, or at least the Gentile men, would recognize a
commonality between their own psychological difficulties
and those of the Jews. The misogyny of the *shadchen* jokes,
certainly, was included in his book because he knew it
would appeal to the misogyny of Jewish and non-Jewish
men alike. The non-Jewish men could think of the Jewish
man as a hero for telling such jokes. Freud must have hoped
they could also relate to such woman-fearing concepts as
"penis envy" and "castrating woman." As we saw in Chapter
4, Freud was a master of "sublimation."

"Penis envy" and "castrating female" are two catch phrases that may be seen as witness to Freud's insecurities and his attempts to generalize them as a universal human problem. In *Annie Hall*, the Woody character, Alvy, discusses Annie's first session with a psychoanalyst:

Annie: Penis envy: you know about that?
Alvy: Me, I'm one of the few males who suffers from that.

Could it be that Freud suffered from it, too? However that may be, his inventing the concept of the "castrating female" has often, and I believe justifiably, been said to have been an attempt to project male insecurities onto women. The "castration" metaphor was perhaps subconsciously reinforced by the popular humorous equation between castration and circumcision, of which we spoke earlier.

Up until Soon-Yi, Woody was, like Freud, following the hidden agenda of turning the neurotic Jewish male into a universal male figure. In 1992, he gave up and turned to a more common method of male self-affirmation — finding a partner who could bolster his male ego — and he involved himself in a bizarre affair with a quasi-stepdaughter.

Shiksas and Younger Women

What Woody Allen does not share with Freud (but does share with other eji men of Freud's period and of Freud's part of the world: Mahler, Schnitzler, Kafka, Kraus) is his predilection for the shiksa. Woody Allen has never seemed to get along too well as a lover with Jewish women, either on-screen, or off. He married his first steady girlfriend, Harlene Rosen, when he was twenty and she was seventeen. The marriage, which lasted seven years, resulted in a suit against Woody by Harlene for holding her up to "scorn and ridicule." But during the years of his greatest fame he seems to have associated (at least as far as the gossip columnists have been able to discover) only with shiksas.

In this, too, Woody is typical of many eji men. One cannot, perhaps, control whom one falls in love with. But when people *always* fall in love with someone not of their own background, then there is a pattern that needs explaining. In *Annie Hall*, Woody says that the most important joke for him and his relationships with women is the famous saying used by Groucho Marx but mentioned even earlier in Freud's book on jokes: "I would never want to belong to a club that would want someone like me as a member." Most Jews have understood the Freud–Groucho witticism to imply that the exclusive club is one that does not admit Jews. Woody adds another twist to the joke: in the context of the film it is clear that the club he is talking about is controlled by — women. Not only does the Woody character worry about not being "admitted to the club" as a Jew, he tells us that he also feels rejected as a man who cannot please women.

The eji man as Jew fears that he is unattractive to Gentiles. And the eji man as man fears that he is unattractive to women. What better way to fell both fears with one blow than to secure the love of a Gentile woman?

Of course, many Jewish women prefer non-Jewish partners. The inclination seems, however, stronger in eji men. This is strikingly so in the fictional world of television. The nineties ushered in a spurt of shows with explicitly Jewish characters: "Seinfeld," "Homefront," "L.A. Law," "Love & War," "Murphy Brown," "Northern Exposure," "Sisters,"

"Flying Blind," and more. All of the Jewish stars were men; none was married to, or even dating, a Jewish woman. Off screen, the situation is not quite as drastic, but statistics do show with some consistency that more Jewish men than women marry Gentiles.

This has two unfortunate consequences for Jewish women. First, the number of Jewish women who never marry is greater than that of Gentile women. Second, since more Jewish men than women prefer non-Jewish mates, some Jewish women will be forced to marry a Gentile even if that is not their preference. Were this not so, the gap between intermarrying Jewish men and intermarrying Jewish women would be even greater than it is.

Certainly, it seems that when Jewish men go out with non-Jewish women, they prefer as shiksa-looking a woman as possible: that is, a blonde. (This partly explains the choice of such women to play Jewish roles in films directed by male Jews who don't like the look of Jewish women.) The symbolic example of such a relationship is that between Arthur Miller and Marilyn Monroe (Monroe converted to Judaism for the marriage), but others are easy to find in our own time and place. Few eji women have a corresponding predilection for the Aryan type of man. This might well mean a greater insecurity on the part of the eji man, who feels he must be able to advertise the goyishness of his mate for everyone to see.

If indeed eji men are more likely than eji women to consistently choose Gentile lovers, then the explanation is easy to find. But the crux of the matter is that while both Jewish men and women may be motivated to marry out, the men have an additional source of motivation. Being loved by a non-Jew proves to both men and women that they are not a "typical Jew" (i.e. an unattractive rich-Jew Judas). But to an eji man it also proves that he is not a "typical Jewish man," that is, a nerd and a sexual fumbler. It is something the Jewish woman, who, as we have seen, still has a considerable reputation as a sex object despite the JAP jokes (most likely invented by Jewish men — is this some kind of sex envy??), need not worry about.

The Brain as a Sex Tool

There are actually two ways open to the nerd who wants to make himself more attractive to women (for nerds are just as desirous of the love of women as other males). One thing the nerd can do is to work on becoming a "real man": popular culture makes the telephone booth where Clark Kent changes into Superman the symbol of this transformation. Perhaps a more realistic approach is to use one's intellect rather than body to do the job. For, as mothers like to say to their sons, a woman can fall in love with a man's mind — falling in love with his body can come later. In this respect, it is indisputably the intellectuals (and artists) who have the sexiest minds. In Chapter 3, we spoke of how the eji have elevated intellectual and artistic culture to a religion. There we spoke of this from the point of view of spiritual needs. But there is an aspect to the intellectualism of the Jewish man that is more physical.

Intellectually inclined male Jews, like all intellectual men, attempt to compensate for the un-macho image of the "brainer" by appealing to women's appreciation of the intellect. Indeed, their pursuit of women can become obsessive, overshooting the simple aim of finding a partner in love, and turning the admiration of women into a badge certifying genuine masculinity. That such behaviour is not always of the kind approved by moralists and psychologists was known quite some time ago to W.H. Auden, who delivered the following verdict in his "Note on Intellectuals":

To the man-in-the-street, who, I'm sorry to say
Is a keen observer of life,
The word Intellectual suggests straight away
A man who's untrue to his wife.

To secure his "conquests," the intellectual, of course, uses his strongest point, his mind. Who could doubt that it is his mind that attracted the many beautiful women Woody has been involved with? (It is typical that he never chooses a homely woman.) That Woody knows the seductive power of intellectual conversation is shown in the scene in *Love and Death* where at the end of a long conversation about subjectivity, objectivity, and immanence Sonia, whom the Woody character loves, interjects, "Let's not talk about sex all the time."

Sonia confides to Boris (Woody) that she wants a man for his intellect, his soul, *and* for his sensuousness. Boris thinks he might fit the bill. But then she reveals, to his deep disappointment, that it is his brother Ivan whom she has in mind. Boris protests that Ivan is a "moron" who can hardly trace his name in the sand with a stick. But, replies Sonia, "he has such animal magnetism." It appears that of intellect, soul, and sensuousness, it is sensuousness that is the most important.

"Sex with you is really a Kafkaesque experience," a woman declares to the Woody character in *Manhattan*. And although she quickly adds, "I mean that as a compliment," we know that Woody himself is not so sure. To the insecure male a woman's assurances that his intellect turns her on sexually are always suspect. Such a male fears that she is still missing something that he cannot give her.

So the ultimate flattery received by a Woody character occurs not in *Broadway Danny Rose*, where Tina tells him that she only gets turned on by intellectuals, but in a fantasy Woody has in *Play It Again, Sam*. Here Woody imagines Sharon, a woman with whom he is planning a first date, whispering to him after sex: "When Dick and Linda spoke of you they used terms like brilliant, genius, but they didn't say that you were also an animal." Unfortunately, that remains a fantasy. The date with Sharon turns out to be a dismal failure. And not because Sharon has any reason to doubt that "Woody" is a genius.

So the Woody character has to make do with the woman who loves him for his mind. This is the way Tina, Danny Rose's *Italian* girlfriend, confesses her weakness:

> Handsome men never did anything for me. You know what really turns me on? Intellectuals. I'm not just saying this to you to make you feel good or any-thing. You're a smooth talker. Angelina [a fortune-teller] once even predicted that I'd marry a Jew.

Fortunately (perhaps) for middle-aged Jewish men, the advantage with some women that is enjoyed by intellectu-als is similar to the one enjoyed by older men. The older man, like the intellectual, is thought to be wiser. There is a strong element of the teacher-student relationship in affairs between an older intellectual man and a younger woman, and since traditional, patriarchal society has long approved of the teacher-student metaphor for the male-female couple, men can easily feel romantic about being teachers, and women about becoming their students, even in love. The tradition of the younger man learning from the older woman is, it is true, a strong undercurrent in Western culture, especially in some continental European countries like France, but it is thought of as something of an exciting aberration rather than a normal, even laudable relationship. In the Victorian period, marriage manuals insisted on the importance of the man being a good teacher to his wife.

It is typical that in both films where a Woody Allen character gets romantically embroiled with a young woman (*Manhattan* and *Husbands and Wives*) the woman is very explicitly portrayed as a student. In *Husbands and Wives*, a film that was still being made as Woody's relationship with Soon-Yi developed, Woody himself plays a professor, making the teacher–student relationship clear. But it is a relationship that is part of any cross-generational love affair. Both lovers feel that the older person has much to teach, and the younger person much to learn.

To the older intellectual the attraction of an affair with a young person is that it combines sex for intelligence with sex for body, albeit in an odd way. The younger person is in it for the intelligence, and the older for the body. She shares with him her body in return for his sharing with her his mind. But if she ends up happy, the intellectual man's pride (like that of any man in the same situation) is flattered: he can satisfy a young woman, who prefers him to men of her own age. He is a real man, after all. And if he is Jewish, he can tell himself, "I am not just a wimpy Jew."

In *Manhattan* the young woman, Tracy, is the only person in Woody's films that says she loves sex with the

Woody character, and we do not laugh; she means it. In
Husbands and Wives he resists the temptation of getting
involved with Rain, but we know once again that her attraction to him is serious. Of course, these are all silver-screen
fantasies. With Soon-Yi, Woody was finally able to try it out
for real. It was something he had apparently considered for
a long time, and now, after much agonizing, he seems to
have given in to the urge.

There is hardly a Woody Allen film in which no allusion
is made at all to sex with the younger generation. Some of
them are subtle, as when in *Manhattan* Woody-Isaac goes
out to a restaurant with his young son, points to two young
women, and jokes that they should pick them up. Or when
in *Broadway Danny Rose* Woody-Danny asks a twelve-year-
old girl if she's married. Others are more blatant. In
Bananas Woody-Fielding is trying to buy a copy of a magazine called *Orgasm* in a news store. When the shopkeeper
loudly calls attention to him by asking his colleague how
much *Orgasm* costs, Woody tries to explain: "I'm doing a
sociological study on perversion, up to advanced child
molesting."

In the same film, Fielding becomes president of a
banana republic, and is in the United States on a fund-
raising tour. He tries to amuse his audience with an anecdote: "I'm reminded of a farmer who had incestuous
relations with both his daughters . . ." then catches himself
and adds, "it's the wrong joke for this crowd." The doubling
of the young female is, by the way, a relatively persistent
theme. In *Annie Hall* his friend Max calls Woody-Alvy Max
as well. He enthuses about a recent sexual experience:
"Twins, Max, sixteen-year-olds. Can you imagine the mathematical possibilities there, Max?" And finally, the whole

"wisdom" is summarized by the old priest (unmistakably recalling a Hassidic rabbi) consulted by Sonia in *Love and Death*. Following Sonia's imploring questions about the meaning of life, we have the following dialogue:

> Priest: I have lived many years and I have come to the conclusion that the best thing is . . .
> Sonia: Yes . . .
> Priest: Blonde twelve-year-old girls . . .
> Sonia: Father!
> Priest: Two of them, whenever possible.

A Struggle Lost

Although Woody's fascination with sex with young women is beyond denial, Woody is not known to ever have acted on it before. On the contrary, his films demonstrate that he is fully aware of the moral issues, and the psychological traps involved. "I understand, sixteen-year-old, no possible threat at all," the Diane Keaton character comments on Woody's affair with young Tracy in *Manhattan*. And we know that Woody agrees. In *Husbands and Wives* Woody, the professor, is sorely tempted by a young woman with a penchant for the "mid-life crisis set." But he resists her advances, and feels good about himself. He is being stronger than in *Manhattan*, where, it is true, he breaks up with Tracy and seeks the love of a woman more his own age, but the film ends with him running to see Tracy before she takes off to study in England, and is lost to him forever. He seems to realize that it was the young woman he really needed; only this time it is she who is determined to go.

As a famous and respected personality, Woody has no doubt always had the opportunity to take advantage of not a few young women's adoration. His movie characters, however, never took advantage of the situation. Woody's films bared to us, in minute detail, the futile inclination to buttress one's manhood by taking advantage of the admiration of overly young women. He knew it was a cop-out. He resisted the temptation, both on screen and in real life. He was right when he protested to a *Newsweek* interviewer that, in spite of what happens in his films, he was not in the habit of dating much younger women (Mia Farrow is nine years younger):

> Where, where are these young women? It's absurd, a stupid perception. It just doesn't bear out against the realities, the relationships of my life. I've been married twice, and have a long-term relationship with Diane Keaton and Mia Farrow. So the four most major relationships of my life are all age-appropriate relationships.

He is quite right that his real-life relationships have not, until Soon-Yi, mirrored his film plots as far as his love affairs are concerned. It is, however, impossible to accept that they have not mirrored his thoughts.

It is interesting that among recent authors who stress the gap between life and fiction in an author's life no one is more outspoken than Milan Kundera, the author of *The Unbearable Lightness of Being,* whose hero is an inveterate womanizer. Understandably, no author would wish to be identified with characters whose sexual behaviour is open to reproach or at least to scandalizing gossip. But we would have to be extremely naïve to accept that Woody's filmic fantasies had nothing to do with his affair with Soon-Yi.

Almost as naïve as if we took his word for it that there is
nothing to explain about that relationship: "The heart
wants what it wants. There's no logic to those things. You
meet someone and you fall in love and that's that."

Too bad. A major point of Woody's films was to bare,
without camouflage, the logic of the male "heart" (is "heart"
really the right word here?) that longs for a young woman,
and to reject it, to teach the moral lesson that mid-life fantasies were best not lived in real life. But Woody is a mortal
human being. The struggle was too hard. He failed.

The debate as to the extent of his transgression will not
soon end. Did he only fall in love with a woman that could
be his daughter? (Nothing unusual about that, for a middle-
aged man.) Or was he actually committing moral, if not
legal, incest by romancing the adopted daughter of a
woman who was more or less his common-law wife —
perhaps to punish, in some perverse way, the mother by
preferring her daughter? Or worse yet, did he really molest
his little daughter, Dylan? In other words, did he commit
an indiscretion, near-incest, or real incest? The courts
cannot close the matter; the controversy is sure to live on
for a long time. But, whatever his real guilt, here is a man
who has long waged an honest battle against the shame of
being an un-macho Jew. Laughing at his own insecurities
ultimately proved not enough. He lost the fight, and made
us all ashamed of him.

So does that invalidate his work? To some, it will. But I
think not. It is common knowledge that great men and
women have often been scoundrels in their personal lives.
Woody raised issues of male identity that speak deeply to
the men of his generation, and perhaps the generations to
come.

His films' message is that trying too hard to be macho is ridiculous. It is not worth the trouble to try not to be a (Jewish) nerd. It is Woody's bungled attempts to be macho that make us laugh, as he ineptly trics out an all-purpose exercise machine *cum* work space for executives in *Bananas*, or as he feigns heroism to conquer Sonia's feelings in *Love and Death*. The lesson is to forget about the unnecessary strains of Shylock's Defence. Accept yourself, he is telling men, and Jewish men in particular, for the man you are. *And* the Jew you are. Too bad Woody was not able to follow his own advice.

Future generations will remember his films, not his sins.

Postscript: The Death of Superman

The demise of Woody as a moral authority occurred in the same year as the ending to a rather different story. It was also in 1992 that DC Comics announced the death of Superman. The coincidence was an interesting one. Here, along with Woody's good-guy image, went another great American symbol of masculinity: the superhero in blue tights and red boots who had for half a century symbolized the male's quest to turn from sissy to macho. Superman was originally the brainchild of two young Jewish friends in their late teens, Joe Shuster and Jerry Siegel. Shuster, like Superman, died in 1992.

The man under whose black-rimmed glasses was the coiled sexual power of a jungle cat — the fantasy image of the Woody character in *Manhattan* — was clearly a version of Superman. Clark Kent, who turns into the superhero with a change of clothes, did have black-rimmed glasses. He shed them as he donned the leotards and boots and became Superman. In the sixties there was a popular poster, which showed an Orthodox Jew opening up his traditional coat to reveal a Superman outfit with the Hebrew letter *shin* in place of the "S." The idea that Superman was a Jew was seen as a joke. It was the blackest of black humour when Lenny Bruce once reportedly flung himself out of the window, crying, "I am Super-Jew!"

But would there have been anything funny about portraying *Clark Kent* as a Jew? Studious, somewhat awkward, and dedicated to his work, and yes, wearing black-rimmed glasses, he looked (except for his strong build) every bit like a "nice Jewish boy." One thing responsible for the "Jewish Superman" poster's success was perhaps that it subconsciously expressed what Jewish boys and men, including Superman's creators, have felt: as Clark Kent turned into Superman, he represented not only the nerd turning hero but also the Jewish male turning real man — a goy.

Notice, however, that Superman was macho only in the good sense, like the ideal Zionist. He was decisive, he fought the enemy, and he commanded lesser beings, but always only in the name of good: "Truth, justice, and the American way." The story of Lois Lane, the secretary who adores the unapproachable Superman but despises the wimpy Kent, follows traditional stereotypes of the female, and is to that extent rather sexist. But Superman never takes advantage of this adoring woman. For years he refuses to reveal his true identity to her. His "coiled sexual power" is expressed only symbolically, by his muscular body, his upward thrusting flight (Freud says that in dreams flying symbolizes the erection), and perhaps by his ejaculation of the beam of light that overcomes everything in its path. But it is a power that is never uncoiled, used only to tantalize Lois Lane and to spark the fantasies of the reader who longs for a Lois of his own. For years, Clark Kent suffered Lois's neglect rather than reveal to her the truth that the hero she adores is really himself.

The clean and clear male heroism of Superman was becoming unfashionable by the time Woody began to entertain the public with films representing the sad funniness of trying to be super-male. People laughed because Woody was funny, but they laughed too because the Superman type of masculine heroism could no longer be taken seriously, even in fantasy. It was the stroke of genius of another New York Jew, Stan Lee, the celebrated comicbook writer and originator of Marvel Comics, to understand this. Stan Lee created a new kind of super-hero, still clearly bearing the marks of the Superman role pattern, but lacking Superman's single-minded trust in his masculine values. In 1962 Marvel introduced Spider-Man.

Spider-Man, like Superman, needs a special outfit to perform his battles against evil. His mask has large insect-like eyes, and like a spider, he can spin webs. In these he catches the "bad guys" and delivers them to justice, and he has some other tricks up his sleeve as well. In "civilian" life he is Peter Parker, a newspaper photographer. (His publisher, J. Jonah Jamieson, cannot understand how he gets such good pictures of the scenes of Spider-Man's exploits, but never of Spider-Man himself.) Like Superman, Spider-Man loves and is loved by a woman, Mary Jane.

So far Spider-Man is very much like Superman. But his woman, Mary Jane, soon discovered his identity. In fact, they got married and have lived happily ever since. Spider-Man often considers his work a burden. He would much rather be home with Mary Jane and his live-in aunt, May.

He does not like to fight, though he feels he must. He often wishes he could go back to being a student. In short, he is a reluctant and angst-ridden super-hero. He even loses battles sometimes. A macho still, but one who has problems with being one.

In one of the incidents where Spidey's masculine image is put on the spot, Mary Jane, an aspiring actress, is offered a major Hollywood acting job. There is a catch, though: she has to take off her clothes. How will Peter Parker — Spider-Man feel about it? This is the sort of thing one could hardly imagine Superman and Lois having to deal with. But it is a tough one for Spider-Man as well, as the tension mounts through several issues of the comic book. Spidey admits that he does not like the idea. Not only might it be demeaning to Mary Jane, but imagine all his buddies seeing her in the nude!

Is this sexism, possessiveness, or the healthy jealousy of a true lover? The point is debatable. It must be said, though, that Spider-Man never forbids Mary Jane to take the job. He expresses his feelings, but threatens no sanctions. It is Mary Jane who must make the decision. What is more important to her — her career or her husband's feelings? What should a woman value more — her independence or her family? Finally, Mary Jane decides not to compromise either her personal goals or her values. She approaches the producers and agrees to take on the role, but demands they let her keep her clothes on. The movie moguls dismiss her derisively. She returns home in tears. It was not her acting skills they wanted but her body! As she sobs on hubby's shoulder, he assures her that a more worthwhile, and equally big, offer is sure to come in soon.

So we never have to find out what Spidey would do if

she did show up on the screen in the nude. His male power is not compromised, and he even gets to use it comfort his wife, who now sees the foolishness of her ways. But the episode shows that Spidey, who is no less macho than Superman, does, unlike his colleague, have to deal with serious problems as a man.

Marvel Comics managed to use the "web-slinger" to outsell rival DC Comics' Superman. Young men just had no more use for the old-fashioned, no-questions-asked hero. It was all right to admit to having problems, and even to *talk* about them, as Spidey regularly did with Mary Jane.

Despite some successful movies and the final admission of his identity to Lois, Superman never caught up again. At the end of 1992, Superman died (though he will be revived by DC in a hardly recognizable form). But for Spider-Man, Superman's death was a hollow victory. As Gorbachev learned in Russia, the nineties were not an age of compromise. To the comic fans, Spidey began to look the way reformed communism looked to the Russians: not going far enough. After all, Spider-Man was but a Superman with a more human face. The kids increasingly turned their attention to other heroes, including the Marvel team of "X-Men," headed by a woman. Many began to follow the new breed of comic artists who left both Marvel and DC to form a new association known as Image Comics.

Image, a goyish outfit if there ever was one, has no use for either Superman's clear-cut transformation from nerd to hero or for Spider-Man's wishy-washy compromises. The hottest Image artist is Todd McFarlane, whose masterful renderings of Spider-Man, often reminiscent of Japanese woodcuts in style, had made him tremendously popular among Marvel fans. McFarlane's chief character at Image, Spawn, has many of Spidey's visual character-istics, as well as the classic cape so familiar in Superman and Batman. But the story (also created by McFarlane) has more to do with popular science fiction retellings of classic fantasy tales than with boys' fears of masculine inadequacy.

Spawn is a secret agent for "the government," who gets killed in action. He makes a Faust-like deal with a Mephisto-like demon to come back to life, though it is not clear just what he promised the demon in return. His chief motivation (and here is the nod to new manhood!) is to be able to see his wife again. But that part of the story soon runs aground when he discovers that his loving wife, who still misses him badly, has remarried in the justifiable belief that Spawn would never come back. What makes things worse is that although Spawn and his wife were both black, he is now "revived" as a white man, so she cannot recog-nize him. He gets used to the disappointment, however, and his wife is no longer the issue in the subsequent instalments of the comic dedicated to Spawn's struggle to free himself from the demon's control. It is a gripping tale of a man's single-minded fight against an all-powerful, invisible, controlling enemy, in the classic tradition of Orwell's Big Brother. What matters here is that Spawn has no nerd aspect; to become a hero, he does not need to change his clothes.

Both Jewish and non-Jewish boys avidly followed the adventures of Superman and Spider-Man. But the charac-ters were created by Jews, who sublimated a particularly Jewish problem into one that all men could recognize and relate to. Like Freud and Woody Allen, Shuster and Siegel,

as well as Stan Lee, played the ultimate role of the twentieth-century eji: to speak as Jews to the heart of all people.
For in the twentieth century, the problems of the Jews
were, as we have seen, a sort of a metaphor and an exaggerated version of the problems that everyone else suffered
from, too. So it is perhaps significant that now, once again,
Jewish boys like non-Jewish ones are becoming excited
about new super-heroes, but these are no longer created by
Jews, nor do they express the old eji male dilemma of how
to turn from nerd to super-man. If that means that the
dilemma itself no longer torments the young Jewish male,
then losing out to the Gentiles in the world of comic-book
production is a small price to pay.

While the aging eji in black-rimmed glasses struggles on
desperately with the fantasy of a coiled Superman within,
the young ones will have, let us hope, better things to
dream of. And moreover, let us hope there is time for the
men to learn from the boys.

12

RELATIVISM, RELATIVITY, AND TABLE MANNERS; OR WHY DO JEWS LIKE CHINESE FOOD?

But have we ever wondered why we attach such extraordinary importance to quiet eating? . . . We have changed our table manners, then, and adopted others, the norm of which at least has been generalized throughout the Western world, where different ways of chewing no longer denote national or local traditions: they are merely good or bad. In other words, and contrary to what we have observed in exotic societies, eating habits, for westerners, no longer constitute a free code: we opt for some habits and prohibit others . . .
— Claude Lévi-Strauss, *The Origin of Table Manners: Introduction to a Science of Mythology*

Most anthropologists would probably agree that their discipline has a number of moral agendas. One of them is to convince people that what we think of as "good" and "bad" is not thought of the same way in other cultures, and, more importantly, that there is no solid reason for saying that our way of looking at it is better than theirs. Lévi-Strauss points out that before eating quietly became a universal value in Europe, eating with your mouth open was quite acceptable in some countries, including France. Indeed, the French viewed with some amusement the Germans, who ate with their mouths closed. What goes for food goes for many other habits of behaviour and even of thought, that is to say, it goes for culture in general. There are, most anthropologists agree, no objective grounds for viewing one culture as "better" than another. This attitude has been called "cultural relativism." The term "relativism" has fallen into disfavour, because it can be taken to denote the extreme position that *everything* in the world of values and of thought is relative (to culture in this case). Such extreme relativism leads to obvious pitfalls. For example, it would result in our having to agree that human sacrifice is not "bad" if done within the traditions of a culture. And if someone could convince us that Nazi anti-Semitism was integral to German culture, then we might have to accept the Holocaust as not "bad," either. So I must make it clear that here I am using the term "relativism" in a milder, less extreme sense. A relativist in this weaker sense might concede that there are *some* absolute values or truths. But he or she will challenge vehemently and wherever possible the idea that anything is good or true simply because habit, tradition, or authority maintains that it is. In this sense, anthropologists are mostly relativist, and all eji are anthropologists — particularly those enjoying their meal in a Chinese restaurant.

Except for those who are worried about MSG, almost every eji could be said to love Chinese food. Often when I am eating Chinese with a mostly Jewish crowd, the Jewish predilection for the cuisines of Canton, Peking, and Szechwan becomes a topic of light-hearted discussion. Indeed, it appears the Jews don't just love dipping into a bowl of hot-and-sour soup, they also love talking about the fact that they love doing so. Yet the puzzle of why Jews like Chinese food still remains, I believe, to be solved.

To start with, one might note that we Jews like both to talk and to eat. We will leave it to the psychoanalysts to decide whether we are an "oral people." What is certain is that eating has nearly as central a place in the life of the eji as in that of the traditionalist, who anchors much of his or her Jewish identity in eating kosher. "A good bowl of chicken soup never hurt nobody" is probably as important a slogan of Ashkenazi Jewishness as any quotation from the Bible or Talmud.

Non-Jews have always found Jewish eating habits peculiar. Shakespeare presents Shylock as eager to interact with the Gentiles, but refusing to eat with them: "I will buy with you, sell with you, talk with you, walk with you, and so following; but I will not eat with you, drink with you, nor pray with you." Of course, the reference here is to traditional religious rules of diet. But the completely non-religious eat "different," too. Back in the sixteenth century, Spanish satirists loved to lampoon the peculiar eating habits of the most "assimilated" of Jews, those who had converted to the Christian faith. More recently in the cosmopolitan cities of the West, the Jews have been in the forefront of the public experimenting with exotic foods. All New York professors are prone to eating Ethiopian or Jamaican food, but the Jewish ones more so than the rest. The less sophisticated Jew will stick to Chinese. The average uptown lower-middle-class Jew, whose Gentile neighbours (if there are any) consider chow mein an adventure, will delight in mushu pork and bird's nest soup.

The eji wants to say to the non-Jew: "Don't think that your food is superior." But it would seem too self-interested to add, "Jewish food is just as good." So the Jew says, "Chinese food is just as good." Exotic Chinese cuisine can be just as fine as the "dignified" cuisines of the West! It follows, of course, that Jewish cuisine can also be just as good, but the eji need not say so.

The Jewish diner in Chinatown is making a relativist statement similar to that of the anthropologist in his or her exotic "field." The diner is saying that no cuisine is inherently better than any other. The anthropologist is saying that no culture is inherently superior to any other. Both relativist statements can serve indirectly to validate the eji's self-respect as a member of a cultural minority.

I will go even further. The attitude of the Jewish guest in a Chinese restaurant has its parallels not only in anthropology but even in physical science. The diner who says that hot-and-sour soup can be just as good as Yorkshire pudding, depending on your culinary preferences, is saying that there is no privileged cuisine. The anthropologist who says that spirit possession among the Comoro Islanders can be just as meaningful as psychoanalysis, depending on your cultural background, is saying that there is no privileged culture. And the nuclear physicist à la Albert Einstein, who says that objects have different dimensions and that time passes at a different pace, depending on where we observe them from, is saying that there is no privileged point of observation in the universe — that in addition to our vantage point as slow-moving objects on the surface of a single planet, other points of observation yielding other views of things are conceivable.

All three attitudes, of the diner, of the anthropologist, and of the physicist, can be summed up under the one relativist proposition: "There is no single truth." It is true that Chinese food is good, but it is also true that Western food is good. In the world of cuisine, there are multiple truths. It is

true that spirit possession can offer valuable knowledge if
you are a Comoro Islander, but it is not true if you are an average Westerner. And in physics, under some conditions the
"true" length of a rocket is less if you're looking at it from a
"stationary" position on Earth than its equally "true" length
would be if you observed it from another extremely fast-
moving rocket. There are multiple truths in anthropology
and in physics, as in cuisine. Indeed, what I am claiming is
that, to the eji, there are multiple truths everywhere.

This relativist attitude to the truth is exemplified by the
rabbi in the following anecdote:

> A man comes to the Rabbi, complaining about his
> marriage. "All our problems are my wife's fault. She
> doesn't look after the children. She doesn't cook. She
> doesn't clean." "You know what," answers the Rabbi,
> "you're right." The man's wife comes in, and grum-
> bles, "My husband doesn't work. He doesn't go to the
> synagogue. He doesn't study. It's all his fault." "You
> know what," the Rabbi replies again, "you're right,
> too." A rabbinical student, a *yeshiva bokher*, who has
> been observing the proceedings, can no longer hold
> his peace. "But, Rabbi," he exclaims, "you said the
> husband is right, and the wife is right, too. They can't
> both be right!" The Rabbi reflects for a while,
> scratches his beard, and then says to the *yeshiva
> bokher*, "You know what, you're right, too!"

It is typical for the early-twentieth-century jokers who
made this up to locate the scene in a traditional rabbi's
quarters. There is every reason to believe, however, that it
was told by the "assimilated" eji rather than by the old-fash-

ioned Orthodox. I heard it from my father, who has had
little contact with *yeshiva bokhers*. European Jews of his
generation tell such jokes with an attitude of benign contempt, like the Americans who tell Polish jokes, or the
French and Dutch who tell jokes about the Belgians. It
would be worth exploring the extent to which jokes about
rabbis and their disciples served to project the eji's own
insecurities onto the "real Jews," the "backward" traditionalists from whom the eji attempted to distance themselves.

The joker who tells the anecdote does not — need it be
said — consciously aim to make a statement about plural
truths. The eji who dips his shrimp in black bean sauce is
even less aware of any significance the act may have beyond
giving pleasure to the palate. But our daily actions carry a
multiplicity of meanings we do not always perceive ourselves. In the case of the Jewish diner in a Chinese restaurant, for example, we are dealing not only with an
unconscious statement in support of relativism, but also
with an interesting symbolic relationship between the Jew
and the Chinese.

The Jew and the Chinese

In an earlier chapter, we spoke of the popular equation
between the Jew and the Italian. Although in a very different sense, the Jews have also been compared to the
Chinese.

In Asia, colonial authorities used to refer to the Chinese
as the "Jews of the East." What they had in mind was their
dedication to business and their social and cultural pride,
cohesiveness, and distinctiveness, as well as the fact that
they had a large diaspora beyond the borders of China.

European racists have long feared the "yellow peril,"

much as they trembled before the prospect of Jewish world domination. In both cases, they perceived a secretive cabal plotting to rule everyone. It might be said that the fear of the Chinese has something to do with their enormously large numbers, while the Jews are only a small group. However, there has always been in anti-Semitism a streak that claims that there are many more Jews than are visible. Recently in Poland, anti-Semites have been claiming, despite all the statistical evidence, that the country still has hundreds of thousands of Jews. There is a curious parallel here. The Chinese multitudes, so feared by the racists, are out of sight in far-away China; while it is purported that huge numbers of Jews are out of sight right here because the Jews hide their true numbers by suppressing the relevant figures — and by exaggerating their losses during the Holocaust.

The Jews themselves, however, draw a parallel of another sort between themselves and the Chinese. It is common for Jews to interpret anti-Chinese prejudice, particularly in Asia itself, as paralleling anti-Jewish prejudice here. When the defeat of South Vietnam occasioned a largely Chinese exodus from the country, Jewish communities everywhere adopted "boat people" and participated enthusiastically in charitable events. Israel instituted its first refugee assistance program for non-Jews, among other things bringing into the country its first genuine Chinese restaurateurs, and making the Chinese food craze an Israeli as well as a general Jewish phenomenon.

The appearance of Chinese restaurant owners in Israel, by the way, added to Israelis' feelings of being "a normal country just like others" (as had the arrival of Filipino guest workers). Similarly, eji diners in the Diaspora feel more like everybody else in a Chinese restaurant, because they believe that the Chinese probably cannot tell a Jew from a non-Jew (nor would they care to), so that they "mistake" the Jew for a "normal" American, Canadian, etc. A popular New York Jewish anecdote speaks of a Chinese waiter in Brooklyn, who goes back to China and means to show off his English. He is devastated when he is told that he has learned Yiddish instead.

Add some little things. Older Jewish women are famous for their love of the Chinese gambling game mah-jong. And older Jewish couples were conspicuous among the first North American visitors to China when that country opened its borders to tourists following the demise of the cultural revolution.

Among younger Jews, especially professionals, a certain amount of animosity against the Chinese has developed as a result of recent competition from highly educated immigrants from Hong Kong, and one can detect a corresponding rise in anti-Jewish sentiment among the Chinese. However, on the whole, relations between the two communities are pleasant, if not close. So the choice of Chinese food as the favoured exotic food of relativism-bent Jews is not purely the result of its greater availability or superior taste; the choice is reinforced by the symbolism that makes a parallel between Chinese and Jews.

Manners

In the symbolism of our visit to the Chinese restaurant, what matters is not only *what* we eat, but also *how* we eat it: with our mouths open, some of us. The Chinese restaurateur may confuse us with WASPs. The guests at the neighbouring table might, on the other hand, be very much aware that they're sitting next to Jews. As some of the Jewish guests wolf up their orange duck, they make no effort to hide their culinary ecstasy. Those who can, fence triumphantly with their chopsticks. The adults never stop tormenting the waiter for more rice or more water. The children express without restraint their contempt for some of the parents' culinary choices. To many a Gentile onlooker, the Jewish diners exemplify the lack of manners said to be characteristic of their "race."

Naturally, many, and probably most, Jews dine with perfectly genteel restraint. Yet it is an easily observed fact that many don't. Unrestrained gluttony is proverbially associated by not a few Jews with Jewish celebrations. Some overly sensitive Jews complain when Jewish novelists draw pictures of oral barbarism at a bar mitzvah or other function. They call the authors anti-Semitic. They deny that some Jews are loud eaters, contradicting themselves the next minute by pointing out that others (Italians!) can be loud eaters, too. Yet the same Jews may complain about bar or bat mitzvahs where they themselves witnessed such behaviour.

Everyone but the most hardened anti-Semite must agree that some Jews are among the most polished ladies and gentlemen. So was Monsieur Haas, the French socialite on whom Proust based his Swann character in *Remembrance of Things Past*. In more recent times, so is Henry Kissinger. But it is doubtful that even such elegant individuals place the same value on good manners that some Gentiles do. It is not likely that Kissinger remembers his youth in the way Joseph Alsop, a well-known journalist and self-declared WASP, does:

If you were sufficiently unfortunate as to have to wear a white tie, a whole series of other strict rules came into severe force. First and foremost, the waistcoat could not show a white line beneath the two side-wings of the coat, yet it must not be too short to cover amply the top of the trousers. For an evening suit a double line of braid on the trousers was required, whereas a mere single line of broader braid was needed for a dinner jacket.... (It was highly desirable for the stiff shirt and collar, which were absolutely essential with evening dress, to be washed in such a way that when ironed, the starched line was glossy.)

This excerpt from a much longer discourse given by Alsop on the informal dress code of the WASP of yore is remarkable not so much in its detail as in its importance to the culture of the WASP. Alsop devotes to clothes more space than to anything else in his depiction of what it felt like to be a WASP. But he dwells also on linen, table habits, and the pronunciation of certain words. In short, he associates WASPdom with the loving observance of exacting rules of manners.

There is, to be sure, no greater ritualist of food and attire than the Orthodox Jew. Among Jews, the traditional men can be distinguished by their garb and hairdo and the women by their shaved heads covered by a wig, and their diet is regimented by the laws of *kashruth*. But observing tradition is never thought of as a sign of good taste, any more than kosher food is an example of fine cuisine.

Among the Jews, the equivalent of the WASP preacher or schoolmaster sternly admonishing children on their manners simply does not exist. "It is noisy here like in a

Jewish school," an international simile we have mentioned earlier, captures the difference. Even the most liberal WASP schoolmaster must find it a struggle to fight the feeling that some of his Jewish pupils are culturally predisposed to bad manners.

Some Gentiles do not even make the effort. They equate Jewishness with bad manners, period. It is debatable if "mild" versions of anti-Semitism exist, but if they do, one of them is the sort that does not necessarily blame the Jews for any religious or economic crimes. It simply complains that they are too loud.

The more sympathetic non-Jews would not put it that way, however. They say, instead, that they are impressed with the honesty of Jewish feeling. Jews appear to be less "uptight" about protocol, they express their likes and dislikes, they joke freely about embarrassing topics, they are less fazed by authority and protocol. And it is not only the North American Gentiles, long accustomed to the Italian Jew as a figure of their popular culture, who think that way. If Sartre is any indication, the French share this view. In the Jew, writes Sartre,

> the rationalist is constantly overwhelmed by a fresh and powerful mass of passions and emotions. He joins crude sensibility to the refinements of intellectual culture. There is a sincerity, a youth, a warmth in the manifestations of friendship of a Jew that one will rarely find in a Christian, hardened as the latter is by tradition and ceremony.

Typically for a non-Jew, Sartre considers Jewish sensibility to be refreshing, but crude.

Jewish tactlessness was the central topic of John Cuddihy's brilliant book, *The Ordeal of Civility*. To the New York sociologist, the work of Marx, Freud, and Lévi-Strauss derived largely from a Jewish inability to cope with Gentile society's emphasis on "good manners." The Jews, says Cuddihy, were late to modernize, and when finally they entered the secular world, they brought with them the "crude" manners of a closely knit, patriarchal society.

But the basis of Jewish hostility to "good manners" is not, or not essentially, a kind of sour-grapes feeling in those whose upbringing did not prepare them for the best of society. Jewish "crudeness" is not so much a survival from before modernization as it is a half-conscious response to what many Jews see as Gentile snobbery.

Sartre came closer to the point when he remarked that the Jew "has as much natural tact as anybody, if by that is understood a basic comprehension of others, but he doesn't seek to have it." The Jew does not seek to "have manners" because, as a cultural outsider, he or she knows that the idea of "good manners" is a relative one.

One attraction that Chinese food has for many Jews is that eating it does not seem to require the strict, WASP-derived table manners that some associate with "fancy" restaurants serving Western food. In choosing a Chinese dish, the eji are making a statement: There is no privileged point of view on food, there is no privileged point of view on etiquette. In their personal lives, these eji display the same relativism and the same equation of cuisine, table manners, and culture that have been characteristic of the thinking of Lévi-Strauss and other great anthropologists, many of them from the ranks of the eji.

Beyond Anthropology

We have said, however, that eji relativism reaches beyond anthropology. Relativism has pervaded eji creativity throughout the arts and sciences. Paul Simon's "world music," which incorporates elements of many musical traditions (a style not of his own invention but which he helped to popularize), is an example that is relatively close to anthropology itself. In the past there have been some bizarre manifestations of eji artistic relativism, such as the films of Dziga Vertov. Vertov was a Soviet Jewish cineaste of the 1920s, who filmed indiscriminately anything the camera saw, without editing. The point was an ideological one: there were no grounds for preferring one visual experience to another. The boldness of such ultimate relativism hides a fear of making a solid choice and standing behind it. It follows from it, that (since *everything* is essentially just like everything else) the Jews are just like everyone else; but it robs all things and people totally of their individual distinctiveness. Predictably, Vertov's films excited some other avant-garde artists, but bored most viewers to death.

A more sophisticated approach to relativism would have been to recognize that although there are no grounds for preferring one thing (a cultural practice, a cuisine, a race) to another *in general,* there are distinctive contexts in which each is more appropriate than the other. Christmas turkey and *gefilte* fish are inherently of equal worth; equally tasty if equally well made. But the turkey is more suitable for Christmas and the fish for the Jewish Sabbath meal; moreover, through each meal's association with culturally distinctive festivities, the Christian may have developed a special taste for the turkey and the Jew for the fish.

In other words, the two kinds of food are equally "good," not because there is no difference between them at all, but because on some occasions, the turkey is more appropriate, and in others, the fish.

Perhaps the most consistent and the most intelligent expounder of this multiple-truth point of view has been Sir Isaiah Berlin. Berlin, a Jewish native of Russia, has devoted an astonishingly productive lifetime to disproving that "to all genuine questions there is one true answer" and that "these true answers cannot clash with one another." As a substitute, he offers a philosophy of many, and often contradictory, truths. Each truth is grounded in a particular context and a particular experience, in which alone its truth is more valid than that of another.

Relativism in Physics
However, it was not Berlin, the philosopher, but Albert Einstein, the physicist, who said, "Everyone sits in the prison of his own ideas." Einstein's relativity can be viewed as an example of relativism applied to the physical universe.

Einstein's genius resembled others in that it was based on something that we had all vaguely fathomed when we were little, but learned to forget as we grew up. As children, most of us have had the exciting experience of boarding a train for a trip, and looking out the window as the train on the next track began to move. We were convinced that it was *our* train that was moving, while the other one stayed behind. We were convinced, that is, until our parents persuaded us otherwise. Soon we learned to think of our train as being "at rest."

Relativist physics sides with the child against the

parents: one of its basic tenets is that there is no absolute rest. The other train is moving only from our point of view, or "frame of reference." From the train's point of view, *we* are moving. The proof was supplied by calculations involving motion at very high speeds. In such cases, problems could be solved more effectively by giving up the old assumption that the observer is "objectively" at rest.

To laymen, perhaps the most fascinating conclusion of Einstein's "relativity" is that even time is relative: clocks can go faster in one frame of reference than in another, if they do not both move at the same speed. Einstein's best-known brain teaser has astronauts leaving the planet at a speed nearly that of the speed of light. Their clocks run more slowly than those on Earth, and when they return, the astronauts are younger than their contemporaries who stayed behind.

What fires the imagination of the public in such examples is not only the near-absurdity of Einsteinian thought experiments. It is also their moral message: how you see things depends on your point of view, and no one point of view is superior to any other. If more than one "framework of reference" can be valid, so can more than one opinion, more than one religion, more than one way of life. This must have been in part what drew an unprecedented number of Jewish scholars into the study of nuclear physics. Einstein was only the most prominent, followed perhaps by the great Danish-Jewish physicist, Niels Bohr. In the first ranks of the science, there were hundreds more. The relativist attitude gives the answer to the question we asked early on: why has *this* branch of science, as opposed to many others, attracted so many Jews?

In his own life, Einstein exemplified the double

commitment to relativist physics and relativist morality, typical of many nuclear physicists. During World War I, Einstein was a committed pacifist. He was one of the first Germans to visit, in deepest sorrow, the graves of the French fighters at Verdun. After the visit he and his companion settled at a restaurant table. Among the guests were two French ex-officers. When they learned who Einstein was, they got up to shake his hand. It was perhaps the first attempt at genuine forgiveness between the French and the Germans after the devastating war.

In Switzerland, in Germany, and in America, Einstein consistently supported ideals of peace, justice, and equality, the same ideals that attracted many other Jewish and non-Jewish scientists to his vision of the universe.

To the "little Jew" eji, Einstein became a source of tremendous pride, a symbol both of "Jewish brains" and of the moral (i.e. not "rich") Jew. When my family and I arrived in America, a Jewish immigration agency helped us to rent a house in a lower-middle-class, then predominantly Jewish area of Philadelphia known as "Logan." Across from our white, wood-frame row house lived Mr Levi, an eccentric senior citizen, originally from Poland. I had, for a young man in my late teens, the rare ability to genuinely enjoy the prattle of the very old. Mr Levi sensed this. He lived alone in what had once been his barber shop, in a dark, permanently messy environment strewn with books and his amateur sculpture. I think I was among the very few to whom he was willing to open the door to this obscure little world. I visited him now and then, and he told me of the things he discovered through long-time, systematic self-study. One day he invited me out to a restaurant, however, and it was there that he told me his proudest secret. He was, he whispered, one of only a dozen people in the world who understood Einstein: he meant both his physics and his moral philosophy.

The restaurant was a Chinese one. With hindsight, I think that was a logical choice.

Postscript: Hiroshima

Unfortunately, the lofty relativist ideals that surrounded the research in relativist physics did not ultimately prevent it from serving as the scientific foundation for one of the worst man-made tragedies in history.

On August 6, 1945, like an evil genie emerging from the bottle, the fateful mushroom cloud rose over Hiroshima. It set off not only the death and maiming of thousands of Japanese victims, but the fear and trembling of generations to come. Here was terrifying proof of the folk wisdom that the road to hell is paved with good intentions. The French Revolution led to the guillotine and Napoleon, the 1848 German Revolution, with much delay, to Hitler, the Russian Revolution to Stalin. The relativity revolution led to the Bomb.

It all started in 1939, when the Austrian Jews Otto Frisch and Lise Meitner carried out experiments bombarding uranium atoms. They discovered that splitting one neutron created more of the same, increasing mass and releasing a spectacularly large amount of energy. Leo Szilard quickly recognized the potential of this reaction for creating destructive weapons. As Germany was already well on its way to its goal of dominating the world and "solving the Jewish problem," Szilard felt compelled to act, and to act quickly. He contacted Einstein, who was then in the United States at Princeton University. Szilard had drafted a letter to President Roosevelt, and Einstein readily added his signature.

It was this letter that is thought to have made up Roosevelt's mind. The "Manhattan Project" to develop the Bomb was initiated in 1942. The premier test had the Christian-sounding name of "Trinity," yet many of the scientists on the team headed by Robert Oppenheimer were Jewish. A number of them had ties to countries fighting against the United States — and persecuting their Jews. Szilard was there, collaborating with a fellow-Hungarian Jew, Isidor Rabi. Enrico Fermi (a Gentile married to a Jew) came from Italy. His compatriot, the Jewish-Italian Nobel Prize winner Bruno Pontecorvo, was then still in the United States. (After the war he helped to build the nuclear program of the Soviet Union.)

There was no time to lose. Everyone feared that the Germans might have the Bomb first. (They might have succeeded, in fact, had they not compelled their Jewish scientists to emigrate.) But the first nuclear test did not take place until July 16, 1945, when Germany had already been defeated.

Arguably, the project could then have been scrapped, but it was not. By this time the details about Auschwitz were out, and although Japan had not been cruel to the Jews (indeed a sizeable European-Jewish population survived as emigrés under the Japanese occupation of Shanghai), the behaviour of the Japanese towards prisoners of war recalled the Nazi concentration camps. Americans were outraged. Perhaps some racism was involved as well. At any rate, most people on the Manhattan Project, as in the U.S. military in general, supported the idea of destroying Hitler's stubborn ally quickly, and at a minimum cost in *American* lives.

After the devastation of Hiroshima and Nagasaki,

however, the scientists who had helped to make the Bomb dedicated themselves to its destruction. (An exception was the Hungarian-American Jew, Edward Teller. Unrepentant, he played a major part in developing the hydrogen bomb, even more destructive than its predecessor.) Einstein was the founder of a committee of concerned physicists who demanded that the Bomb be banned. Rabi, Szilard, Oppenheimer, and Einstein all spoke out forcefully for disarmament. Their part in the development of the Bomb was, to them, a personal tragedy. Their roots were in an intellectual culture of relativism and understanding, in an ideology of peace among all peoples. They were forced by the Nazis, sworn enemies of tolerance, to offer their services to the cause of what they could not but see as a just war. They then used relativity, a physical theory that has its roots in the tolerant philosophy of relativism, to develop the most lethal weaponry ever made.

Hiroshima made them aware of the dangers nuclear weapons posed for the future of humanity. They saw no reason to continue producing them now that the monster had been beaten — and beaten indeed without the brute weapon it had forced them to invent. History may yet show that humanity was able to avoid suicide, and live with the benefits of a scientific revolution wrought by these men and women of peace.

13

OF GRAMMAR AND THE HOLOCAUST; OR WHY DID A JEW DEFEND A HOLOCAUST-DENIER?

If we happen to be Jews, we make a point of trying to understand the anti-Semite's point of view.
— Marcel Proust, *Jean Santeuil*

It is hard to pinpoint the time when serious Chinese food (i.e. beyond foo-yong and chow mein) became *à la mode* for the eji, but it was probably during the sixties, the coming of age of the baby boomers. The period represented a flowering of eji culture — its last bloom, perhaps — that deeply affected (and was firmly a part of) the ferment in the greater society "outside." Bob Dylan and Leonard Cohen turned into verse the baby boomers' needs. Woody Allen made them laugh at their insecurities. But there were many things they did feel secure about: their intelligence, their ideals of a more just world, their contempt for the bores of the "establishment." The individual who, perhaps more than any other, embodied their self-image of intellectual vigour and their optimist idealism was Noam Chomsky, a Massachusetts Institute of Technology professor, a linguist and political activist.

Indeed, Woody seemed to be aware that he was a sort of Chomsky-in-negative, the comic, self-conscious twin

brother of the self-assured leftie intellectual represented by
the strident language scholar. Woody's characters sometimes converse about the intricacies of syntax (a field of linguistics that Chomsky revolutionized and at the same time
made incomprehensible to most, even educated people).
In *Manhattan* the Woody character has a psychoanalyst
named Chomsky. A brilliant way to represent himself as an
eji intellectual: a group of people among whom Chomsky
was once almost as popular as Freud.

In the "sixties" (to use the popular term for the period
of the Flower Children, which culminated just around
1970), Chomsky had been the hero of all "progressive intellectuals." No one had spoken with more assurance against
the war in Vietnam, his reputation brightened by his
success as a scholar. His style of linguistic analysis, known
as "generative grammar," was the hottest item in Academia.
What came to be called the "Chomskian revolution" influenced not only linguists but psychologists, anthropologists,
sociologists, and philosophers as well.

An enormous number of Chomsky's devotees were
Jewish. They stayed with him over the years, as the
American involvement in Vietnam, Chomsky's first political passion, receded into the past, and Chomsky chose
other targets, including above all Israel, which he criticized
severely for its wars with the Arabs and later for its han-
dling of the Palestinians under its control. Some of his
friends might have thought that he was being a little too
zealous, but most thought he was simply using astute political and moral judgment. Yet, even to many of his most
sincere admirers, Jewish or otherwise, his defence of an
apparent Nazi sympathizer was too much. For Chomsky
came out repeatedly in defense of the "right to speak" of a

little-known French professor of literature at the University of Lyon in France, who was under censure for his denial of the Holocaust. Eventually, the French courts convicted Robert Faurisson of "willingly falsifying history," and he was suspended from his university job. In 1980, he wrote a book to justify himself. To everyone's astonishment, Noam Chomsky chose to write the preface.

"How could he do it?" many of his followers wondered. An issue of the *Village Voice* was devoted to a largely negative appraisal of Chomsky's step.

Of course, to the general public Chomsky's fame has never approached Freud's or Woody Allen's (so when Woody used his name for his psychiatrist he was making an intellectual in-joke that not everyone would get). Whatever Chomsky did would stay out of the tabloids, which is not a comfort available to a Woody Allen. At any rate, the "cheap" press is sure to consider a personal transgression, such as Woody's, more exciting material than a questionable intellectual judgment, which is the most one can blame Chomsky for. But as far as the symptoms of the eji's decline are concerned, the Chomsky incident was the more serious. For if Woody's actions were symptomatic of the troubles of the eji male, Chomsky's located a problem in the very foundations of eji culture: a problem with Shylock's Defence itself.

The idea that the Jews are like everyone else does not go a long way to explain the Holocaust. The Nazis certainly thought the Jews were quite different, and a lot of people, unfortunately, seemed to see their point. The Holocaust has, consequently, been the thorniest issue facing the eji. The eji are supremely uncomfortable with the idea that the Holocaust was in any sense a unique event, because if so, it would support the view that says that the Jews have a destiny different from other peoples. Many of the eji who lend their voice call for a cool, calm, and collected "scientific" look at the event, free of interference from an irate Jewish community and from the courts; in other words, for an investigation that treats the Holocaust as any other incident in history.

We shall see that Chomsky's scientific work is a celebration of the universal characteristics of the human mind, as opposed to differences among human groups. As such, it provides subtle but effective support for Shylock's Defence. (If the differences among all peoples are trivial, then so is the difference between Gentiles and Jews.) It is not surprising, then, that it was Chomsky, of all people, who should be the one prominent eji to stick his neck out for the "right to speak" of those who deny the Holocaust, the one recent event that might justify the claim that the Jews are very really "different."

Certainly, it has been argued that Chomsky only defended the freedom of speech of an individual, not his ideas. But a Holocaust survivor with whom I discussed the matter put his finger on the right spot when he asked, in his Yiddish accent, "So he got nothing better to do?" Chomsky has stood up admirably for a number of causes he considered just. But surely, there are still plenty left that he could have chosen to champion, over this one.

No, his choice was not a coincidence. And there was more at stake here than freedom of speech.

Chomsky Speaks

One afternoon about a year after he wrote Faurisson's preface, I heard Chomsky speak to a captive crowd on a

typical American university campus. He had lost some of
the aura of the days when his linguistics was almost unchal-
lenged by any linguist under thirty-five, and when his
speeches set the intellectual tone of the anti-Vietnam
movement. Still, he inspired reverence, and the hushed
exuberance in Lecture Hall 3 reminded one of a Joan Baez
concert in the sixties. Chomsky, a tall, imposing figure,
made quick forays to the blackboard, in between leisurely
offered morsels of wit. Even more than his pleasant,
slightly angular face, it was his manner that charmed the
crowd. Shirt-sleeved and bespectacled, he derided his
opponents in the most unflattering terms, but with a generous touch of the well-meaning, amused sort of indul-
gence of which only the supremely self-confident are
capable — a Clark Kent certain that everybody knows he
is Superman.

"But, Professor Chomsky," a daring soul asked, "what is
your opinion of the recent article in *Language,* showing
"transformational generative grammar" to be useless to
deal with most sentence types in French?" *Language* was
at the time the most prestigious publication in linguistics.
Transformational generative grammar was the name of the
linguistic theory that made Chomsky famous. And the
article in question was one by Maurice Gross, a French linguist. After ten years of trying, Gross still could not make
transformational grammar describe more than a fraction of
the French language. First Chomsky jested charmingly
about the "low level of sophistication" of the editors of
Language, who stooped to publishing the article. Then he
replied, "I am not a butterfly collector."

The audience of professors and graduate students was
delighted. Before Chomsky, linguists used to walk the back

roads of foreign lands, paddle down jungle rivers, dog-sled through tundra, and ride camels through deserts with their large battery-operated, reel-to-reel tape recorders, cajoling natives to speak into the microphone. These scholars believed that a linguist's work should always start with collecting a "corpus" of real, recorded language. They treasured their recordings the way butterfly collectors cherish their display boards of colourful *lepidoptera*. To Chomsky, on the other hand, language was not in any important way about "the corpus." He believed that the legitimate object of linguistic inquiry was not what people actually said, but people's intuitions of what *might* be said: not linguistic performance, but linguistic competence. He was not interested in language as most people think of it, that is as speech or writing. He was interested in what in past centuries was called the "linguistic faculty."

Crucially, Chomsky believes that this linguistic faculty is (1) innate, and therefore (2) universal, that is, the same in all people regardless of what language they speak. Consequently, he devised a way to describe the grammar of each language ultimately in terms of the "universal grammar" that is the same for all. He distinguished between the "surface structure" and the "deep structure" of languages. There are intermediate stages as well, but the most shallow of structures is unique to each language (English, French, Swahili), while the deepest of deep structures is common to all. To use Chomskian terminology, universal deep structure "underlies" particular surface structures.

Notice what all this means for the relative status of those who study universals and those who study particular languages. The students of universals are devoting themselves to something absolutely essential about the human mind — in fact, Chomsky's linguistics gave an important impetus to "cognitive science," a multidisciplinary field that is today perhaps most popular among psychologists. But what of those who study particular languages (that is, "real" languages like French or Swahili, rather than the linguist-made constructions of "universal grammar")? Those researchers that are accepted by Chomskian linguists are like reporters in the field, sending back bits and scraps of footage to the news room to authenticate the view of the world presented by the anchor, who in our case would be a "universal grammarian." But woe to those who forget the universalist news room and wish to collect linguistic data simply out of a curiosity about the diversity of languages as such, for they will be labelled butterfly collectors.

To put it another way, to Chomsky the universals of language are interesting, but the individual languages, not particularly. Whatever is unique about languages is laughably trivial compared to what unites them.

This has important consequences for the study of human thought processes. Modern philosophers have showed us how almost everything we think is influenced by language. If "language" is essentially the same regardless of which particular language we speak, then it follows that differences among our languages do *not* make us think differently in any important sense. Essentially, all humans think alike. Samuel Johnson said that language was the dress of thought. If Chomsky is right, then when it comes to thinking, we all wear a uniform.

Now anthropologists have long maintained that differences among cultures are very much a matter of differences in thought patterns. If such differences are trivial, then what fool would dare to suggest that there could be

anything but unimportant, superficial differences between
cultures? And who would dare to make much of the difference between Jew and non-Jew? Shylock's Defence has
never been given such powerful support.

Chomsky's thought was widely admired. It became an
intellectual fashion. Chomsky's success was no doubt due
mostly to his great scientific significance and originality. It
did not hurt, however, that Chomsky, the linguist, was also
known as Chomsky, the leading "progressive" political
author, pamphleteer, and orator. The link between his linguistics and his politics was often stressed by Chomsky
himself. Moreover, his writing style was infused with the
cadences of political polemic: the stridency of his attacks
on other linguists was unprecedented. The combination of
brilliant argumentation with merciless belligerence gave
his scientific prose an aura reminiscent of the best political analyses of a Trotsky or a Luxemburg.

To many young people, getting a job teaching linguistics meant involvement in an intellectual revolution associated, through its leader, with the "real" revolution
sweeping the Western world's campuses. Young Ph.D.'s
began to emanate in concentric circles from Chomsky's
department at the Massachusetts Institute of Technology,
and set off other concentric circles wherever they arrived.
The late sixties and the early seventies were a time of plen-
tiful academic jobs, but Chomskian linguists — "transformational grammarians" as they were then called — were
especially welcome everywhere. By the time even East
Germany and the Soviet Union boasted transformational
grammarians, in the West "Noam" was in neck-in-neck
competition with "Albert" as a name for household pets
owned by the intellectually minded.

Among the young Chomsky enthusiasts, the number of Jews was astonishingly high. Due at least in part to their background as wanderers, which allowed them to learn languages, Jews had been prominent in linguistic science ever since emancipation and even before. But among the leading transformational grammarians, with their rejection of differences in favour of unity, the odd non-Jew stuck out nearly as much as they had among the disciples of Freud.

Chomsky's linguistics was a genuine movement with a largely Jewish leadership and with a wide and energetic non-Jewish following, a situation that has always filled the hearts of an eji activist with exaltation. Though here and there one heard the yet faint voices of black and Third World anti-Semitism, Jewish and non-Jewish activists marched together, arm-in-arm. This seemed like the eji's finest hour.

Chomsky and Faurisson

Though the late seventies took much of the steam out of the Flower Revolution as well as the Chomskian, Chomsky was still the hero of the eji intellectuals when he wrote his preface to Faurisson's book. Faurisson, like Chomsky, had little respect for detail unless it confirmed some very general opinion he held to be a truth. And he, too, liked to uncover the "deep" facts that lay beneath surface appearances. But there the similarities ended. Unlike Chomsky, Faurisson was not Jewish and the son of a Hebrew scholar — not at all. He claimed that the greatest Jewish tragedy, the Holocaust, did not happen. According to Faurisson, the gas chambers were really hygienic establishments. They were dedicated not to "racial hygiene" but to disinfecting prisoners' clothing. The Germans, said Faurisson, built them to save Jews from falling victim to the typhoid epidemic that raged in the camps. (Faurisson admitted that typhoid fever killed many Jews, although nowhere near the number "mainstream" historians say were murdered by gas.)

After his conviction for knowingly falsifying the truth in the matter, Faurisson was unrepentant, as he wrote in his book:

> . . . I do not believe for a moment in the existence of a single homicidal 'gas chamber,' no matter what concentration camp it was supposed to have been in. Better still: I have many proofs that the 'gas chambers' are a myth.

In his preface, Chomsky insisted that Faurisson had the right to explore the issue and publish his opinions, though he (Chomsky) did not take a position on the merits of the issue.

Chomsky had previously signed a petition protesting the "intimidation" directed at Faurisson, including the then as yet unrealized plans to bar him from teaching. The petition described Faurisson as a "respected professor of twentieth-century French literature and document criticism" and "strongly" protested the efforts "to deprive Professor Faurisson of his freedom of speech and expression." It condemned the "shameful campaign to silence him." The signatures of Noam Chomsky and Alfred Lilienthal were soon singled out by Faurisson's defenders, to show that there were Jews who did not wish to keep him quiet.

The defend-Faurisson camp also appreciated the participation of another individual with a Jewish background: Jean-Gabriel Cohn-Bendit, the brother of "Danny the

Red," the leader of the 1968 student unrest in Paris. Jean-Gabriel was one of the editors of the publishing house La Vieille Taupe, whose sole purpose was to publish works that deny the Holocaust. The editorial board included people belonging to the radical French left. It may be one of them, if not Cohn-Bendit himself, who solicited Chomsky's involvement.

Chomsky was fully aware of the objections against his action. He decried the critics who had described his participation in the defence of Faurisson, and described their position as "scandalous." After all, Chomsky pointed out, he had signed petitions defending the freedom of speech of Russian dissidents whose views he found deplorable: "partisans of American savagery as it ravished Indochina, or of policies favoring nuclear war, or of religious chauvinism that recalls the Middle Ages. No one has ever raised an objection to that." So he could not see why people would object this time.

With his usual self-assurance, Chomsky declares that among

> people who have learned anything from the eighteenth century (viz. Voltaire), it is a matter of course, and something that one wouldn't even dream of discussing, that the defense of the right to free speech cannot be limited to ideas that one approves, and that it is precisely in the case of ideas that one finds the most shocking that this right needs to be most vigorously defended.

Chomsky is no doubt right. Moreover, forbidding Faurisson to speak was not only a violation of free speech, it was also an ineffective and possibly dangerous way to fight those who deny the Holocaust. Silencing such people by force is an oblique challenge to the evidence of Nazi murder. If the Jews are right, many people ask, then why are they worried so? Muzzling the likes of Faurisson only makes some people wonder whether they might not, after all, have something to say.

It is not Chomsky's defence of Faurisson's freedom to speak that is disturbing. It is his attitude to Faurisson's message. It is that he does not say that he finds Faurisson's ideas "shocking," as he did those of reactionary Russian dissidents, for example. It is that the petition he signed was "neutral" on Faurisson's "findings." It is that he gives no indication that he himself was any less neutral than the appeal he supported.

How is it that Chomsky had "no particular insights" ("*pas de lumières particulières*") on the Holocaust — he who spoke with a passion on the Middle East, Southern Africa, and later Central America or Iraq? It is totally inconceivable that he, a Philadelphia Jew, has never met a Holocaust survivor or the children and relatives of survivors, people who claim to have seen the gas chambers with their own eyes. The message of the survivors is at any rate so well publicized that no one, even the most lukewarm Jew, could have missed it. Yet Faurisson can continue to demand, "show me one proof!" and Chomsky can sign a petition that is "neutral."

Chomsky is not saying that the Jewish community, including those who have survived the camps, are liars, but his "neutrality" implies that they might be.

What should concern us most here, however, is not Chomsky's views as an individual. More worrisome is that in the context of eji thinking, Chomsky was being perfectly coherent. The moral bankruptcy of his action was not due to the idiosyncrasies of his personality, nor, necessarily, to any "Jewish self-hatred." It was due to his exaggerated adherence to Shylock's Defence. Chomsky simply took the idea that the Jews are not singular to such an uncompromising extreme, that even a suggestion that there may be something unique about the Jews is suspicious. And nothing makes the suggestion more powerfully than the Holocaust.

How Unique Was the Holocaust?

How is a universalist to deal with the terrible fact that while differences between Jew and non-Jew are supposedly trivial, they were held important enough by huge numbers of Gentiles to support an anti-Jewish policy of mass segregation and murder?

One way to answer the question while maintaining Jewish "non-uniqueness" as much as possible is to insist that the Holocaust was not that much different from horrors inflicted on other people. Those who argue this way cite the very true fact that the Jews were not the only victims of the Nazis. Hitler's henchmen (and their allies in the different areas they occupied) also persecuted many non-German Gentiles, as well as communists, democrats, gays, and anti-Nazi Christians of all nationalities. They not only killed the Jewish Six Million, but also perhaps another six million Gentiles.

The eji who argue this way easily find allies among some Gentiles who, likewise, criticize the "Holocaust was a unique event" theory. Many Poles, for example, feel that they have suffered just as much as the Jews. They point out that six million Poles died, too (although they often forget to add that half of these "Poles" were Jews). Seen in this light, the Nazis were just another, but more efficient, cruel oppressor in the history of Europe, causing the deaths of countless Slavs, French, Gypsies, Greeks, etc., as well as political opponents, supposed moral undesirables like gays, and the severely handicapped not deemed fit to live. In other words, even as victims of genocide, the Jews were essentially just like everyone else.

Immediately after the war, this was the favoured position on the victims of Naziism of the great majority of Jews as well as non-Jews. Indeed, the Biblical term "Holocaust," which immediately suggests the Jews, was not in use then outside Israel. People preferred to speak of "Nazi persecution" in general. If absolutely necessary, "racial persecution" was used, still mercifully avoiding the terrible word "Jew." The Jews were often listed in the category of "victims of German fascism" along with the persecuted political opponents of the Nazis.

In Paris, near Notre Dame, there is a "Memorial to the Deported." The monument is graced with a number of inscriptions about the struggle between freedom and oppression, all quotes by Gentile French writers. Nowhere is there one word in Hebrew; in fact, the word "Jew" does not appear anywhere. If future archaeologists not familiar with the Holocaust dug up the place, it is hard to see how they would know that most people deported from France by the Germans were Jews. Even the word "deported" is meant to obscure the difference between Jew and non-Jew, and the fact that while political refugees were also destined for the horrible camps, only the Jews were gassed. The monument was certainly built with the knowledge and official support of the large French-Jewish community.

Visiting the Paris site, I was reminded of the memorial in

Kremnička, Slovakia, the resting place of my grandparents
Max and Elisabeth Kalmár to whom this book is dedicated.
Kremnička had a number of tank trenches that had been dug
there by soldiers, either Germans or members of their allies,
the Slovak army. On three different occasions, Slovak fas-
cists of the "Hlinka Guard Emergency Service" took Jews to
the trenches, shot them in the back, and allowed the bodies
to fall in, to be covered up later. A total of more than three
hundred people were killed in this way. The nearby museum
claims that people of many nationalities were murdered
here. However, I challenged one of the officers of the museum, Mr Tóth, to give me the name of a single victim who
was not either a Jew or a Gypsy; and I have asked a number
of other historians and interested Slovak people to do the
same. To date, I have received no names. An elaborate cover-
up seems to have taken place, with officials (this was before
the communist takeover) making efforts to minimize the
number of Jews killed. This started right after the war. My
father, who went to identify the bodies of his parents, was
shocked when the officials attempted to declare the unrec-
ognizable body next to his father, whom he thought must be
his mother, to be a Gypsy woman — a statement for which
they had no evidence whatsoever. In the event, a monument
was erected near the sight of the murders, with three huge
crosses and a red star representing the communist partisans.
Nowhere a Star of David, nowhere a declaration that most
of the victims were not partisans but Jewish civilians. The
official Jewish community made a mild protest, but were
told that the presence of a Star of David might cause vandals
to desecrate the monument. They agreed it was better for
the peace of the dead to rest under crosses than under hostile graffiti.

In many European countries after the war, the eji willingness to be equated with resistance fighters was reinforced by the fact that compensation for Jewish victims was
more easily accepted by the population if they were presented in the same light as non-Jewish anti-Nazis. My uncle
in Prague has even quite recently received an extra-large
state apartment (two rooms for two adults, plus kitchen and
bath), to which he was entitled as a former "resistance
fighter" (as a Jew he qualified, even though he had spent
the war as a civilian refugee in Palestine). Otherwise he
would only have gotten one room.

Exaggerating the Jewish resistance was, as we have
seen, also the policy of the early Israeli authorities. The relatively passive death of Jewish millions was an embarrassment to the male sensibilities of the *sabra*. But there was
also a matter of psycho-political strategy. Whatever other
arguments there may have been for recognizing the State
of Israel, it is clear that the victorious allied powers recognized it in large measure out of the feeling that the Jews
had been the Nazis' chief victims. It helped Israel's image
when people who had fought the Nazis saw the Jews as
having been on their side, and people who had suffered
under the Nazis saw them as having gone through the same
ordeal, and to an even greater extent. It would not have
done much for Israel to stress that Jewish suffering had
been different not only in degree but in kind. The allies
had not fought for the Jews, but against the Nazis, and they
preferred to see the Jewish victims as proving the horrors,
not so much of anti-Semitism *per se*, but of Naziism in
general.

Though, for reasons to be explored later, the organized
Jewish community and Israel eventually swung to the view

that the Holocaust was a uniquely Jewish tragedy, many eji intellectuals, particularly those opposed to or lukewarm on Zionism, continue to voice views that deny the uniqueness of the Holocaust. So Chomsky says of the Indonesian invasion of East Timor, which according to Amnesty International may have claimed 200,000 victims, that it was "the worst slaughter relative to population since the Holocaust." And so Abraham Serfaty, the Jewish leader of Morocco's Left, makes the following comparison: "Tazmamart and Auschwitz . . . True, the numbers are different, but a transgression against a single human being is also a crime against humanity."

Serfaty is right in the sense that the suffering of the inmates may have been equally terrible in both places. He, a Moroccan opposition leader, knows well what he is talking about; at the time he made the comparison to Auschwitz, he had just been released after years in prison. In Tazmamart political prisoners were shut into a ridiculously small prison cell, never to come out alive. They were given an inadequate ration of food every day, until they slowly died. By comparison, a gas chamber may have appeared as an act of mercy.

Sadly, since East Timor and Tazmamart we have witnessed more and more examples of inhuman intolerance. The atrocities committed are every bit as reprehensible as the Holocaust. But one crime is not like another. East Timor was mass murder. Tazmamart was savage political repression. Auschwitz was an attempt at genocide. Between these crimes, there is a difference not of degree but of kind. Only the Holocaust was an attempt at true genocide.

The word "genocide" has been used loosely to refer to

any large-scale murder carried out by some more or less official group: a government, or a guerrilla army. The
Rumanian dictator, Nicolae Ceauşescu, was accused of
genocide against his own people. His son was tried for the
same crime. But, strictly speaking, the charge could not be
true. Genocide means the murder of an entire people (a
"genus"). Genocide against Rumanians would mean the
extermination of the entire Rumanian people. To be truly
genocidal, the Ceauşescus, as Rumanians, would have had
to kill themselves as well as all their compatriots.

Genocide was, however, what the Nazis wished to
accomplish against the Jews. They may have planned the
same fate for the Poles and some, or all, of the other Slavic
peoples. Fortunately, history did not permit us to know for
sure. As it is, the Germans killed millions of Slavs, but never
began a campaign to wipe them all out, men, women, and
children, of whatever age, and wherever they lived.

The aboriginals of the Americas and of Australia are
another example of people who have suffered unspeakable persecution, including mass extermination. The
calamities that have resulted in the disappearance of
entire native nations as the result of the invasion by
Europeans have been just as bad as (and obviously have
had the same results as) genocide: attacks by the
Europeans themselves or their native allies; diseases
brought by the Europeans; forced migration to other
native areas or to European-dominated cities, resulting in
intermarriage and loss of cultural and linguistic identity.
Yet there has not been a truly genocidal campaign even
against the native peoples. White settlers in America and
Australia would go to any lengths to chase natives off the
lands they wanted, and would not shy away from killing

all of them if they did not go. But they did not pursue them. They did not investigate everyone who lived in their own communities to see if their veins contained any native blood, in order to have them murdered. In other words, their goal was to "get rid" of the racial minority, but "only" to gain possession of the territory they coveted. On the other hand, to the Nazis the Jew was a threat to the very health of humanity. After toying with the idea of quarantining the Jews on the isolated island of Madagascar, they decided to kill them all, regardless of where they lived. World War II, from the Nazi point of view, was in one sense a worldwide exercise in "racial hygiene," designed to eliminate the Jew, like tuberculosis or polio, from the face of the Earth.

None of this makes the murder of a Pole, a Gypsy, or an Amerindian one bit less reprehensible than that of a Jew gassed in Auschwitz. Nor does it mean that as individuals, the Jewish victims necessarily suffered worse than the non-Jewish ones. The "who suffered more" competition between some Jews and non-Jews (particularly Slavs) is one of the most distasteful elements of the debate about the Holocaust. But the fact remains that the Jewish case was different. Had Hitler succeeded in ruling the whole world, every Jew, and many others with only part Jewish blood, would have been killed, regardless of where they went, how they lived, whom they married. There is no conclusive evidence that Hitler planned true genocide against anyone else, except, apparently, the Gypsies, who lost the same proportion of their population as the Jews. And that should not be surprising, given the Nazi view of the Jews as a *unique* enemy, posing a danger of a singular nature.

It Could Not Have Been Someone Else

This, too, has come under challenge by those who would minimize the uniqueness of the Holocaust. To exaggerate their view just a bit, they see Hitler as a demagogue who wished to exploit the German people's unhappiness during the Great Depression, and was looking for a scapegoat to give them so they would see him as the way out of the economic morass. Hitler was, they say, looking for a suitable group to be such a scapegoat, and he happened to choose the Jews. Generally speaking, people who argue this way do not go very deeply into why it was the Jews and not someone else. What matters is, they say, that it could have been anyone.

It is actually true that the Jews were offered up as a scapegoat. But it could not have been someone else.

In their analysis of what had brought on the Depression, the Nazis spoke for some of the victims of capitalist modernity — particularly the tradition-bound shopkeeper class, but also some of the marginalized rural and urban workers, as well as some of the aristocracy. All of these felt, and with good reason, threatened by a new society where money counted above personal connections to the privileged, and above loyalties based on kinship, place of origin, and — "race." The socialists in the Marxist tradition called for a fight against capitalism in terms of the class struggle. The Nazis, who also called themselves socialist, substituted for the class struggle the struggle of races (which is what eventually allowed them to make a cozy peace with non-Jewish capitalists, happy to rid themselves of the Jewish competition). Both the Marxists and the Hitlerites talked of fighting the rich. But for the majority of the Marxists who avoided the temptation of anti-Semitism, the "rich" were the capitalists. For the Nazis, it was the ages-old human metaphor for ill-begotten wealth, the people of Judas — the Jews. There is no other ethnic group in Europe who could have fitted the bill.

To the transformed image of the anti-Christ Judas as the unfeeling capitalist, a transformation that had already taken place among the anti-Semites of the nineteenth century, the Nazis, however, added a new, pseudo-scientific veneer. They claimed that the Jews exploited the ills of urban civilization to their own benefit. Like vermin, they thrived on urban chaos. The Nazis vowed to purify the city environment, and to get rid of the money-minded, libertarian milieus, which they saw as the "cesspool" of the Jew. The Jews were, to them, parasites who survived by threatening the health of other races. As Robert Jay Lifton showed masterfully in his book *The Nazi Doctors*, the Nazis thought that their discovery of the "Jewish bacillus" was on a par with Robert Koch's discovery of the anthrax bacillus, the first disease-causing bacterium known to medical science. When the Nazis called the Jews a parasite on the body of the "Aryan race," they were not just using some nasty figure of speech. They believed that they were dealing with scientific fact. Their institution for segregating and eventually murdering the Jews was called "Office of Racial Hygiene." One of the top Nazis, Reinhardt Heydrich, declared that "Naziism is all about biology."

In other words, the Jews were parasites who could do no more to stop being harmful than a beakerful of streptococci. Like bacteria, they had to be exterminated by disinfection. This sort of thinking may have led the Nazis to choose Zyklon-B gas as the agent for mass murder in the death chambers of the concentration camps. It was a rat poison and a disinfectant (the use of this agent made Faurisson claim that the gas chambers were really rooms for disinfecting prisoners' clothing). The Nazi ideologists believed they were not cruel sadists in killing Jews, but were simply protecting humanity from a pest. They hired engineers to make continuous improvements in the gas chambers, ensuring that the Jews died as painlessly as possible.

In the light of such horrors, the idea that the Jews are just like everyone else, and its more general version as propagated by the eji of whom Chomsky is a prime example, that all differences between one people and another are trivial in comparison to the similarities, seems like something of a pipe dream. As an ideal, the idea is not, of course, new. The apostle Paul preached that in paradise there would be no distinction between Jew and Gentile (as there would be none between male and female, or slaves and free citizens — such a paradise would be heaven for many an eji!). During World War I, pacifists often argued that national differences were a red herring, used by demagogues to whip up the emotions that precipitated the bloody conflict. The pacifists were often members of well-established organizations that aimed to abolish as much as possible the differences among peoples. Esperanto flourished briefly as an international language. In New York, the Society for Ethical Culture, founded in 1876, preached a gradual elimination of national and religious boundaries. It seems that most of the members, however, were Jewish.

In the hippie era, we believed that paradise could happen here on earth, if only we wanted it badly enough.

While the war in Vietnam raged, young people everywhere hung banners in their windows, with John Lennon's famous words: "Peace is here." (Lennon also equated the heaven-on-earth he pictured in "Imagine" with "no religion, too.") Peace Beatles-style would be a universe in which everyone *was* (as far as ethnic and religious backgrounds are concerned) the same.

But peace is not here. Since World War II, the guns have never fallen totally silent. And the Holocaust remains a rude reminder that a paradise without human differences is, even if we should wish for one, not yet for this earth. And an equally rude challenge to the universalism of Chomsky et al.

Increasingly, more and more Jews have had to admit that in the light of the Holocaust, the insistence that we are not different seems to make little sense. (Other things happened to bring forth that admission as well, however, and we will deal with those later.) Even Chomsky's rhetoric has become less focused on the implications of his linguistic universalism for our political future. For example, his critique of capitalism has come to focus quite markedly on what he sees as the struggle of particular industrial powers (America, Europe, Japan) against each other. But, predictably, although he is still listened to with great respect, he does not excite the same allegiance as when his scholarship lent itself to a now no longer so fashionable messianism of universal non-difference.

The "Chomsky Lectures," a series of pronouncements on politics in the late twentieth century, developed something of a following among left-wing youth in the early nineties. But the youths who came to watch a film based on the lectures were not a particularly Jewish crowd. It is very doubtful that many of them remembered Chomsky's defence of Faurisson, or that they would have cared much if they did. Wearing neo-hippie scarves or post-punk black, they were revering a living memory, a yesterday's hero, a Rolling Stone of Academe.

14

FROM PROPHETS TO PROFITS; OR WHY DID THE GOYIM SWALLOW BOESKY AND THE REICHMANNS?

"Don't ever use my helicopter again for a stunt like this,"
Mulheren said angrily. "Are you fucking out of your mind?
Revolutions are made of this. People get put in gas ovens."
— James B. Stewart, *Den of Thieves*

In the age of air travel, there is no practical use for a ship like *Queen Elizabeth II*. The last of the great ocean liners has been outfitted purely for the pleasure of the monumentally rich. One of them, the developer and hotel owner Gerald Guterman, rented it on a September day in 1986 to give a party that would outdo them all. Guests arrived at the pier in New York to be greeted by the pleasing sounds of a salon orchestra. Later, the music was taken over by a big band under the direction of Peter Duchin. To add to the atmosphere, there was a fifty-one-member company of mimes and roving entertainers, and clowns to amuse the littlest ones. And above it all hovered a giant banner with the words, MAZEL TOV, JENNIFER, ROBIN AND JASON. Of the three Guterman children, Jason was just the right age for a bar mitzvah: thirteen. The girls were a little older. But there is no firm rule on when a bar or bat mitzvah must take place. Why not synchronize the rituals so that a really good party can be had by all?

The ship was out at sea, the band was playing, and the guests were, by the looks of it, all enjoying themselves. Suddenly, those on the deck turned their gaze towards the sky. A twin-engine helicopter, drowning out the music, was landing on the ship's helipad. The doors opened. Out stepped a dapper grey-haired gentleman in tuxedo and black tie. It was Ivan Boesky, the notorious billionaire. He was known to never be on time.

The helicopter belonged to John Mulheren, head of Jamie Securities. Boesky had not told him he was going to rent it. When Mulheren, who was not at the party, found out, he was beside himself. He told the pilot never to let Boesky do "that kind of thing again." To him, Boesky's excuse, that he had missed the ship's departure, was hogwash. He was sure Boesky just wanted to show off. But Boesky did not care. For him, it was a last fling. Two days later he turned himself in to United States officers, and agreed to help to uncover what was perhaps the biggest financial scam of the century, and one in which he himself had participated to the fullest.

Mulheren, a non-Jew, was warning Boesky that such ostentatious displays of wealth by Jews would bring a serious anti-Semitic backlash. As he was yelling at Boesky about gas ovens, he was perhaps in one of his explosively angry moods. One day, after Boesky had implicated him along with other suspected participants in the financial scandal, police arrested Mulheren on weapons charges. His car was packed with arms, and he told police he was out to kill his former friend. Mulheren may have been unstable; however, his concern with an anti-Semitic backlash was not unrealistic. It was shared by his Jewish colleagues in the investment community. There was a joke going around about the B'nai Brith offering a $250,000 reward to anyone who could find a non-Jew involved in the scandal.

But both Mulheren and the jokers were wrong. There was to be no backlash.

So far, we have dealt mainly with eji artists, scientists, and intellectuals. We have not said much about those who had perhaps most to fear from the "rich Jew" image; that is, the Jews who actually *are* rich. Eji in the money business used to have to be particularly careful not to appear to be "too" Jewish, and too rich. It was another sign that the eji era was coming close to its end, when Jews like the Gutermans and Boesky were willing to practically smoke dollar bills in public. Unlike Mulheren and unlike many embarrassed Jewish financiers who heard about his exploits, Boesky himself worried little about extravagance. The free-wheeling spirit of the eighties meant, for many moneyed Jews, that the stops could be pulled out on ostentatious consumption. No longer did they feel that a Jew had to refer to the Prophets for self-respect. Profits would do. Boesky did not think that his lifestyle would expose him to anti-Semitism. If events had not caught up with him, he would have carried out his dream of building an oversize replica of Jefferson's famed residence (depicted on the obverse of the U.S. nickel), Monticello.

And Boesky was right. Since the eighties, the "rich Jew" image has no longer been bringing out anti-Semitism the way it used to; not, that is, among the "mainstream," white Gentiles in the Western world. The reason has to do with the new image of Money introduced in the Reagan-Thatcher era. It is not only Deng Xiao-Ping who declared, in the eighties, that getting rich was glorious. The middle classes of the West, after two centuries of capitalism, have finally accepted that Money was fine.

Jews had been labelled — unfairly — as the people of Money. To more and more white, middle- and upper-class people, that began to sound like a compliment. These were the people that really mattered. Those left on the sidelines (and too often the sidewalks) during the New Right revolution of the eighties were not likely to witness the bar mitzvah on the *Queen Elizabeth*. Nor were they able to understand the headlines that dealt with the havoc Boesky and his associates wreaked on the New York stock market and, consequently, on the American and world economy.

It is widely believed that the Boesky revelations led to the painful stock market crash in October 1987 — Black Monday. Stock market participants were shocked to find out that a clique of leading financial players had traded insider information, misused the trust of their clients, defrauded the Internal Revenue Service, ruined corporations, and caused major losses to investors who were playing by the rules. Not everyone that seemed to be involved was eventually convicted of illegal trading practices. Mulheren was, at first, but was later acquitted. Chief among those found guilty were, along with Boesky, Michael Milken of Drexel Burnham Lambert Inc.; Martin Siegel of Kidder, Peabody & Co.; and Robert Freeman of Goldman, Sachs & Co. — all Jews. The extent of the damage to the public can be glimpsed only in part by the fines imposed. In addition to receiving a jail sentence of three years, Boesky agreed to pay $100 million — and that was considered especially light punishment, part of the deal to get Boesky to be a government witness. Milken, who probably benefited most from the sham, paid $600 million, and got ten years in jail. Milken's firm, Drexel, paid $650 million plus various charges.

Hurt and disenchanted investors complained loudly about the individuals involved, but not about the Jews in general. It was an unprecedented signal that in this group (mostly white and at least middle class, it is very important to note) anti-Semitism was on the decrease.

If B'nai Brith had really declared a prize for turning in a Gentile involved in the scam, it would, of course, have been easy to earn. Apart from Mulheren, many other non-Jews were implicated. And, even though it was true that the chief culprits were, as far as could be known, Jewish, there was no rational reason to single out the Jews for blame. The entire scandal was, notwithstanding its capital importance, really just one large case, the handiwork of a single network of criminal friends. As statisticians would say, the sample was too small to generalize, not only to all Jews but even to all Jews on Wall Street. Nor is the record of the non-Jewish Wall Street players a shining monument to honesty and fair play.

"Jewish" Scandals in the Past

However, the history of anti-Semitism is hardly a showcase for human rationality. Did Anne Frank not lament that "What one Christian does is his own responsibility, what one Jew does is thrown back at all Jews"?

The Boesky case would not have been the first to be blown up into an anti-Semitic campaign. In fact, the history of anti-Semitism as a political movement could justifiably be dated to a financial scandal almost a hundred years before the Boesky affair of 1987. Because of its capital importance, it is necessary to look at that incident in some detail.

In the fall of 1888, the passions of ordinary French people were whipped to a frenzy as the result of the famous "Panama scandal," in which leading figures of the Third Republic were implicated. Ferdinand de Lesseps, the flamboyant builder of the Suez Canal, convinced the government to support his project to build a similar canal in Panama. When the public learned that the government was going to guarantee the Lesseps company's obligations, people simply began to throw their money at him. Unfortunately, it was not the lot of the French to complete the canal. Unbeknownst to the public, the badly managed project became bankrupt soon after its inception. However, in order to pay the interest on the huge debt incurred, Lesseps's people covered up the fact. For years they went on raising more and more money, paying the old debt with the new. Like most struggling speculators, Lesseps no doubt hoped that his luck would eventually turn, the Panama project would start paying the huge dividends that had been expected, and all creditors would be paid off. But people were beginning to catch up with him. To prevent censure by the National Assembly, Lesseps hired two Jews, Jacques Reinach and Cornélius Herz, as intermediaries to oil the palms of important deputies. This was a costly affair. Eventually, the greatest part of the public's investment went to those to be bribed (none of whom were Jewish) and to these Jewish middle men.

The pressure turned out to be too much for Reinach. When his colleague, Herz, took to blackmailing him, it was the last straw. Reinach wrote down a list of the parliamentarians who had been bribed, and gave it to La libre parole, the mouthpiece of the anti-Jewish fanatic, Edouard Drumont. Then he killed himself.

Drumont published the list in tantalizing, small instalments. Each instalment raised the public's anger, and deepened the despair of the myriad of investors who were never to see their money again. Many, egged on by Drumont and his cronies, blamed the Jews. It was the dress rehearsal for all the anti-Semitic madness to come, including, a few years later, the notorious Dreyfus Affair.

Subsequently there were other "Jewish" affairs, each adding fuel to the anti-Semitic campaigns that soon spilled well beyond France's borders. In 1912, the British Post-Master General, who was Jewish, accepted a huge tender for building a telegraph network throughout the British Empire. The beneficiary was the English Marconi Wireless Telegraph Company, headed by a Jew, Godfrey Isaacs. Godfrey seems to have slipped some useful information to his brothers Harry and Rufus, for they were found to have bought an oversized lot of Marconi stock just before the public announcement of the deal drove Marconi shares to the sky. The Liberal Prime Minister and Chief Whip had also bought some of the stock "just in time." This was clearly insider trading, although the law did not condemn the practice quite the same way then as it does now. One of the loudest critics of the deal was Cecil Chesterton, brother of the well-respected author G.K. Chesterton. But even G.K. was emotionally involved, to put it mildly. In his *Autobiography*, he writes that "it is the fashion to divide recent history into Pre-War and Post-War conditions. I believe it is almost as essential to divide them into Pre-Marconi and Post-Marconi days." Aided, sometimes ambiguously, sometimes not, by people of G.K.

Chesterton's calibre, the conspiracy theorists made the most of the affair. It was seriously considered that an international Jewish cabal was acting as a grey eminence, pulling the strings of the British and other governments.

The Public Response to the Boesky-Milken Scandal

It was as clear as day, however, that in the Marconi affair important Gentile personalities were as involved as the Jews. In the Panama scandal, indeed, the really big fish were all non-Jews. A century later in America, on the other hand, Jewish swindlers not only played the main roles, but wrote the script. But no backlash.

It's not that people were not interested. News of the scandals was lapped up by an eager public. The motion picture *Wall Street* featured Michael Douglas, who is of some Jewish background, as the lead character, a crooked manipulator misusing insider information. But the film was totally free of even a hint of anti-Semitism. The same was true of *Den of Thieves*, a book by the Pulitzer Prize-winning journalist, James B. Stewart, which, five years after Boesky began to "talk," made number one on the *New York Times* bestseller list. Stewart avoided any suggestion of anti-Semitism with a consummate skill that did honour both to his moral integrity and his writing talent. (Had he not done that, one might find the title of the book objectionable. "Den of thieves" is what Jesus called the Jewish money changers and traders that he chased out of the Temple.)

For the most part, the public responded the same way: curious but not quite outraged, interested as much in the glamour as in the moral corruption of the affair, and not really blaming the Jews. When Milken's company, Drexel Burnham Lambert, went bankrupt as the result of the scandal, one of the bidders rummaged through the lot offered at an auction of the firm's office. "What's his name? Mitchell?" he asked. "Milken" is not widely known as a Jewish name, but "Mitchell" is hardly the kind of name one would come up with if one were struggling to recollect the name of someone whose Jewishness one thought of as important.

A few years after the Boesky affair, in 1991, the British publisher Robert Maxwell was found drowned, off the Canary Islands, where he had been vacationing on his boat. Maxwell was born in a *shtetl*, in a part of Ukraine that then belonged to Czechoslovakia. In the wake of his death, it was discovered that he had used the savings of his employees to prop up his failing business empire, and that large sums had disappeared from various of his companies without trace. Maxwell's wrongdoing did not seem to approach the seriousness of the Wall Street insider information scandal. But there were again fears of a major anti-Semitic campaign, and once again they did not materialize. There was endless controversy about how the publishing magnate died: did he suffer a heart attack, did he kill himself, was he brutally beaten and thrown overboard? The circumstances of his death made sure the story would stay in the news. But for the most part, talk about the affair was of the sort one can always expect when a rich man dies in mysterious circumstances. Whatever anti-Semitic feeling was raised seemed to remain within the confines of polite restraint.

In Canada, in the winter of 1992, Julius Melnitzer was sentenced to nine years in prison and to repaying a debt of $20 million, after what was called Canada's biggest ever bank fraud. Melnitzer became famous through honest work as a criminal lawyer in London, Ontario, an exclusive WASP town said to have the highest per capita income in the country. He successfully represented a developer whose family had tried to prove for more than seventy years that they, and not the province of Ontario, owned a mile-long stretch of beach in the area. In the wake of the trial, colleagues and clients flocked to him for help. It was at this point that Melnitzer saw the opportunity for getting richer more quickly. He borrowed millions on his good name or on false securities, which towards the end of his criminal career included huge numbers of forged stock certificates.

To pay the interest, Melnitzer defrauded clients and friends by convincing them to invest with him. Some of the investments turned out to be in bogus schemes, of which the most notorious was a non-existent investment program in Singapore. In the end, Melnitzer's indebtedness totalled more than $20 million. He had spent the huge amounts he had collected, apart from some genuine investments, on opulent residences, art, mistresses (not long before his arrest he dropped off $100,000 for his current *liaison*), and, best noted by his — mostly Gentile — peers, lavish parties.

It could be argued that so many of the big-time swindlers of the high-rolling eighties were Jewish because risky and even illegal practices were the only way they could break down the barriers put in their way by the hostile, anti-Semitic, old-money establishment. Indeed, there is evidence that Melnitzer, for one, thought of himself as an outsider. In an interview with a local newspaper, he said he moved into criminal law because "criminals, well, you don't have to break into their clubs." The theme of Melnitzer the outcast was picked up by the press. A feature article summing up the affair a year after the judgment headlined the story as follows:

> Julius Melnitzer, a brilliant young trial lawyer, craved riches and respect in a stuffy town whose old-money families aren't generous with either.

Yet there was no evidence at all that Melnitzer had been kept out of either the clubs or the boardrooms. On the contrary. His is a story of a man who generated almost unlimited, even foolish trust in his money-making abilities. And one who had no trouble at all making up the guest list for his parties. If anyone refused to come, the press did not say.

Like Melnitzer, Boesky, Milken, and their cronies embarked on large-scale fraud only *after* they (and Jewish business people in general) had finally gained a foothold in the old-money establishment. Patrician securities houses had for the first time accepted them and other Jews. It was the big goyish banks that lent them money with a vengeance. No one refused to have lunch with Boesky, no one snubbed Melnitzer's megabashes, and the annual "predator parties" organized by Milken in Los Angeles pulled in the top of the business and finance community, regardless of religion or pedigree.

No, these criminals did not have the excuse of having to resort to shady practices in order to counter discrimination. Their crimes were the result not of frustration but of euphoria. Drunk with their economic *and* social success, they did not develop the prudence, restraint, and simple decency that should have accompanied their new position. It had all just happened too fast, and they wished, in the spirit of the racy eighties, for it to keep on happening, and ever faster. It is the measure of the acceptance of the Jews by the Gentile élites that, for reasons we looked at earlier, the actions of this small but visible group of criminals did not bring with it a reinstatement of anti-Jewish discrimination.

This was so even in the financial establishment of North America, which not long ago had been so anti-Semitic that Jewish bankers, accountants, and brokers were for the most part segregated in "Jewish firms," whose reputation seldom equalled that of the old Gentile institutions. The people involved in the eighties scandals were among the first Jews to be allowed into some previously very Gentile firms, such as Siegel's Kidder, Peabody & Co. "You see," one might expect the greying WASP gentlemen at the patrician banks and brokerages to say, "We should never have let in the Jews." It's possible, indeed likely, that some did say something more or less like that, but they were not much heard. The opening up of top financial careers to the Jews, which began full steam in the eighties, has since continued unabated.

Not that anti-Semitic rhetoric was good and dead. I have already mentioned David Duke. The predictably unsuccessful candidate for the 1992 Republican nomination for President had gathered quite a large minority of votes in the Louisiana gubernatorial race the year before, despite — or because of — his proven record as an extreme racist and anti-Semite. But the mystery deepens: even Duke did not misuse the Boesky-Milken and Maxwell scandals to make an appeal to the anti-Semites. (Surely it could have been done without explicit anti-Jewish references, in keeping with Duke's new "moderate" image.) Given the history of two centuries of "economic anti-Semitism," the quiet was gratifying.

The *Embourgeoisement* of the North American Jews

Curiously, this was happening at a time when economic anti-Semitism could have had a field day. The rise of the Jewish upper middle class in North America was nothing short of a quiet revolution. Children and grandchildren of lower-middle-class immigrants from the Russian Empire and Poland have moved up into the upper middle and even upper classes. Statistics now show the Jews as the wealthiest religious group in the United States, having overtaken the élite Episcopalians. In many of North America's major cities, neighbourhoods where money screams rather than talks are known to be largely inhabited by Jews. Tennis clubs are often a very Jewish affair. Wherever luxury tours go, there tends to be a gift shop or two selling locally made or "antique" Stars of David and menorahs.

While this is a new experience for North American Jews, it is in many ways a replay of the *embourgeoisement* of the Jews of Central and Western Europe, which had taken place a generation or two earlier. My father describes with amusement the scene at prewar Carlsbad (Karlovy Vary), an elegant spa in what is now the Czech Republic. The townsfolk were mostly German. The clientele, on the other hand, was very Jewish. My grandfather once decided to confront a spa attendant with the issue. "Are there many anti-Semites here?" he asked. "Oh, no," replied the German politely, "not during the season."

The anecdote neatly illustrates the limits of money's power to buy social acceptance. Economists know that they oversimplify things when they look at the world as made up of individuals, each of whom struggles to gain as much wealth as possible. People do not seek wealth for its own sake, but as a means to an end. Even among the poorest of the poor, goods serve not only to satisfy necessities but also to provide status symbols. (By goods, we mean not only material things but also intangibles that can be acquired by purchase: education is the best example.) We buy goods for their function — to feed and clothe ourselves, to keep warm, or to ease our labours — but we also buy them for what the anthropologists Mary Douglas and Baron Isherwood called "marking." Social marking is the process of classifying things and particularly people. People are classified in great measure by the goods they own. The importance of money is that it can purchase, as long as they are available, the goods that will bring their owner a desired classification.

Since the Jews are *on the average* wealthier than most other groups, they potentially have easier access to the goods that will classify a person as élite. But only potentially. The existing élite can frown upon the attempts of another group (the "new" rich) to acquire the goods that mark élite status. They can and do change the "fashion" so that the goods bought by the upstarts are no longer recognized as right. Failing that, they can refuse to allow the upstarts to come to the occasions where possession of the right goods is certified: parties, funerals, clubs, or lectures (once again remember that goods include education and therefore bits of knowledge and information as well as things). As Mary Douglas and Baron Isherwood have pointed out:

> Goods are endowed with value by the agreement of fellow consumers. They come together to grade events, upholding old judgments or reversing them.

Each person is a source of judgments and a subject of judgments; each individual is in the classification scheme whose discriminations he is helping to establish. By the presence of his fellows at his family funerals and weddings, by their regard for his birthdays, in their visits to his sickbed, they render marking services to him.

In the famous Kwakiutl institution of the potlatch, natives of northwestern North America used to conspicuously give away much of their wealth at public rituals designed to enhance their élite status. But members of the old élite resented the efforts of the newly rich to organize potlatches. They made it clear that they just wouldn't come. Élite anti-Semites similarly refuse "marking services" to the Jews. They do not invite or visit them, they forbid their children to marry them, they avoid neighbourhoods, resorts, clubs, and educational institutions where there are many of them.

Mercifully, there are not many such anti-Semites left; but there used to be plenty of them everywhere, and they abounded in the Vienna of Freud, Mahler, Wittgenstein — and Hitler.

Let us remember, however, that even during the centuries when anti-Semitic social discrimination was the rule, the very richest of the Jews were accepted in high society. The Gentile élite simply needed their money-making expertise too much. In Baroque Germany, practically every prince had his "court Jew," a high-level financial administrator who was generally welcome at all court functions, and who was often known for giving lavish parties attended by the *crème de la crème*. Later, the Rothschilds won their battle for acceptance by Europe's gentry, earning themselves a peerage here, a baronhood there. Despite exceptions like these, however, most wealthy Jews were barred from occasions where the élite could provide the "marking services" that would legitimize the status of their wealth: club memberships, charitable events, and the like.

To a much larger extent than they had done in Europe, the rich Jews in North America responded to discrimination by founding their own élite, and their own marking services. Apart from the injunctions of the Torah and the Talmud, this is what explains the absolutely extraordinary success of Jewish charities. It explains the network of excellent Jewish schools and hospitals. And it explains the rise of leading "Jewish" legal, accounting, and securities firms, a refuge for many brilliant practitioners excluded by the fancy Gentile institutions. Without the development of separate Jewish marking services confirming the separate prestige of a separate Jewish élite, the eventual entry of the Jews into the "mainstream" élite would never have happened.

Ultimately, the Jewish élite as a whole was able to become indispensable to the Gentile élite in the way that the court Jews and the Rothschilds had once become indispensable as individuals. The gamble has paid off. The annual Israel Bonds gala and a few similar events have come to be a major marking service at which the Gentile establishment certifies, by its presence, its acceptance of the Jews. The non-Jewish élite started to come when they realized that the Jewish élite simply held too much economic clout and expertise to be ignored. If young Jews finally began to enter the bastions of the corporate establishment in the eighties, it was because the preceding generation forced the corporate establishment to recognize the achievement of the Jewish firms, and through them, the potential of Jewish professionals.

Gold Rehabilitated

One might be tempted to celebrate, if it weren't for the existence of another, rather inelegant way in which the middle class and the upper crust came to accept the Jews. The economic indispensability of the Jewish élite tells only part of the story. It may explain why top corporations might now want to deal with the Jews. It does not explain why not only the upper classes but also the rising middle class whose small-scale economic operations certainly do not need the Jews, seem to have finally rid themselves of the worst forms of anti-Semitic bigotry. (I deal with the important exceptions in the next chapter.) The reason is not an improvement in the image of the Jew as such. It is an improvement in the image of money.

The Jews used to be falsely accused of being the servants of the arch-enemy, Gold. But in the eighties, Gold was — to white, middle- to upper-class people — looking more and more like a friend. A scapegoat to blame for its evils was no longer needed.

The new attitude to Money is as important as any collective influence of the Jewish élite in explaining why the patrician firms of Wall Street opened their gates to the Jews. The Establishment brokers had once raised to perfection the old bourgeois game of aristocratic airs. It was a game that required you to put breeding above money, and the Jews, so the stereotype held, had the second but not the first. Now that Money was OK, there were fewer bigots left who worried that hiring Jews might make the company look as though it cared too much for Gold.

An anecdote of the period tells of a Hollywood producer who meets the devil. The devil suggests a deal: he
will make sure that the producer lands all the most glam-
orous and lucrative deals, making him a famous millionaire.
In return, the producer must offer the devil his soul.
"What's the catch?" replies the startled producer.

"Selling your soul to the devil" was as ancient a parable
on the demonic powers of Gold as Western mythology had
to offer. In the eighties it became a joke. The ancient foundation myth of anti-Jewish hatred, the cosmic battle of
Good and Gold, began to lose its power in the era of communism's collapse. If there were no Jews, medieval
Christian fanatics would have invented them as a bodily
reminder of the anti-Christ. The enemies of modern
society would have reinvented them as an incarnation of
the evils of capitalism. But in the eighties the evils of capitalism began to look comparatively tame. Socialism in its
extreme form seemed to lead only to repression and line-
ups in Eastern Europe, and poverty and public debt in the
Third World. Even in its moderate forms, collectivism
seemed to be losing its former attraction. The social democratic traditions of Western Europe were turning into a gov-
ernment-managed and union-supported policy of
controlled but aggressive capitalism, à la Japan. In the
United States, the old spirit of individualism manifested
itself in the free-wheeling, relatively uncontrolled capitalism of the Reagan years.

People correctly estimated that the crimes of Boesky
and company were a symptom of the ills of unchecked capitalism, rather than the "fault" of one population group, the
Jews. But there was no sign of a revitalized Left. The people
and Money seemed to have made their peace for good.

This revolution of attitudes was wrought by what was referred to in the eighties as the "New Right." The old patrician conservatives were being replaced by people of a modest background, like the shopkeeper's daughter Margaret Thatcher, or the actor Ronald Reagan whose profession was traditionally associated with left-leaning sympathies. They stood for the frankly and proudly *nouveaux riches*, as opposed to the snobbish, exclusivist families of the Old Right. In their movement, the Jews were not merely welcome; the Jewish neoconservatives in fact formed its ideological vanguard.

The more conservative Israelis and American Jews never had a better friend than President Reagan. In the 1992 campaign, George Bush's Secretary of State, James Baker was reported to have said about the Jews: "Fuck 'em. They didn't vote for us." (The comment was supposedly heard by an unnamed acquaintance of the Jewish former mayor of New York, Edward Koch. Baker denied having made it.) But in fact, 30 per cent of American Jews had voted Republican at the close of the Reagan era in 1988, an astonishing number if one considers how dogmatically Democratic the American Jews once had been (they became nearly so again when the old-fashioned Republicans represented by Bush and Baker came back).

Margaret Thatcher, Reagan's staunchest ally, was perhaps less friendly to Israel than Reagan, given the constraints of Britain's links to the Arab world. Nevertheless, she, too, was able to tap a swing to the right among British Jews. Her riding, Finchley, was as heavily Jewish as any in England. Her cabinet included a disproportionate number of Jews. It had such ministers as Michael Howard and David Young. Recalling Disraeli's idolization

of the famous Jewish banking family, Thatcher appointed
Lord Rothschild to be the head of her Think Tank. But
perhaps the most famous (or infamous, depending on
one's politics) was the Chancellor of the Exchequer, Nigel
Lawson.

Lawson epitomized the "New Right," "free-marketeers
with libertarian social attitudes," who often came into conflict with the old-style, insular traditionalists whom political fortunes happened to join them with. Lawson ended
up resigning in protest against Thatcher's over-reliance on
Alan Walters, her economic adviser. Walters spoke for the
good old British tradition of keeping aloof from the
Continent, an agenda that had little appeal to a Jewish
Tory, whose background dictated a more international
outlook. This was one issue on which Lawson and
Thatcher did not see eye to eye. The anti-European
rhetoric of the "Iron Lady" irritated Lawson almost as
much as it was upsetting to the Euro-bureaucrats in
Brussels. (Much more positive on Europe, the next Prime
Minister, John Major, rehired Lawson.)

The Fall of the Reichmann Empire
"Ronnie" and "Maggie," friends of Money, were friends of
the Jews; and so were more and more of the rich. That even
the old-money, goyish Establishment was loosening up was
best illustrated by the story of the Reichmann brothers. In
1992, a number of major real-estate corporations controlled by the prominent developers applied for court protection against their creditors, shocking the ranks of the
choicest "Gentile" investors and banks. All had given the
Reichmanns money with the greatest confidence.

The Reichmanns were one of two Canadian-Jewish

families whose interests came to span the world. The other was the Bronfmans of Montreal. But while the Bronfmans (some of whose companies experienced their share of trouble in the nineties' recession as well) "looked like everyone else," the Reichmanns, Orthodox Jewish Canadians of Hungarian background, looked unambiguously like Jews. Always in dark suits and wearing yarmulkes, they were devoted to their semi-private little synagogue in Toronto. (It was known as the "boat *shul*," because the building had previously housed a motor boat dealership, and once the big sign with a boat had been pulled down, no new sign was put up.) The family were surrounded by the strictest of the Orthodox, whom they financed generously. Partly under their influence, a new ultra-Orthodox community developed in the vicinity of their rather modest residences near Lawrence Avenue and Bathurst Street.

For such people to be major business players contradicted previous history. From the late nineteenth to the late twentieth century, the turf of the Orthodox business person shrank steadily. The Orthodox seemed to be confined to marginal, speculative trades whose markets were open and as such required no private contacts with the élite, such as the commodities futures markets. They sometimes became active in areas geographically removed from "where it was at" in international finance and business (as well as from the major Jewish communities). The classic example is the heavy involvement of Lithuanian Jews in the early, "frontier" days of the South African gold and diamond trade. (The trade gained respectability, however, when Sir Cecil Rhodes obtained a large chunk of it from the Jew Sir Alfred Beit. In recompense, Rhodes got for Beit — neither had at the time been knighted yet — member-

ship in the exclusive Kimberley Club, and promised to
"make him a gentleman.")

Small Orthodox communities continue to this day the
business of buying and selling in regions remote from the
main centres of both international commerce and of the
established Jewish communities. One of the oddest sights
I have ever encountered was an ultra-Orthodox Jew on a
snail-paced local train in rural Mexico. He was making his
trading rounds as his ancestors must have done in Ukraine
or Poland, peddling his wares among the villagers.

The Reichmanns, who had moved from Hungary to
Austria in 1922 to avoid political unrest, also at first concentrated on a rather exotic area. They made their initial
fortune in the Moroccan free port of Tangiers. It was logical
that when they moved to Canada in the 1950s, they did not
join the thriving "mainstream," and rather assimilated,
Jewish community of Montreal, where most Canadian
Jews lived. Instead, they went to Toronto. In the seventies,
heavy immigration from abroad and from increasingly
"French only" Quebec — including tens of thousands of
Montreal Jews — made Toronto "number one" in the
country. But until then English Canada was mostly a
goyish place. Here a shrewd Orthodox Jew saw unexplored
opportunities. After all, the founders of the Bronfman
dynasty (whose first flagship was the Seagram company)
had made their fortune in the Prairie centre of Winnipeg.
They had started there by exploiting the whisky trade
"while skating to the very edge of the U.S. and Canadian
prohibition laws designed to kill it." Perhaps the former
remoteness of English Canada from the centres of business
action in North America and Europe made a good base for
the Reichmanns, as it had for the Bronfmans, from which

to gather the strength needed to expand worldwide, and to build an empire unrivalled in wealth and influence by practically any United States Jew in recent memory.

The business the Reichmanns started with was entirely legitimate: a ceramic tile dealership. It was from here that they moved on to build their giant development company. The fact that they succeeded in "invading" the very nerve centres of international business and finance without donning the secular garb of the Bronfmans and the rest of the Jewish business magnates was an unambiguous sign of change. In the eighties, entrepreneurs with yarmulkes no longer had to be confined to peddling in the rain forests of Venezuela (I know of one Jewish trader who sold his wares up and down the Orinoco River) or risking all in the jungle of securities and commodity speculation. An Orthodox Jew could make it big, and make it big centre stage. The Reichmanns were, until their troubles began in 1992, a living example to eji business people. Their message was: "You need not mask your Jewishness any more." They were living proof that anti-Semitic prejudice was on its way out in the international community of business and finance.

It was under Thatcher's rule that the Reichmann brothers were given the go-ahead on Canary Wharf, perhaps the most ambitious real-estate development in world, and certainly British, history. The idea was to develop an entirely new area as a serious alternative to London's congested centre as the focus of business activity. Unfortunately, it proved too hard to convince enough British firms to give up the comforts of their traditional quarters for the Reichmann's monument to neoconservative modernism. Offices at Canary Wharf yawned empty, waiting for tenants who were not arriving. As time went on, things were not improving. What seemed like a minor tremor turned into a major quake: the mighty Reichmann edifice soon came crashing down. The Reichmanns' Olympia & York Developments Ltd. (popularly known as O&Y) and its associated companies had formed the world's largest real-estate empire. No more. The family fought valiantly to arrange a restructuring of the debt, but the creditors were merciless. In the spring of 1992, the pious brothers went to court on behalf of a number of Canadian companies and their American affiliates, asking to protect these corporations against their creditors. Religious officials financed by Reichmann money must have begun to worry about their next meal. So did personnel at many secular hospitals and educational institutions. For the Reichmanns' acceptance by the secular and Gentile élite was, despite their famous secretiveness, reciprocated by the family's generous involvement in charity well beyond the confines of the Jewish community.

When troubles came to the Reichmanns, they were not due to discrimination because of their Orthodoxy, let alone their Jewishness. Many of the triumphant capitalist dreams of the early eighties eventually turned into nightmares. A sobering recession set in, causing the profit margins of businesses, big and small, to drop like flies in the late fall. Many of the more prominent business failures or near-failures involved Jewish firms such as the Maxwell and Reichmann empires as well as those implicated in the Wall Street scandals. The reason is obvious. Jews, enthusiastic about playing the capitalist game without any of the old hindrances, supported by ideologists who were also often Jewish, and spurred on by philo-Semitic governments, threw themselves into the waves of the speculative mania with even less restraint than their non-Jewish colleagues.

True, the recession of the early nineties brought some moderation. "Greed is all right, by the way," Boesky had told the 1986 commencement class at Berkeley. In the nineties, he would have had to speak in softer tones. People wanted a more caring society. Basic morality will never approve of ill-begotten wealth, or even of simply putting greed before compassion. "Money is not everything," declared the title of an autobiography published in the late eighties. It was written not by a Marxist but by Baron Philippe de Rothschild. Once, he would have been considered arrogant; now, he only appeared cute. Wealth was never to be approved of unconditionally. But both the socialists and the reactionary nostalgics had taught that money was an evil as such, even if a necessary one. The capitalists, on the other hand, thought that money was basically a good thing. They won.

The recession might have been expected to bring in an enormous backlash against the "forces of the free market." After all, for the first time since the Second World War, the standard of living suffered a significant decline. People wondered where all the homeless might have come from. The middle classes watched their prime asset, the family home, plummet in price. If all this caused people to seriously revolt against capitalism, there would as usual have been those whose anti-capitalism was misdirected against the Jews. But no one called for riots, either against the capitalists or against the Jews, as the culprits of Black Monday were being brought to justice at last. For the most part, the news did not even make it to the front page.

The troubles of capitalism were overshadowed by the historic events in Eastern Europe. The communist façade collapsed, revealing an economy rotted to the foundations, and a system of government utterly detested by the people. A few diehard Western socialists mounted platforms to broadcast that it was not socialism but its misuse by the communists that had failed. But the public was not in the mood for what seemed like a tired old tune. In spite of the recession, and despite frustration with the human cost of the free market, Money maintained its attractiveness.

In America, Bush continued and even expanded Reagan's emphasis on helping the rich. Clinton changed the tone, but began his Presidency with the one conservative agenda Reagan and Bush had actually ignored: a serious effort to balance the budget. Economic conservativism was not to go easily, in America or the world at large. And economic conservativism has a respect for Money. It has always been wrong to accuse the Jews of greed, and incorrect to describe them collectively as "rich." But if the accusation was now becoming less effective, it was not only because people were getting more rational about the Jews, it was because being called rich was turning, from an unearned curse, into something like an undeserved praise.

This is why neither the scandals nor the honest bankruptcies led to the anti-Semitic "backlash" we feared. This is not the way, perhaps, that most of us would have wanted to tame anti-Semitism. But history chooses its own ways.

PART IV

THE MORNING AFTER

15

ANTI-SEMITISM OF
THE MARGINS

*We wish that they would understand that we too
are victims, yet it's understandable why they may think
otherwise.*
— Tikkun Passover Haggadah Supplement

"Anti-Semitism tamed?" I hear some of my readers declaim
at this point, shaking their heads in disbelief. Almost every
day we hear of disturbing anti-Semitic incidents some-
where or other in the world. Thugs paint swastikas on synagogue walls. Ex-communists in Eastern Europe join
nationalists in blaming the Jews for their country's failure
to catch up with the West. A black intellectual or politician
reproaches the Jews for the ills of racism today or for the
crime of slavery in the past. Young people on television
declare their admiration for Adolf Hitler. How then can I
speak of an increased acceptance of the Jews? Is it not the
case that anti-Semitism is on the rise?

Yes and no. The white, privileged Gentile élite accept
us more than ever. But at the same time, anti-Semitism is
growing, in both numbers and intensity, among those who
get less than their share of the pie. If more of the disenchanted — the poor, the blacks, the Hispanics — did not
express shock about Milken and Boesky, it is simply

because the stock market was just too far removed from
their concerns. They did not read the business pages.

The racial minorities of the West have not shared
equally in capitalist prosperity. They have not made their
peace with Money, and they find it as convenient as ever
to blame the Jews for Money's ills. Among them, anti-
Semitism has grown. It has grown also among the frustrated "white trash" of working-class slums in Europe,
where short-sighted governments have been depositing
thousands of non-white immigrants, increasing racist
attitudes in general and conjointly anti-Semitism. It has
grown in the countries of origin of these immigrants: the
Third World, which has also for the most part been left
out and ignored by the dominant groups of the West. It
has grown in the ex-communist countries, whose people
missed out on the postwar boom, and now find it hard to
catch up. And it has grown in some marginalized areas of
white America, such as — if David Duke's campaigns
were any indication — the rural white population of the
South.

Throughout the last two centuries, when we complained about discrimination, we aimed our protest at the
privileged, white élite. Eji ideology — Shylock's Defence
— eji lifestyles, the eji character all were formed in the
furnace of that struggle. It seems that this is one fight we
have won, uneasy and temporary as our victory may possibly be. In the twenty-first century, our problems are more
likely to come from the underprivileged than from the no
longer seriously discriminating white, Western élite. The
language of the eji, designed for talking with the élite, will
no longer do. To talk with the less favoured, we will need
to find entirely new words.

Some sociologists divide populations into the privileged "Centre" and the underprivileged "Periphery." The sociologists mean to contrast the city versus the country, the important metropolis versus the rest of the country, and the First World versus the Third. But the distinction can just as well be applied to the white race versus the black, or, in the post-communist era, to the First World versus the ex-communist Second. To clarify that I am expanding the meaning of the term, I replace "Periphery" with "Margins." In this sense, the virus of anti-Semitism can be said to have moved from the Centre to the Margins.

The urgency of our finding a way to deal with the Margins is that its importance is increasing. It is the Margins that, in the future, we as Jews will increasingly have to address. We are living through a period when peripheral groups maintain a relentless pressure not only to break down the privileges of the Centre, but also to become part of it — as we have become.

It is likely, indeed in justice it is desirable, that the underprivileged should gain their place in the sun. Blacks, Arabs, Moslems, and Africans will soon be, both literally and metaphorically, "everywhere." As the Margins strengthen, however, we Jews are faced with some increas ingly embarrassing problems. We wish justice for the oppressed and equality for the discriminated against, but not at the expense of our own rights. Unfortunately, it is a fact that the Margins include the Arab world, much of it hostile to the very existence of the Jewish State. And it is a fact that a vocal and growing minority among some peripheral groups, such as the African Americans, uses anti-Semitism to achieve their goal.

The situation sorely tests the liberal and pluralist

sentiment of most Jews. Indeed, some Jews have become irreconcilably hostile to the aspirations of the Margins, discarding without a thought the egalitarian, humanist ideals which are the one part of the eji heritage that is worth keeping.

Let us, as our sage Maimonides counselled, follow the Golden Mean. We have every right to defend our social and economic achievements, which we won only by a concerted struggle against discrimination and for personal and communal betterment. We shall never be ashamed of our victories in that long fight. The self-doubt, the guilt, the compulsive denial of our importance and our distinctiveness must go. But the values of universal understanding, of "cosmopolitan" artistic and intellectual inquiry, and of challenging entrenched but irrational ideas must not be discarded, but adapted to the new realities. After exploring our current situation versus the "Margins" and how it will direct our thinking in the future, I will close this chapter, and this book, with some suggestions on what we can do to assert ourselves positively as a unique people, yet become neither unfeeling nor arrogant.

Why Do They Hate Us?

At first glance, the anti-Semitism of the Margins is surprising. Black Americans do not see as many Jews, one would imagine, as do urban white Americans. The rural whites of Louisiana hardly see any; the Poles whose parents may have come into frequent contact with Jews now live in a virtually Jew-free country; and there are not many Jews in the non-Arab parts of the Third World. Let us stress that the great majority of all of these populations are not anti-Semitic. But many individuals among them are, and often in a context that has come to be known as "anti-Semitism without Jews."

Why do they hate us? The answer has to be the same as always. Anti-Semitism can never be understood as long as we refuse to understand that to anti-Semites the Jew above all represents all that is undesirable about Money. To be frustrated about money is a prime requirement for anti-Semitism. To know any Jews is not.

To be frustrated about money means, primarily, not having enough of it. But it can also mean being resentful towards those who have it, but — in our opinion — do not deserve it. The Jews have only recently entered the Centre from the Margins. Some of the other groups who are still there resent them for it. "Why do you accept the Jews," they say to the elite, "and you do not accept us? Can't you see that their money is *Jewish money?*"

Anti-Semitism in the East
One place where such noises come from are some of the ex-communist countries of Europe. East Europeans dreamed through decades of communism of re-entering the Western world. But since the Iron Curtain was torn down, they have seen themselves as the West had long ago come to see them: poor, *déclassé* cousins, not to be invited to dinner except out of charity. Rightly or wrongly, they perceive the Jews as one of the few groups able, through business activity, to immediately benefit from reintroduced capitalism, and to purchase the goods required to certify them as "Western." Many of them equate the "gangsters" and "speculators" (terms East Europeans often use to designate any enterprising person, however legitimate) with the "Jews." In countries like Russia or Rumania, the

anti-Semites think of the government as beholden to "cosmopolitan" Jewish interests allied to the West.

The noisy neo-Nazi groups in Germany are justifiably
viewed with concern, particularly by Jews. One cannot take
lightly the danger of a Nazi revival. Yet it seems that the
neo-Nazi skinheads are quite a different breed from what
the brown shirts once were. Although they use the shocking paraphernalia of the Nazis, these young thugs, former
East Germans for the most part, are reacting much more
out of frustration with the after-effects of communism
than out of nostalgia for what to them is a rather distant
past. In 1992 it was reported that about one in every nine
hundred foreigners were attacked in eastern Germany as
opposed to one in every 12,000 in the western part of the
country. Despite some virulent rhetoric and some grue-
some attacks on Jewish graves, the neo-Nazi violence has
focused on non-white immigrants (including dark-skinned
Rumanian Gypsies) and asylum seekers, and not on Jews,
and this may be an indication that Nazi outfits are more
important to the young extremists than Nazi ideology.

The phenomenon is not really confined to Germany.
Nazi salutes have been photographed by newsmen in
Lithuania. In Prague, a city that suffered Nazi occupation,
Czech youths have beaten non-white residents and even
tourists. In Slovakia and to a lesser extent in Croatia, significant minorities treat the newly won independence of
their countries as the second coming of the discredited
puppet regimes who first established their nominal independence, during the Second World War, by grace of Hitler.
Anti-Gypsy slogans abound in the region. It may well be
that the violence in Germany is worse only because in the
other countries, non-white immigrants are rare. For the

same reason, however, should the riff-raff in Eastern Europe turn nasty, it may be the Jews that they would attack. Truly serious anti-Semitism is, despite appearances, potentially a greater danger east of Germany than in Germany itself.

Anti-Semitism in the South

It is, unfortunately, not only from the East that worrisome anti-Semitic noises are heard. We also hear them from the South. In 1975, the United Nations adopted a resolution that equated Zionism with racism. Such vicious nonsense would never have passed in the General Assembly had it not been for the votes of the Third World, organized by the Arabs. It was a time when poor nations suffered from sky-rocketing oil prices, and the Arab producers used their leverage to the fullest. The UN as well as other international agencies, dominated by a Third World "tyranny of the majority," saw an orgy of anti-Israeli discrimination that equalled in the virulence of its rhetoric the worst anti-Jewish speeches of Nazi and Stalinist demagogues in the past.

Those who defended this outpouring of venom argued that anti-Zionism was not to be confused with anti-Semitism. They were wrong. True, Israel is not and should not be beyond criticism. The idea that all anti-Zionists are anti-Semites has all too often been used by Israeli governments and their supporters to ward off legitimate objections to their policies. Nevertheless, in many, and perhaps most cases, anti-Zionists bring to Israel complaints whose farcical absurdity is matched only by their unrestrained malice. In the years following the Zionism-is-racism resolution, Israeli delegates were hounded out of sporting

events, women's conferences, and children's aid organizations. Israel is not faultless. But what could be more inane
than when delegates from Arab countries where women
were not allowed to drive ganged up with Third World
countries to censure Israel's treatment of Palestinian
women? Or when the same anti-Zionist block removed
Israel from an organization whose aim is to help needy children, without even bothering to tie the reason to the status
of Israel's children?

A telling example of the crass racism that often hides
under the anti-Zionist veneer of the Third World government was Malaysia's banning of Steven Spielberg's Oscar-
winning film about the Holocaust, "Schindler's List." It
was condemned by the Malay government as "propaganda"
for "a certain race" and as tarnishing the Germans. No
official even bothered to suggest that the ban had anything
to do with Zionism or Israel.

The Anti-Racism of the Fools

Perhaps the most disturbing aspect of Third World anti-
Semitism was not what it represented but the boost it gave
to the growing anti-Jewish feeling among American blacks.
The Palestinian movement as we know it followed the Six
Day War of 1967. (The Palestine Liberation Organization
was formed in 1969.) This happened to be the period of a
rapid rise in black consciousness in the United States,
expressed by the most frustrated of the black youths in
sporadic, violent riots. Many blacks perceived a kinship between their fight and that of the Palestinians. In the rhetoric
of their leaders, the Third World was coloured and the West
was white. According to this naïve, race-based vision, the
blacks of America should therefore ally themselves with the
Third World, including the Arabs. In actual fact, of course,

it is very often hard to tell an Israeli Jew from a Palestinian Arab. Palestinians are seldom very dark, and Israelis, more than half of whom are of North African or Near Eastern origin, are often considerably darker than the average New York Jew. Nevertheless, it became common among blacks to think of the Jews as white and the Arabs as people of colour. The Black Muslim movement strengthened this identification, and added anti-Jewish touches of its own.

Since this period in the late sixties, anti-Semitic rhetoric, both among Muslim and Christian blacks, has been on the rise almost steadily. It got worse in the nineties. Anti-Semitism was once referred to as the "socialism of the fools." It has become the anti-racism of the fools.

There have been complaints that a number of African American entertainment personalities are anti-Semitic; including such stars as the brilliant film-maker Spike Lee and the rappers Public Enemy and Ice Cube. However, we need not take a position on personalities here. It may be that Spike Lee is not an anti-Semite, but the fact that anti-Semitism is growing among blacks is beyond doubt.

"A recent survey finds . . . that blacks are twice as likely as whites to hold anti-Semitic views," wrote the black Harvard University professor Henry L. Gates, Jr. in an influential New York Times article. The primary example Gates used was a publication by the Nation of Islam, one of the major Black Muslim organizations, which claims that the Jews bear a special responsibility for slavery. This is, of course, a particularly vicious permutation of the legend of evil Jewish Money. This time Judas is pictured as a slave driver, or rather, a slave trader. Historically it is true that a minority among the slave traders were either Jewish or of Jewish origin, former forced converts to Christianity who were expelled from Spain and Portugal because the

Inquisition accused them of continuing Jewish religious practices. Only a minuscule number of these so-called *marranos* became engaged in the slave trade. As for the plantation owners who bought and exploited the African slaves, practically none were Jewish. On the whole, the Jews had much less to do with slavery than the Gentile English, French, Spanish, and Portuguese, and certainly less than the Arabs, supposed friends of black people. For among the Arabs, black slavery was a centuries-old institution.

The idea that the Jews are somehow responsible for the evil of slavery makes it hard for black Christians to cope with the fact that Jesus was a Jew. They find considerable attraction in the theory, articulated by Spike Lee's Malcolm X, that "God was black." Malcolm X's claim was not new, though it was a strange thing for a novice Muslim to refer to Jesus as God. The idea is that Jesus must have been black because he appeared in a vision to John as having hair "white as white wool," and "feet like burnished bronze"(Revelations 1:12). This might appear to be a rather harmless assertion — though probably a mistaken one, for it is likely that John understood the woolly hair and bronze feet to be aspects of the supernatural apparition he saw, rather than of Jesus when he was alive. (In the same vision, John also saw that Jesus' eyes "were like a flame of fire . . . from his mouth issued a sharp two-edged sword, and his face was like the sun shining in full strength".) The problem is, unfortunately, that all too often the Jesus-was-black argument is taken to the next step, which is much more worrisome. As educated a body as the African American students' organization at the University of California at Los Angeles declared, in their campus paper, that Judaism was a religion stolen by the Jews from people of colour. In other words, the Jews are not the real Jews. The real Jews were black, or at least coloured, while the current would-be Jews are not. Their theft of the religion from black people certifies the Jews as racists, and at the same time as phonies whose claim to Palestine rests on a lic.

The black UCLA students also recommended the *Protocols of the Elders of Zion* as a primer on Jewish underground plotting. This discredited, libellous pamphlet, proven long ago to be the product of the Tsar's secret police, formed an important pillar of Nazi propaganda. It records an alleged conversation among Jewish leaders about their campaign to use both capitalism and communism to dominate the world. The Jewish students were understandably upset. But the black students refused to retract.

It may be surprising that educated people could believe such rubbish. But Henry Gates points out that anti-Semitism is actually more prevalent among educated, younger blacks than the rest. He attributes this to the struggle of a new black élite to take over from the old. The symbol of the old élite was Martin Luther King; the symbol of the new is Malcolm X. The new élite, Gates implies, is exploiting anti-Semitism as demagogues have always done, to whip up emotions that would garner it political support.

Gates's insight should be supplemented by a look at the difference in background between the old and the new élites. The leadership around King was a political one. It did not have behind it a black business or intellectual network, but rather a grouping of political and religious activists. The new élite, the product in many ways of a generation of partially successful programs to promote education and enterprise among blacks, can hope to find support in a much more genuine black middle class. This middle class demands recognition for its own "goods," the same recognition the élite accords the "goods" of the Jews.

The Black Power advocate Eldridge Cleaver once mused that it was the "insult" that hurt most in racism. It is a sentiment that Jews can certainly understand. The insult is the message that though you might have the money, the knowledge, and the education, you still do not count. It is hard to say if the hopelessly poor care as much about the "insult" as the better-off members of a discriminated minority. But we can understand Spike Lee's motivation when he declares that "race is more important than class." Spike Lee is simply describing his black middle-class experience: an experience of being snubbed on the basis of race, even though in terms of class you are much like those who do the snubbing.

Anti-Semitism among the black élite could not, however, be due totally to jealousy about the Jews' acceptance by the white élite. Friction between the black and Jewish middle classes has, at least historically, some foundation in economic interest. Possibly because the Jews are less prejudiced against blacks than other whites, it was largely Jewish business people who until quite recently ran the little shops and owned the decrepit housing, in black slums. During the early riots, black anger and violence were openly focused against Jewish shopkeepers and landlords. Elijah Muhammad invited black people to start their own businesses, rather than rely on the Jews. For that, he was called an anti-Semite. That he was not. The Black Muslim leader was probably right that real equality for blacks will come only after they establish their own economic base, as the Jews have done. (Unfortunately, the agitation did expel the Jews, but only to be replaced by the Koreans, victims of the next round of rioting.)

Much as Jewish liberal activists had been allies to King, Jewish business people were competition to would-be black entrepreneurs. And Jewish students were competition to those blacks who wished to better themselves through education. The most contentious issue between Jews and blacks in America has become that of affirmative action, or "affirmative discrimination," as the sociologist Nathan Glazer called it. Preferred places for blacks are seen by many whites as discrimination against them. For twist the facts as you may, a black person not admitted purely on merit disqualifies a non-black person who is at least equally qualified. Jews feel particularly sensitive about the issue. Above all, it was access to education that enabled us to gain admission to the Centre. We remember only too clearly when well-qualified Jews were refused admission to university by anti-Semitic quotas designed to keep them out of these preserves of white Gentile privilege. No sooner have we won that fight than we find ourselves once again discriminated against, this time in favour of integrating the black élite and would-be élite. Our politicians and intellectuals have done much for the advancement of black people. And now our very own efforts are turned against us. No wonder many of us have become confused and disappointed.

What is to be done? It has been said that there are only two things we know for sure about the future. First it will not be the way we think it will be. Second, it will not be the way we want it to be. Nevertheless, we need a strategy for navigating the treacherous waters ahead. The following may be some of the things that we need and some of the things we do not need:

We Do Not Need Shylock's Defence

Certainly, Shylock's Defence won't do any more. When we say "we are just like you" to the dominant, white Gentile élite, we are suggesting they stop excluding us. But if we say the same thing to those who think of *us* as the élite, then we are insulting them, ignoring their unique experience and aspirations.

One way in which we Jews may have hurt the self-respect of the blacks was in the early days of the civil rights movement, when some of our well-meaning activists would lecture blacks on how to succeed by doing as we did before *we* succeeded. Such activists were merely echoing the sentiment one hears time and time again at dinners and barbecues in Jewish homes, whenever the subject of black peoples' rights comes up in conversation: "We made it, so why can't they?" But of course they can't make it just like us. They are *not* just like us. They are more visibly marked by race, and they, descendants of people who were forced out of Africa to become slaves, lack a tradition of education. In such circumstances to maintain that we are just like them would be not only ridiculous, it would be insensitive and offensive. Our suffering and their suffering have both been terrible; they have not been the same.

We Do Need Chutzpah

Even as discrimination by the Centre no longer pressures us to argue that we are like everyone else, resentment by some at the Margins *forces* us to admit our distinctiveness. Everything points to a need to assert our individuality without apologies, without guilt, without worrying inordinately about what others will think about us.

In 1992, Dershowitz's *Chutzpah,* a book exhorting the

Jews to become more self-confident, made it to the top of the *New York Times* bestseller list for non-fiction. Some of its success no doubt had to do with the colourful personality of the author. At the time *Chutzpah* was published, Dershowitz had not yet been appointed to defend the boxing champion Mike Tyson against his rape charge, nor to be one of Mia Farrow's attorneys against Woody Allen. But his career had always kept him in the limelight. As a young man, he had worked on the defence of the Chicago Seven. But what turned him into a celebrity outside the court rooms was his defence of Claus von Bulow who was accused of attempting to murder his wife. Dershowitz turned his experience during the trial into a successful book, which became an even more successful motion picture, *Reversal of Fortune*. Still, Dershowitz's fame alone could not explain the popularity of *Chutzpah*. Rather, the book was celebrated because it encouraged the Jewish reader, long tired of eji self-consciousness, to assert without guilt the value of his or her Jewishness. The title, *Chutzpah*, told it all. Dershowitz was telling Jews to like themselves, and to like how they were different from others:

> American Jews need more chutzpah. Notwithstanding the stereotype, we are not pushy or assertive enough for our own good and for the good of our more vulnerable brothers and sisters in other parts of the world. . . . We worry about charges of dual loyalty, of being too rich, too smart, and too powerful. Our cautious leaders obsess about what the "real" Americans will think of us. We don't appreciate how much we have contributed to the greatness of this country and don't accept that we

are entitled to first-class status in this diverse and heterogeneous democracy.

The very popularity of Dershowitz's book is proof that the timidity he criticizes has become largely a thing of the past. Even in the nineties, of course, not everyone has come around to the Jewish liberation proposed by *Chutzpah*. (If you are a Jewish reader of this volume, ask yourself some questions about how far you personally have come. Would you feel any qualms about reading this book in a public place? Would you require some courage to recommend it to your Gentile associates?) In 1992, the well-loved comedian Robin Williams still complained that he was getting a cold reception to his idea to film Saul Bellow's *Humboldt's Gift*: "I've heard executives say that it's too Jewish. Funny, but so are most of the executives. I think it's fear." And yet, things *have changed*. A decade earlier, the fear Robin Williams speaks about would probably have prevented Dershowitz's editors from publishing *his* work. They would have worried about offending the Jewish public, then religiously attached to Shylock's Defence.

As I have argued, we will need chutzpah not as much with the "real Americans" (or, for those of us who live outside America, real Canadians, French, British, or the like) as with those who are thought of as even less "real" than ourselves: racial minorities, foreigners. To a powerful minority among us, centred around the "neoconservatives," we ought not go too far out of our way to help the non-Jewish poor, the victims of racial discrimination, etc. To them, it is naïve to forget that among such groups there are elements that are viciously hostile to the Jews. Why, they ask, feed the mouth that will bite your hand?

It would be foolish to pretend that the argument made by these apparently heartless Jews is not a powerful one. It is. The child our money helps might indeed grow up to confront the Jews or Israel. The same legitimate fear applies to politics. Is it not silly to support even worthwhile and morally impeccable aspects of the black, Palestinian, and other such causes, when those whom we would benefit might include our worst enemies?

The answer is that if all blacks and all Third World countries (and all white poor?) were anti-Semitic, then we would be fully justified to leave them to their own devices. But they are not all anti-Semitic. To equate, in a blanket fashion, black and Third World activism with anti-Semitism is just as ridiculous and morally and factually just as wrong as to claim that Zionism is racism. Maintaining contact with, and concern for, the disadvantaged is not only morally right. It is a guarantee that the Jews remain an actor on the inter-racial and international scene.

The alternative to involvement is to withdraw without a fight into the bosom of the existing élite of the democracies and particularly America, hoping that *they* will protect us against the evil tendencies of the Margins. It is disappointing to see how some of our best minds waste their talents on composing, mainly for Gentile consumption, odes to old-fashioned virtue, which are supposed to win us the favours of the conservative élites. They sermonize theatrically about the baseness of our enemies, no doubt as a means of moral blackmail should the "moral majority," as it was once called, think of abandoning us. Such a strategy resembles more closely the passive-aggressive antics of the stereotypical (not the actual!) Jewish mother, rather than real chutzpah.

We in the Diaspora should take our cue from Israel. From the start, Israel, although hardly a rich country, has maintained an extensive assistance program for the Third World, although naturally there has been no aid for the most virulent enemies of the Jewish State, who would not take it anyway. After the awful Zionism-is-racism resolution, Israel did not, in righteous anger, cut off all contact with the Third World. Instead, informal contacts continued. Israel took a pragmatic approach, continuing its aid wherever possible, patiently working to minimize Arab oil influence, and to appeal for American pressure to gain back old friends. The strategy has worked. The odious UN resolution was withdrawn in 1991. Today a great many African and other Third World states once again have friendly relations with Israel.

In the United States, the main Jewish community rightly took up a posture towards black anti-Semitism that combined uncompromising opposition to offensive statements and behaviour with leaving the door open for reconciliation. The Rev. Jesse Jackson, one of the leading African American politicians, caused serious damage to black-Jewish relations when he referred to New York as "Hymie Town." Jewish organizations protested. Instead of cutting themselves off from Jackson behind a Jewish Iron Curtain of righteousness, however, they witnessed the Rev. Jackson attending the 1992 meeting of the World Jewish Congress. There Jackson spoke out forcefully against anti-Jewish rhetoric among American blacks. His speech encouraged other blacks, like Henry L. Gates, to speak up in the same sense, and did much to slow a very dangerous trend.

The anti-Semitism of the Margins is something we will have to face in all its complexity. We cannot wish it away, in the classic fashion of the eji. But neither can we deal with it by withdrawing into a moralistic, self-righteous matzah ball. There is no more poignant statement of real chutzpah than the famous aphorism of Rabbi Hillel, *im ein ani li mi li,* "If I am not for myself, who will be for me?" But let us not forget that the sage followed this by a cautionary second line: *vekesheani leatsmi ma ani,* "And if I am for mine own self alone, what am I?"

EPILOGUE

DIFFERENT,
LIKE EVERYONE ELSE

It is only because we are now, slowly and shyly, emerging from our eji past that we are able to begin looking at it objectively. Like an individual's actions, historical periods only become transparent with hindsight. It was impossible to write about the eji era when we were in the midst of it.

What we are beginning to discover is this: the lives of millions of Jews have until recently been dominated by a desperate wish for acceptance by the Gentiles who kept the gates to economic and social success. The responses of the Gentiles varied from compliance to violent rejection, eventually culminating in the Holocaust. Feeling excluded, most Jews became eji: Embarrassed Jewish Individuals. They suffered from a collective neurosis: rejected as inalterably "different," they insisted at all costs that they were just like everyone else. Shylock's Defence informed all of the eji's intellectual life, both in the sciences and in the arts. It led to the development of counter-stereotypes: the Fiddler, the Brooklyn Jew, the Jewish Princess, and the like.

As we have seen, these popular images, some of them rather romantic, others quite vicious, were all meant to neutralize, sometimes in ways that are less than obvious, the one image all eji feared most: the "Rich Jew," the traitor Judas who sells even God for money. The battle between Good and Gold has been one of the great themes of our civilization. The anti-Semite accused the Jew of being the embodiment of Gold. The eji will do almost anything to deny the charge.

Somewhat to our surprise, in the eighties, Gold finally became accepted by the white, Western élite as a "good thing." They no longer needed a scapegoat to blame for the evils of capitalism. Although in the recession of the early nineties one might have expected a new reaction against those who were rightly or wrongly perceived as rich, such a backlash did not happen; perhaps because of the collapse of communism in Eastern Europe. Anti-Semitism among the élite began to whittle away: a process that is still going on in the more sober nineties.

In the meantime the populations of the "Margins," those left on the sidelines of affluence — much of the Third World and Eastern Europe, and in particular important segments among the American blacks — have seen a surge in anti-Semitism. It is their challenge we have to answer now.

Shylock's Defence cannot do the job. The different populations of the Margins insist on their own distinctiveness. They would not accept the absurd argument that we are just like them, even if we wished to make it. Shylock's Defence had plenty of other problems; the anti-Semitism of the Margins finally finished it off.

We can now appreciate at last that we are different —

just like everyone else. Like all people, we Jews, even the supposedly "assimilated" among us, have a distinctive culture and history. Jewish history used to be coloured by the prejudices and insecurities of the eji era. In Arthur Schnitzler's panoramic novel of Jewish Austria at the time of Freud, *The Way Into the Open*, the Gentile aristocrat Georg laments that "wherever he appeared, he saw nothing but Jews who were ashamed of being Jewish, or Jews who were proud to be Jewish, and feared that one might believe them to be ashamed." I think we now have the chutzpah to see that shame is irrelevant. We can dare to look at our past the way it really was, not the way it might look good to the goyim or to the sentimentalists among us.

We now see 1) that modern Jewish history depended, more than on the religious organizations, on the great masses of the "unaffiliated," eji Jews; and 2) that these modern "unaffiliated" Jews have had their own distinctive culture, largely shaped by their insistence that such a culture did not exist.

Eji culture was not all bad. No price is worth paying for the mental anguish due to the eji's fearful denial of anything specifically Jewish — other than romantic shmaltz about the *shtetl*, or sexist jokes about Jewish women. But in truth, the eji neurosis was a creative one. Certainly, we are better off without it. But are we still going to win the Nobel Prizes now?

Above all, what *was* good about the eji was their regard for other cultures, their challenge to fixed points of view, and their emphasis on what all peoples have in common.

It is up to each and every one of us to live up to the challenge of keeping and developing the good, while rejecting the bad in the eji heritage. If we measure our steps carefully, a healthy, renewed Jewish life might, with luck, be possible in the century ahead. Among the most encouraging signs that this might be so are the current qualified revival of traditional Judaic observances and the effect on both religious and secular Jewish life of the creative new role of women.

The Religious Revival

I was a little late with my Passover shopping this year. When I arrived at my local supermarket, a few days before the Seder, there was no Passover matzah left. Across the parking lot at the liquor store, all the kosher wine was gone: the red and the white, the sweet, the semi-sweet, the dry. I quickly drove to one of the largest liquor stores in the city. Even there, only two kinds of kosher wine were left, an Italian and a Californian, both outrageously overpriced. I shared my irritation with two other desperate and hurried customers. We decided to confront the manager. She explained that this year they had ordered considerably more kosher wine than ever before, but it had all been snapped up very quickly. There was little left to do. I reluctantly plunked down the exorbitant price demanded, and drove off in search of matzah. Eventually, I found two boxes left at the local yuppie specialty food store. I was sure the store had never carried Jewish items before. Either the owner was Jewish and, for the first time, decided to advertise the fact, or she realized that there was now a growing market for the stuff.

However, the unprecedented interest in Jewish ritual ought not to be misinterpreted as a resurgence of Orthodoxy. Of the two people that joined me in talking to the liquor store manager, one was a man who, having considered the prices, decided to simply go for non-kosher wine. The other person interested me in particular. A blonde and blue-eyed woman with a British accent, she was unlikely to have been born a Jew. She appeared to me as one of the growing number of Conservative or Reform converts (the Orthodox conversion process is so demanding as to be almost prohibitive). We struck up a conversation. She was discussing her preparations for making matzah ball soup in tones that one expects to hear in a debate about the rules for serving high tea. She confirmed to me not only that she had converted before her marriage to a Jew but that her husband was a relative of someone I knew. When we found out that mutual friends would be attending her second Seder, she invited me to join them, and I accepted.

When I arrived at their house a few days later, I found a long table laid out in the traditional manner: a white tablecloth, place settings for more than a dozen guests, the special Seder plate on which are arranged, according to custom, the various ritual foods. There was the ornate silver cup filled with red wine. It is offered to the Prophet Elijah, who, we pretend to believe, might come at the end of the Seder to announce the arrival of the Messiah. My new acquaintance's husband sat at the head of the table, wearing the white *kittel*, a long gown worn by the leader of the ceremony. In spite of all these traditional trappings, however, there were a number of significant differences that set this Seder apart from what you might see in the homes of the strictly Orthodox. Not all of the food was certified kosher. I suspect that the hosts did not use a special set of tableware, reserved, as required by tradition, for Passover alone. Some of us could not read Hebrew at all, and only two of us were fluent enough to recite our part of

Haggadah in Hebrew. The rest used English, either entirely or in part. At crucial points in the ceremony, we joined in a discussion of the "contemporary relevance" of the texts. As we ate the traditional parsley dipped in salt water (meant to symbolize the tears of our slave ancestors), we spoke about nature and the ecology. As we read about the exodus from Egypt, we recalled the continuing plight of the Syrian Jews, and of many non-Jewish peoples who still remain "enslaved." One participant's suggestion that the Palestinians were now *our* slaves brought on an acrimonious discussion, which the host skilfully calmed down by getting us all to join in singing the folk song "Yaseh Shalom." The song ("He who makes peace in the heavens shall make peace for us and for all Israel") is based on the conclusion of the *kaddish* — an important prayer, but not one that tradition prescribes at the point we had reached in our Passover ceremony.

Such innovative practices have come under criticism from both the unbendingly traditional and the soberly secular. First, the critics point out that many of the "revivalists'" practices have little to do with the authentic Jewish tradition. Second, they caution that these new forms of Jewish observance may never take the deep roots characteristic of the old-fashioned religious tradition. As Sarah Bershtel and Allen Graubard conclude in *Saving Remnants,* an absolutely fascinating book of interviews with contemporary American Jews: "Jews in America today [and in most parts of the world, let us add] are a people not 'chosen' but choosing." Because their Jewishness is not any longer to a significant extent forced on them by either the Gentiles (who accept them quite readily) or the Jewish authorities (who have no power of coercion), any new

religious observances today's Jews create will never acquire
the community-sanctioned authority of the old tradition.
As such, these practices will probably offer little resistance
to constant revision, in part as a response to trends in the
non-Jewish environment.

These "criticisms" are right. Should we care?

It is, to a large extent, the "revivalists" themselves who
set themselves up to be attacked. Some of them insist that
the changes they are making are actually justified by a more
correct interpretation of the Bible and the Talmud than is
provided by the traditional Orthodox. Nonsense. The
Torah, the Prophets, the Talmud are all products of their
time. They are permeated, along with a great vision of
freedom, love, and justice for the Jews and everyone else,
with sexism, racism, and homophobia. They show disre-
gard for the rights of animals (sacrifice) and of the handicapped (lepers). They support rewarding or punishing
children for the actions of their ancestors. They advocate
collective punishment against an entire people when some
of them have crossed the Jews or God.

I have argued for a frank appraisal of our recent, eji,
past, without resorting to romantic and not-so-romantic
counter-stereotypes. The same argument must be made
for de-shmaltzing our great religious tradition.

I am not advocating assimilation; far from it. But there
are indeed some values that we share with the goyim that
we need not, and should not, give up. These values are universal, or at least universally Western. That means that they
are no more Gentile than they are Jewish. It is the argument of this book that many modern values have been
developed in large measure under Jewish influence — the
influence of the eji. Let us, carefully but without guilt, pick

and choose what we like, both in the Judaic tradition and in our important eji heritage. If this means that our Jewishness will differ radically from that of the medieval model, so be it.

The Role of Women

Judaism has always been marked by diversity. It will probably be even more multifaceted in the future. There is, however, one issue that cuts across all the divisions, from the Orthodox to the most "unaffiliated." I am speaking of the new role played by Jewish women.

The extent of female participation in Jewish ritual and secular life varies, but it is on the rise everywhere. Orthodox women form women-only prayer groups. Many Conservative and all Reform and Reconstructionist women are now regularly admitted to the *bimah*; quite a few have been ordained as rabbis. The "egalitarian" movement embraces Orthodox traditions, but gives equal participation to women in every aspect of religious practice and observance.

At our Seder table, the women wore yarmulkes just like the men. As we read the text, we struggled as best we could with eliminating references to God as male. "He took us out of Egypt" became "God took us out of Egypt." "Our fathers" became "our ancestors." Each of us made up the changes as we went along, laughing self-consciously when we slipped up. True, some of those present did not know enough of the holy tongue to make the corresponding changes in the Hebrew text, so that ironically they left "sexist language" alone in Hebrew, even as they were pruning it from the English. The proudest were those who confidently changed the Hebrew pronouns and suffixes as necessary, displaying their personal concoction of tradi-tional learning and pro-feminist sentiment.

"Non-sexist language" is, to the lay Jew, the most visible example of feminist influence on Jewish observance. However, Torah commentary, the mainstay of Judaic learn-ing, is also beginning to benefit from women contributing a specifically female perspective. To take one example among many, the Torah prescribes segregation and purifi-cation rituals for treating the bodily emissions of both men and women. Yet even the Orthodox today follow only the rules relative to menstruation. The passages on which these practices are based need to be painfully reinterpreted to take into account the female point of view, a process that has been going on for a number of years.

While women are becoming free to fully share in all the domains of Jewish life previously reserved for men, there is plenty of room for reinvigorating the many positive aspects of the traditional role of the Jewish female. Many years ago, I admired Judy Chicago's masterpiece of femi-nist art, *The Dinner Party*. I do not know if Chicago, who is Jewish, was inspired by the festive layout of the Passover table, but it was the first thing that came to *my* mind. Chicago's work is in the form of a triangular table with thirty-nine place settings, each representing a female per-sonality. The objects on the table are artistic variations on the theme of "everyday" items such as a tablecloth, plates, and the like. Together they make a sublime statement, in pottery, lace, and embroidery, on how the products of women's artistic imagination have been unjustly demeaned as "just crafts," while painting and sculpture, dominated by men, were admired as something of a much higher order. The ceremonial traditions and objects of the

Jewish festivals give ample scope to women who wish to give their creative impulse a traditionally "female" venue. Some women find in the holy days a key to both the Judaic and feminine heritage. First of all there is the cooking. The meals need to be served on festive, often decorated plates. The *chalah* is covered by an embroidered cloth, usually made by a woman. Women may wear traditional, lace, head-dress. Many women enjoy sewing clothes for their children, and at the festive gatherings these can be shown off to good effect.

Cooking, pottery, and sewing are, of course, not forbidden to men. Some men find that taking up these activities within a Jewish context gives added moral weight to their determination to challenge the old gender roles.

Certainly, the arrival of women on the *bimah* is of immense benefit to Jewish men. I believe I have shown that all is not well with Jewish manhood: the fondness for JAP jokes and the "Jewish Nerd complex" are among the symptoms. As Jewish women initiate debates on gender roles, they prod Jewish men, too, to question themselves.

For me, seeing Jewish women take on a greater role has had unexpected benefits on the spiritual side as well. One of the most moving religious experiences I have had was a Sabbath visit to a small "egalitarian *shul*." Standing on the *bimah*, a mother was intoning the Torah reading with a quiet, comforting soprano, her sleeping baby strapped on her chest. She was singing as much to her baby as to the congregation and to God. Even when chanted by a male reader, these melodies are presented in a soft and caressing monotone not always associated with the male voice. I had never expected how much these gentle melodies, when interpreted by a female voice, would recall a lullaby.

In the sermon that followed, a man delivered a speech in which he occasionally referred to God as "she." I was briefly tempted to laugh at what might have appeared as a grotesque gesture of political correctness. But I realized how supremely comforting it was for me as a man to be able, for the first time, to think of God as a mother as well as "our father, our king." (David Biale in *Eros and the Jews* argues that at one point the ancient Israelites regarded God as having both male and female features. *El Shaddai*, one of the ancient names for God and a masculine noun, means, according to Biale, "God with breasts.")

In Conclusion

After thousands of years, *yiddishkeit*, Jewishness, is still fully capable of evolution. Its history began thousands of years ago. The last chapter is not about to be written yet. This mysterious, powerful concoction of religion, ethnicity, culture, and collective neurosis, this slippery something that a Freud would identify as his "essence," has a future.

It is too early to see where the "Jewish revival," the increased role of Jewish women, and indeed, the entire complex of post-eji attitudes will land us. What is certain is that the eji, the creature whose difference lay in its will not to be different, will soon be gone. The new, "Chutzpah Jew," will be rid of the old hang-ups, and as ready to affirm a unique destiny as any Italian, German, or Japanese. At last, we Jews will truly become like everyone else, and not more so.

Hopefully, our new self-confidence will also free us of the need to be defensive not only about the achievements but also about the faults of the figures that determined our history. The rabbis tell us that Jews should be proud of the realism of the Torah. Apart perhaps from Abraham, not one of the Jewish heroes was perfect. Moses was reluctant to take on the burden of prophecy. David was an adulterer who did not shy away from causing the death of the husband of his mistress, Bath Sheva. The matriarch Rebecca showed blatant favouritism to one of her sons, Jacob, as opposed to Esau, the first-born.

It was such imperfect men and women who brought the world the message of love and righteousness, spread by Jews, Christians, and Moslems alike.

There is no reason to be any more defensive about the principal figures of modern Jewish history — the eji — than about the characters of the Bible. Marx's thought led to the disaster of communism, Freud's was used to justify sexist attitudes, Einstein's facilitated the invention of the Bomb. But by the same token, Marxists brought increased awareness of social injustice, Freudians bared suppressed truths about the soul, Einstein's followers unlocked untold mysteries of the universe. Without the eji, the modern age would not have been.

GLOSSARY
OF "JEWISH" TERMS

Pronounce "ch" as in German (a velar fricative).
Abbreviations:
Heb. — Hebrew
Pop. — Popular North American spelling or pronunciation, based
on the traditional Ashkenazic pronunciation of Hebrew,
strongly influenced by Yiddish. Younger, more "modern"
(including "modern Orthodox"), and more Israel-oriented
Jews have abandoned many of these linguistic practices in
favour of Israeli Hebrew. For the most part, Israeli Hebrew
is based on Sephardic rather than Ashkenazic usage.
Yidd. — Yiddish

amcho   The "ordinary" Jewish people: those of modest
means and education. (Pop. from Heb. *amcha* "your
— i.e. God's — people.")

Ashkenazi (adj. and n.), Ashkenazim (pl.) Ashkenazic (adj.) A
descendant of, or a follower of the religious rites of,
Jews ultimately from Southwest Germany and
Northeast France (the area referred to in Medieval
Hebrew as *ashkenaz*) who established themselves in
Northeastern Europe and now represent most of
European and North American Jewry. Cf.
Sephardi.

bar mitzvah   The rites of maturation of a boy, involving the
recitation of a religious passage in the synagogue,

and followed by a feast. (Aramaic for "son of the commandment.") A relatively recent innovation is the *bat* or *bath mitzvah* ("daughter of the commandment"), a similar maturation ceremony for a girl. Alternate spelling: *bar/bat mitzva.*

baruch hashem "Thank God." (Hebrew, lit. "blessed be the Name," i.e. God.)

beit hamidrash A space for religious study; often the synagogue. (Hebrew, lit. "house of the Midrash." The Midrashim are religious commentaries on the Bible.)

bimah   The raised platform in a synagogue, where the Torah reading takes place. (Heb.) Also spelled *bima.*

chalah   An egg bread traditionally used for the Sabbath and other holidays. The Sabbath version is made by braiding the dough. (Heb.) Alternate spellings: *chala, halah, hala.* Known in Central Europe as *barches.*

chochem   A person skilled in traditional Jewish study and argument. (Yiddish, from Hebrew *chacham,* "wise.")

chutzpah   Impudence, guts. (Heb. and Yidd.)

frommie   Ultra-Orthodox. (Yidd. *from,* "pious.")

gelt   Money. Also gifts of money given to children on holidays, and the chocolate money used in play at Hanukkah. (Yidd.)

goy, pl. goyim A non-Jew. The term is generally taken, especially by non-Jews, to be derisive, and it is in fact often meant to be so. It is, however, the ordinary and emotion-free (if that is possible) term for Gentiles in Yiddish. In Hebrew, *goy* means a nation. Its Yiddish meaning comes from Hebrew phrases like *yisrael ve-ha-goyim,* "Israel and the nations."

Haggadah   1) The text of the Passover Seder (see Seder below). 2) The books, usually illustrated, that contain the story and that are used by each participant in the Seder. 3) In some communities, particularly among the Sephardim, the term used instead of "Seder." (Heb. *haggadah*, "a tale, a telling.")

halakhah   "The way," the body of Jewish law and custom considered authoritative by the Orthodox. (Heb.) Alternate spellings: *halacha, halachah*.

Hanukkah   The Festival of the Rededication of the Temple, when candles or oil receptacles are lit in an eight-branch menorah, to recall the oil lamp in the Temple that was relit after the defeat of the Graeco-Syrians in 165 B.C.E. Miraculously the tiny bit of holy oil the Jews managed to find lasted the whole of eight days, the period needed until new oil could be prepared. Consequently, Hanukkah lasts eight nights. The first night one candle or oil dish is lit, and on each night following another is added, until, on the last night, there are eight. (Heb.) Alternate spellings: *Hanukah, Hannuka, Chanuka, Chanukah*, etc.

haymishe   Homey, familiarly Jewish, home-made. (Yidd.)

heder   A small, traditional Jewish school for boys. (Lit. Hebrew for "room.")

kaddish   One of the most frequently recited texts of the Jewish liturgy, expressing resignation to, and trust in, God's will and the arrival of His kingdom, and ending with the words, "He who makes peace in the heavens shall make peace for us and for all of Israel. Amen." Even Jews who follow few or no other religious customs often recite, or have recited for them, the *kaddish* when in mourning and on the anniversary of a loved one's death. (Aramaic)

kibbutz   A communal settlement in Israel. (Heb.)

kiddush   A blessing over wine, traditionally recited by a man, that comes at the beginning of many important festivals, including the Sabbath. (Heb.) Alternate spelling: *kidush.*

kittel   A white apron worn by the leader of the Seder.

kohen, pl. kohanim A descendant of the ancient priests of Israel, a hereditary clan that was part of the holy tribe of Levi. Kohanim are said to be descended from the first priest of Israel, Aaron, the brother of Moses. They performed the main ritual functions in ancient Israel, assisted by the non-Kohanim of their tribe, the Levi'im or "Levites." In traditional communities today, they perform a limited number of rituals reserved specifically to them (such as blessing the congregation on the High Holy Days), and are first to be called to perform the ritual reading of the Torah. (Heb.)

Kol Nidrei Opening prayer of Yom Kippur. (Aramaic)

maagen David Star of David. (Heb.) Pop.: *mogen David.*

matzah, pl. matzot Unleavened bread, obligatory during the week of Passover. (Heb.) Also spelled *matza.* Pop.: *matzo,* pl. *matzos* or *matzes.*

mazel tov   "Congratulations," "good luck!" (Pop. from Heb. *mazal,* "luck," *tov,* "good.")

menorah   A ceremonial candelabrum, and especially the sort used for Hanukkah. (Pop. from Heb. *menorah,* "light." The Hebrew term for the Hanukkah menorah is *hannukiyah.*) Also spelled *menora.*

minyan   The quorum of ten Jewish men over thirteen years of age, required for prayers and rituals to count as being performed by a congregation. Less traditional Jews also include women. (Heb.)

Mossad   Israel's secret service.

Ostjude   Broadly, any Jew from the former Russian Empire
              and adjacent areas. A derisive term used by
              German-speaking Gentiles *and* Jews before the
              Holocaust, it referred specifically to Yiddish-speak-
              ing Orthodox Jews in traditional East European
              Jewish garb, even if born and raised outside the
              "East." (German for "Eastern Jew.")

payis   "Side locks," a tuft of hair that male members of
              many ultra-Orthodox groups grow at their temples.
              Also *payes, payot, payyot,* etc. (Pop.)

roshe   An anti-Semite, in the dialects of Yiddish once
              spoken among other places in Austria and Hungary.

Seder   The meal and associated rituals of the first two
              nights of Passover. Reform Jews and all Jews in
              Israel keep only the first night. The term Seder
              means "order" in Hebrew. Its use for the Passover
              feast comes from the expression *seder haggadat
              Pesah*: "the order of the telling of Pesah," which is
              the full title of the Haggadah books read during the
              ceremony — see *Haggadah* above.

Sephardi (adj. and n.), Sephardim (pl.), Sephardic (adj.) A descen-
              dant of, or a follower of the religious rites of, Jews
              ultimately from Spain (Hebrew *sepharad*), who
              established themselves chiefly in North Africa,
              Southern Europe, and the Ottoman Empire.
              (Once there were also many Sephardim in Holland
              and its overseas possessions, and some in Hamburg
              as well as in England and its American colonies,
              including the Caribbean). Popularly (but incor-
              rectly), also any Jew from Iran or Iraq. Today the
              most important Sephardic populations are in
              Israel, Morocco, and France.

shabos

The Sabbath — from sunset on Friday until sunset on Saturday. Traditional Jews refrain during this period from work and from travelling or lighting fires. The injunction against lighting fires is extended to turning on electrical appliances or starting cars. Also spelled *shabes*. (Ashkenazic pronunciation; Sephardic and Israeli Hebrew: *shabbat*.)

shiksa

A non-Jewish woman.

shmaltz

Fat; sentimentality, a sentimental book, film, play, etc. (Yidd.)

shmatta business The textile industry and especially its trade end. (From Yidd. shmatta "rag.")

shmuck

Penis; an incompetent, foolish, and/or disliked person. (Yidd., cf. German *schmuck*, "jewel.")

shnorrer

A beggar; a poor Jew who makes demands for charity on the basis of Jewish law or custom; anyone who takes advantage of other people's charitable inclinations. (Yidd.)

shtetl, pl. shtetlach A small town or village in Eastern Europe with a large and traditional Jewish population. (Yidd.)

shul

Synagogue, especially a small, traditional one, but also used by members of progressive congregations wishing to "connect" to tradition. (From Yidd., "school," "synagogue.")

tallis

Prayer shawl, traditionally blue-and-white or black-and-white, worn by men to prayer and on some ritual occasions. In experimental synagogues today, it may be multicoloured and worn by women as well as men. Alternate spellings: *talis, tales, talles*. (Pop. from Hebrew *talit*.)

tefillin   Phylacteries: a leather band that is ritually wrapped
                around a man's arms, plus a box containing a bibli-
                cal passage that is attached with another leather
                band to the forehead; used in prayer. (Aramaic)

Torah   The first five books of the Scriptures — the
                Pentateuch. Also the parchment scroll from which
                these texts are ceremonially read in the synagogue.
                The Torah scroll is the most venerated ritual object
                in Judaism. Figuratively: Jewish learning and law.
                (Heb.)

tsaddik, pl. tsaddikim A Jew of exemplary religious learning and
                moral qualities; often the leader of a Judaic sect or
                school. Sometimes (probably misleadingly) trans-
                lated as "saint." Alternate spellings: *tsadik, zadik,
                zaddik*, etc. (Heb.)

tsitsis   Fringes of cloth, usually dangling from a kind of
                sash, worn by traditionalist men at all times accord-
                ing to an injunction in Leviticus. (Pop. from
                Hebrew *tsitsit*.)

yiddishkeit   Jewishness, Judaism, Jewish culture, the Jewish
                spirit. (Yidd.)

yarmulke   A skull cap, also known as *kipa* (Heb.) or *kippele*
                (Yidd.), worn by traditional Jewish men at all times,
                and by others on religious occasions (not required
                by the Reform denomination). Also spelled
                yarmulka (Yidd.)

yid   Jew. This is the ordinary Yiddish word (the root for
                the name of the language): it often takes on a
                derogatory or mocking connotation if used in
                another tongue.

Yom Kippur   The Day of Atonement, a fast considered the
                holiest day of the Jewish religious calendar. (Heb.)

NOTES AND SOURCES

In writing the book I have relied on sources in several languages. Unless otherwise acknowledged, all translations are my own.

Prologue
Page 6 — "Special Jewish sorrows": Rosa Luxemburg, *Briefe an Freunde, herausgegeben von Benedikt Kautsky* (Hamburg: Europaische Verlaganstalt, 1950); letter to Mathilde Wurm dated February 16, 1917.

Chapter 1
Page 9 — Freud reported the incident in a letter to his future wife, Martha Barnays, dated December 16, 1883, found in *Sigmund Freud, Briefe 1873–1939, ausgewählt und herausgegeben von Ernst und Lucie Freud* (Frankfurt am Main: S. Fischer, 1980), pp. 83–87. The translation by Tania Stern and James Stern in *The Letters of Sigmund Freud*, ed. Ernst L. Freud (New York: Basic Books, 1960), pp. 77–80, gives, for *Sie müssen das liebe Ich unterordnen*, "You'd better think less of your precious self," instead of "your precious ego," as I do. The Sterns' version is perhaps better English, but it misses the significant fact that to Freud *das Ich* was a technical term. The word means literally "the I," and it was

Freud's term for what came to be known to English-language psychoanalysts as "the ego."

Page 10 — The passage, ". . . completely estranged from the religion of his fathers . . ." may be found in *The Standard Edition of the Complete Psychological Works of Sigmund Freud*, transl. by James Stackey in collaboration with Anna Freud (London: Hogarth, 1955), p. xv. I have altered Stackey's translation somewhat to better reflect the meaning of the original German. The introduction is dated December, 1930. It is reproduced in Sigmund Freud, *Gesammelte Werke, chronologisch geordnet*, ed. Anna Freud and the Princess Georg of Greece, Marie Bonaparte (London: Imago, 1948), vol. 14, p. 569.

Page 14 — The story about the embarrassed professor came to me second-hand from Dr Howard Greenberg.

Page 21 — Matisse's habit of depicting a "Jewish book" is mentioned by Pierre Schneider in *Matisse* (New York: Rizzoli, 1984), p. 27. Matisse may have been alluding to the famous collection of Jewish jokes by Raymond Geiger, *Histoires juives*, 1922.

Page 22 — I owe the information on the Rothschilds' Christmas party to Prof. Peter A. Reich of the University of Toronto, who was told about it by a young Rothschild.

Page 24 — The Russian railways were financed by a consortium that in addition to the non-Jewish bankers Baring of London and Hope of Amsterdam, included the Jewish houses of Mendelssohn in Berlin, Oppenheim in Cologne, the Russian-Jewish bankers Steiglitz in St Petersburg and Fraenkel in Warsaw, and the French-Jewish Pereire brothers who dominated the Crédit Mobilier.

Page 26 — The Dershowitz quote is from Alan M. Dershowitz, *Chutzpah* (Boston: Little, Brown and Company, 1991), pp. 31–32.

Page 28 — Arnold Schoenberg's words are quoted by E. Randol Schoenberg, "Arnold Schoenberg and Albert Einstein: Their Relationship and Views on Zionism," *The Journal of the Arnold Schoenberg Institute*, vol. 10, no. 2, 1987.

Page 28 — The Rumanian graffiti is reported by Jean-Claude Guillebaud and K.S. Karol in *"L'antisémitisme dans les pays de l'Est,"* *Le Nouvel Observateur* 1325 (March 29 to April 4, 1990), p. 9. On Roman's origins, see his *Le devoir de liberté* (Paris: Documents Payot, 1992).

Page 29 — On the treatment of converts by the Jews and non-Jews, see, for example, Ivar Oxaal and Walter R. Weitzmann, "The Jews of Pre 1914 Vienna: An Exploration of Basic Sociological Dimension," *Leo Baeck Institute Year Book*, vol. 30 (London: Secker & Warburg, 1985). On p. 415, the authors refer to a 1903 pamphlet on the subject, written by a Moravian rabbi and quoted approvingly in the official Jewish publication, *Die Neuzeit*.

Page 30 — The quote from Peter Gay is from *The Berlin-Jewish Spirit: A Dogma in Search of Some Doubts*, Leo Baeck Memorial Lecture 15 (New York: Leo Baeck Institute, 1972), p. 6. See also his *Freud, Jews and Other Germans: Masters and Victims in Modernist Culture* (New York: Oxford University Press, 1978); *A Godless Jew: Freud, Atheism, and the Making of Psychoanalysis* (New Haven: Yale University Press, 1987); *Freud: A Life for Our Time* (New York: Norton, 1988).

Page 30 — The remarks on Hollywood Jews are based on Neal Gabler, "The Jewish Problem," *American Film*, July-August, 1988, p. 44.

Page 33 — The collapse of communism in some East European countries has uncovered — or created? — an alarming resurgence of serious anti-Semitism. In my native Slovakia, 20 per cent of those surveyed by an independent

opinion poll in 1991 said that the Jews were a major problem
— at a time when hardly one or two thousand Jews
remained in the area.

Page 34 — Chomsky's remark about paths he had to choose
is from Noam Chomsky, *Chronicles of Dissent: Interviews by
David Bersainian* (Vancouver: New Star Books, 1992), p. 71.

Page 35 — Norman Podhoretz writes of the Columbia
quota in *Breaking Ranks* (New York: Harper & Row, 1979),
p. 10.

Page 35 — Dershowitz's comments on Bok's appointment
are on pp. 73 to 74 of *Chutzpah*.

Page 35 — The Werner Sombart quote is from his book *Die
Zukunft der Juden* (Leipzig: Duncker & Sumblot, 1912),
p. 6.

Page 35 — The Budapest debate is reported on in Zoltán
Novák, *A Vasárnap Társaság: Lukács Györgynek és csoporto-
sulásának eszmei válsága, kiútkeresésük az első világháború
időszakában* (Budapest: Kossuth, 1979), p. 17.

Page 35 — Caran d'Ache was referring to the Dreyfus Affair.
The cartoon is described in David Lewis, *Prisoners of
Honor: The Dreyfus Affair* (New York: William Morrow &
Co., 1973), p. 215.

Page 38 — I am quoting Alsop from *The New York Review
of Books*, November 9, 1989, p. 48. This was a prepublication extract from his memoirs, *I've Seen the Best of It* (New
York: W. W. Norton, 1992).

Page 39 — The famous speech by Shylock is from
Shakespeare's *The Merchant of Venice*, III.i.

Chapter 2

Page 42 — The opening quote from Alfred de Vigny is taken
from his *Le journal d'un poète* (Paris: La Pléiade, 1986),
vol. 2, p. 1258.

Page 47 — The comment on German gymnasien is by Sidney Whitman, *Teuton Studies* (Leipzig, 1896), p. 125 and was quoted by Norbert Kampe, "Jews and Anti-Semites at Universities in Imperial Germany (I); Jewish Students: Social History and Conflict," *Leo Baeck Institute Year Book*, vol. 30 (London: Secker & Warburg, 1985), p. 381.

Page 47 — On Fletcher's Field High, see Mordecai Richler, *The Street* (Markham, Ont.: Penguin Books Canada Ltd., 1985), pp. 4–7.

Page 48 — The remarks about Jews in the Civil War appeared in the January 7, 1862, issue of the *Allgemeine Zeitung des Judenthums* (Leipzig). Benjamin, a prominent lawyer who had once declined a seat on the U.S. Supreme Court, later became Secretary of State of the Confederacy. Subsequently, he emigrated to England, where he became one of the most prominent lawyers, and where he continued to write authoritatively on the law.

Page 49 — The quote about the "Jewish demon" and its vampire wings appears on p. 237 of Konrad Menzel, *Wolfgang Menzel's Denkwürdigkeiten, herausgegeben von dem Sohne Konrad Menzel. Drei Bücher in einem Bande. Mit dem Portrait des Verfassers* (Bielefeld and Leipzig: Bielefeld & Klafing, 1877).

Page 49 — On Wagner's views on "Jewish music," see his *Das Judenthum in der Musik* (orig. 1850) (Leipzig, 1869).

Page 49 — Freud on Wagner is quoted in Theodor Reik, *Jewish Wit* (New York: Gamut Press, 1962), p. 63.

Page 55 — The full text of the Shema is: *shema yisra'el adonai eloheinu adonai ehad:* "Hear O Israel, the Lord, our God, the Lord is One." (Deuteronomy vi, 4). The commandment about when to recite it is in Deuteronomy vi, 7.

Page 56 — Deborah Schiffrin, "Jewish Argument as Sociability," *Language in Society* 13 (1984), pp. 311–335.

Page 58 — I quote the passage criticizing the Jewish egg-seller from an article by Hans Wendland in *Akademische Blätter* 11 (1896/1897), as translated by Norbert Kampe, "Jews and Anti-Semites . . . ," p. 381. Galicia had been a part of the former Kingdom of Poland, and at the time was the home of the largest traditional *Ostjuden* population under Austrian control.

Page 59 — The quote about Richler's school rank is from p. 4 of *The Street*.

Page 73 — "a naive love for a communion of reason": Jean-Paul Sartre, *Jew and Anti-Semite* (New York: Schocken Books, 1965), pp. 114–115.

Chapter 3

Page 75 — The interchange between Le Pen and Stoléru took place on the French television channel, TF1.

Page 76 — The Clermont-Tonnerre speech is recorded in *Archives Parlementaires de 1787 à 1860: Recueil complet des débats législatives et politiques des chambres français, imprimé par ordre du senat et de la chambre des députés sous la direction de M. J. Mavidal* (Paris: Librairie administrative de Paul Dupont, 1878), entry for December 23, 1789.

Page 76 — Napoleon was forced to give certain concessions to the Jewish communities. He created "Jewish synods" as consultative bodies with limited self-government. However, these were organized on principles that recognized that as citizens the Jews were "just like everybody else."

Page 77 — Heine uses the phrase, "aristo*scratchy*," in "Germany — A winter tale" (*Deutschland, Ein Wintermärchen*), Caput 22, in *The Complete Poems of Heinrich Heine: A Modern English Version by Hal Draper* (Boston: Suhrkamp/Insel, 1982), p. 523.

Page 78 — Stoléru's "Breton" remark was reported in the French daily, *Libération*.

Page 79 — The "leopard-ally" woman's remarks on afterlife appear in Jeanne Achterberg, "A Leopard Spirit: An Ally in the Defense Against Cancer," *Shaman's Drum*, summer 1987. The woman interviewed is described as an "Orthodox Jewish lady of some 60 or so years." If she was indeed Orthodox, her lack of knowledge of Jewish teaching on death is remarkable. It may show how the ideology of the eji has in recent years influenced even those who cling to traditional practices.

Page 81 — On the history of the Jews in Freemasonry, see Jacob Katz, *Jews and Freemasons in Europe 1723–1939*. (Cambridge, Mass.: Harvard University Press, 1970).

Page 83 — "Divine Law . . .": Spinoza, *Tractatus Theologico-Philosophicus*, ch. v; see also *The Philosophy of Spinoza*, ed. Joseph Ratner, New York: Modern Library, p. 88.

Page 86 — The statistics on conversions in Vienna are from the *Statistisches Jahrbuch der Stadt Wien*. Cf. Ivar Oxaal and Walter R. Weitzmann, "The Jews of Pre-1914 Vienna: An Exploration of Basic Sociological Dimension," *Leo Baeck Institute Year Book*, vol. 30 (London: Secker & Warburg, 1985), p. 415.

Page 88 — Israel Zangwill's quote about conversions is from his *Children of the Ghetto*: A Study of a Peculiar People (London: Heinemann, 1902), ch. 1.

Page 90 — The verse from Mahler's symphony, translated by Michael Talbot, appears in the booklet accompanyng the Philips compact disc 420 234-2, *Mahler Symphony no. 2 / Wunderhorn-Lieder*. The comment about Mahler's work being "Christian in the broadest sense," which follows later, is by Karl Schumann, from the same booklet.

Page 91 — The quote about "musical cathedrals" is also
from the Philips compact disc booklet.
Page 95 — The quote by Ron Mann is from the *Globe and
Mail* review of his film, *Twist*, by Jay Scott, September 19,
1992.

Chapter 4

Page 101 — The Émile Durkheim quote on the man who
kills himself is from his *Suicide* (Glencoe, Illinois: The Free
Press, 1951), p. 169.
Page 102 — The Fishberg statistics quoted here are given
on pp. 325 and 355 of his book *The Jews: A Study of Race and
Environment* (New York: Arno Press, 1975).
Page 102 — The statistics on the patients at the Vienna
clinic for nervous diseases are quoted by Fishberg (p. 334)
from A. Pilcz, "Geistesstörungen bei den Juden," *Wiener
Klinische Rundschau* xv: 888-890, 908–910, 1901. The
quote on Jews travelling to Vienna to see a doctor is on p.
334 of Fishberg.
Page 103 — The Édouard Drumont quotes are from his *La
France juive devant l'Opinion* (Paris: C. Marpon and E.
Flammarion,1886), pp. 107 and 108. See also p. 132.
Page 104 — Wilhelm Erb's speech was published in *Neue
Heidelberger Jahrbücher*, vol. 4, no. 1, and reprinted as a
pamphlet: *Über die wachsende Nervosität unserer Zeit*
(Heidelberg: Gustav Koester, 1893). The quote given here is
translated from p. 19 of the reprint.
Page 105 — The David Duke comment appears in
Newsweek, November 18, 1991, p. 27.
Page 105 — The Joseph Alsop quote is from his "The Wasp
Ascendancy," *The New York Review of Books*, November 9,
1989, p. 56.

Page 109 — The Kafka passage is known as "Die Bäume," *Franz Kafka, Das erzählerische Werk, vol. 1: Erzählungen, Aphorismen, Briefe an den Vater*, ed. Klaus Hermsdorf (Berlin: Rütten & Loening, 1983), p. 94.

Page 111 — The Ernest Gellner quote is from his *The Psychoanalytic Movement or the Cunning of Unreason* (London: Paladin, 1985), p. 36.

Page 112 — Freud acknowledges that he got the idea of the Jews killing "the Egyptian, Moses" from Ernst Sellin, *Mose und seine Bedeutung für die israelitisch-jüdische Religionsgeschichte* (Leipzig: A. Deichert, 1922).

Page 118 — Among the New Testament passages where Jesus identifies the ritual bread and wine with his body and blood is Matthew 26:26.

Page 121 — The Donne quote is from "To Sir Henry Wotton," l. 46.

Page 123 — The quote by Jonathan Miller appears in *The Macmillan Dictionary of Qutoations* (New York: Macmillan, 1989).

Chapter 6

Page 139 — The incident involving the Byelorussian minister is reported in the Dutch magazine *Vrij Nederland*, December, 1991, p. 37, in "Jiddisje cultuur tegen de vergetelheid," an article by Felix Kaplan.

Page 139 — Kampelman described his decision to rewrite his speech in a conversation with George Urban. "Can We Negotiate with the Russians? (and if so, how?)," *Encounter*, March 1985.

Page 140 — Disraeli's statement about his ancestors as priests in the temple of Solomon was made in reply to Daniel O'Connell, Member of Parliament.

Page 141 — Jacques Derrida's remarks on circumcision are quoted from his essay, "Circonfessions," in Geoffrey Bennington and Jacques Derrida, *Jacques Derrida* (Paris: Seuil, 1991, p.70).

Page 142 — The Lenny Bruce passage is from *The Essential Lenny Bruce* (New York: Ballantine, 1967), p. 292.

Page 143 — The anecdote about Hollywood Jews is from Neal Gabler, "The Jewish Problem," *American Film*, July-August 1988, p. 44. For a lively account of the Jewish influence on the American cinema, see Neal Gabler, *An Empire of Their Own: How the Jews Invented Hollywood* (New York: Crown Publishers, 1988).

Page 144 — Freud's comment on "host peoples" is found in his essay, "Das Unbehagen in der Kultur." The title of this work is commonly translated as "Civilization and Its Discontents," although something like "Ill at Ease in Civilization" might be closer to what Freud meant.

Page 144 — The full reference to Cuddihy's book: John M. Cuddihy, *The Ordeal of Civility: Freud, Marx, Lévi-Strauss, and the Jewish Struggle with Modernity* (New York: Basic Books, 1974).

Page 150 — The Sartre anecdote is from *Jew and Anti-Semite*, p. 102.

Chapter 7

Page 160 — One person who recorded Yiddish-speakers on early phonograph equipment was An-ski, born as Shlomo Rappoport, a playwright who became famous for his *Dybbuk*. Stored at the Ethnographic Museum of St Petersburg since before World War I, An-ski's recordings and the large number of artifacts and photographs he also collected survived two wars and the anti-religous, anti-

Semitic attitudes of the Communists. An-ski's collection was reassembled for the public in 1992 by Ludmila Uritskaya of the St Petersburg Museum and Judith Belifante, the director of the Amsterdam Jewish Museum. The exhibition opened in Amsterdam, then travelled to Germany, and later New York.

Page 161 — The critic quoted on Sholom Aleichem here is Maurice Samuel, *The World of Sholom Aleichem* (New York: Alfred Knopf, 1943), p. 6. The Howe and Greenberg quote is from *A Treasury of Yiddish Stories* (New York: The Viking Press, 1954), p. 74.

Page 162 — "already passing into the collective memory": Joseph Butwin and Frances Butwin, *Sholom Aleichem* (Boston: Twayne Publishers, 1977), p. ii.

Page 163 — The Northrop Frye quote is from his book *The Anatomy of Criticism: Four Essays* (Princeton: Princeton University Press, 1957), p. 97.

Page 163 — The quote on Sholom Aleichem's early writing is from Marie Waife-Goldberg, *My Father, Sholom Aleichem* (New York: Simon and Schuster, 1968), pp. 66–67.

Page 165 — On Gorky's great-aunt, see *The Autobiography of Maxim Gorky, with a New Introduction by Avraham Yarmolinsky* (New York: Collier, 1962), p. 258.

Page 166 — The libretto of *Fiddler* is by Joseph Stein; the music is by Jerry Bock.

Chapter 8

Page 173 — The Lenny Bruce quote is published in *The Essential Lenny Bruce*.

Page 175 — Theodor Reik on Bergler's concept of "psychic masochism" is taken from Bergler's *Laughter and the Sense of Humor* (New York: International Medical Book Corp.,

1956), p. 112, quoted in Theodor Reik, *Jewish Wit* (New York: Gamut Press. 1962), p. 218.

Page 175 — The "Bronx" joke is reported in Reik, p. 56.

Page 176 — Woody Allen's comparison of himself to his affectionate parents was quoted in an interview by Jack Kroll, soon after the accusations of child abuse were made public (*Newsweek*, August 31, 1992).

Page 177 — On the Italians looking Jewish: the Bahn quote is cited in Elisabeth Frenzel, *Judengestalten auf der deutschen Bühne: Ein notwendiger Querschnitt durch 700 Jahre Rollengeschichte* (Munich: Deutscher Volksverlag, 1942), p. 165. I am giving it as translated by Sander L. Gilman, *Jewish Self-Hatred: Anti-Semitism and the Hidden Language of the Jews* (Baltimore: The Johns Hopkins University Press, 1986), p. 148. That Russian Jews referred to their own people as "Italian" is reported by Vladimir Medem in "The Youth of a Bundist," reprinted in *The Golden Tradition: Jewish Life and Thought in Eastern Europe*, ed. Lucy S. Dawidowicz (Boston: Beacon Press, 1967), p. 428.

Page 178 — The "Saturday Night Live" program with Glenn Close was broadcast on December 12, 1992.

Page 182 — Betty Friedan describes both the Jewish and the Italian woman as subject to the same syndrome of protection creating dependence in *The Feminine Mystique* (New York: W.W. Norton, 1963), p. 294.

Page 182 — In her book *Conversational Style: Analyzing Talk Among Friends* (Norwood, N.J.: Ablex, 1984), Deborah Tannen distinguishes between the aggressively talkative "high-involvement speakers" and the more shy and cooperative "high-consideration speakers." Although she does not herself make the point, it is clear that the Jews in her sample tended to be the "high-involvement" kind. The point is more explicitly developed in her *You Just Don't Understand: Women and Men in Conversation* (New York: Ballantine, 1991).

Page 182 — The British Airways video story is reported on in *The Jerusalem Post International Edition*, April 18, 1987, p. 6. In fact, the video seems to deal with conflicts between ritual prayer times and times for serving on-flight meals. It is the *Jerusalem Post* that jokingly interprets it as referring to the Jewish passengers undisciplined behaviour.

Page 182 — I have taken the Totie Fields and Joan Rivers quotes from Sarah Blacher-Cohen, "The Unkosher Comediennes," *Jewish Wry: Essays in Jewish Humor*, ed. Sarah Blacher-Cohen (Bloomington and Indianapolis: Indiana University Press, 1987), pp. 113 and 115.

Page 184 — Woody Allen made the statements on his family background to Claude Weill of the French weekly *Le Nouvel Observateur*. ("Woody et son double," in the July 31 – August 6, 1987 issue.)

Page 184 — See Gerald McKnight, *Woody Allen: Joking Aside* (London: W. H. Allen, 1982), p. 14.

Page 185 — The quote on Midwood is from McKnight, p. 19.

Chapter 9

Page 186 — The exchange between Medem and Trotsky in the opening quote is given in *The Golden Tradition: Jewish Life and Thought in Eastern Europe*, ed. Lucy S. Dawidowicz (Boston: Beacon Press, 1967), p. 441, referring to a debate in 1903.

Page 187 — The Trotsky speech is in Tsvetlana Zelikson-Bobrovskaya's *Pervaya Russkaya Revolutsia v Peterburge 1905* (Moscow, 1925).

Page 188 — On how Levin had to educate the Jewish deputies on the Sabbath, see Shmarya Levin, "In the First Russian Duma," reprinted in Dawidowicz's *The Golden Tradition*, p. 478.

Page 188 — "The atmosphere during the debate . . .": Shmarya Levin, p. 480.

Page 190 — Brouckère's speech is reported in the *Minutes of the Second Congress of the Russian Social Democratic Labour Party*, translated and annotated by Brian Pearce (London: New Park, 1978), p. 117.

Page 190 — That Jewish strikers were a majority in the earlier strikes is underlined by Robert J. Brym in his fascinating monograph, *The Jewish Intelligentsia and Russian Marxism: A Sociological Study of Intellectual Radicalism and Ideological Divergence* (New York: Schocken, 1978), fig. 16, p. 91.

Page 192 — The Lieber quotes are from the *Minutes of the Second Congress*, p. 75, and pp. 77–78.

Page 192 — Lev Deutsch expresses his frustration with his fellow-revolutionaries in his book *Rol' evreev v russkom revolyutsionnom dvizhenii* (Berlin: Grani, 1923), vol. 1, pp. 8–9.

Page 193 — That the delegates laughed at Lieber is reported on p. 223 of the *Minutes of the Second Congress*.

Page 193 — On "personal autonomy," see Lieber's speech, *Minutes of the Second Congress*, p. 79. Lenin's judgment of Bauer's idea is given in "Theses for a Lecture on the National Question (Excerpt)," *Lenin on the Jewish Question*, ed. Hyman Lumer (New York: International Press, 1974), p. 137.

Page 194 — Worries about what non-Jewish workers might think of being led by a Jewish socialist must also have

consciously or otherwise biased Otto Bauer, who solved the
problem — ironically if one considers his influence on the
Bund — by specifically excluding the Jews from personal
autonomy, because, he felt, the Jews were not a "nation." In
the Russian Empire, however, they were recognized as a
nation by law, and were, more than in much of Austria-
Hungary, distinguished from other groups by their language and principal population centres.

Page 195 — The Trotsky-Lieber exchange is given on p. 83
of the *Minutes of the Second Congress*.

Pages 196 and 197 — The Bund platform is given in the
Minutes of the Second Congress as Appendix IV.

Page 199 — Marx's famous aphorism on "the opiate of the
masses" appears in the third paragraph of his "Zur Kritik der
Helgel'schen Rechts-Philosophie. Einleitung," *Deutsch-
französische Jahrbücher* (Paris, 1844). The English version is
to be found in *Critique of Hegel's "Philosophy of Right,"* ed.
Joseph O'Malley (Cambridge University Press, 1970), p.
131.

Page 201 — Trotsky's defence is reported in his "Nasha
Pervaya Revolutsia," *Sochineniya* vol. 2, 1925, book 2, pp.
163–177, translated and quoted by Isaac Deutscher, *The
Prophet Armed, Trotsky: 1879–1921* (Oxford University
Press, 1954), pp. 167–168.

Page 202 — Trotsky's description of how he refused to
head the Cheka is given in his autobiography, *Moya Zhizn'*,
vol. ii., pp. 62–63.

Page 202 — "larger than any of the older leaders": Isaac
Deutscher, *The Prophet Armed*, p. 116. Deutscher identi-
fies Jacques Sadoul's judgment of Trotsky as coming from
Sadoul's *Notes sur la Révolution Bolchévique* (Paris:
Editions de la Sirène, 1919), p. 76. Note that "Stalin," a

pseudonym taken up by the Georgian Bolshevik whose real name was Dzhugashvili, means "son of steel."

Page 202 — Trotsky gives his reasons for refusing to head the first Soviet government in *Moya Zhizn'*, vol. 2.

Page 204 — "Anti-Semitism raised its head . . .": Davidowicz, *The Golden Tradition*, p. 447.

Page 207 — The Russians asked my father to go with them into an apartment building, which they proceeded to loot. They made my father drunk with vodka, and pushed him into the crawl space of the elevator shaft. The Russians escaped, but my father was found by the residents, who beat him badly and then turned him over to the police for "interrogation."

Page 207 — On the murder of Trotsky, see Nicholas Mosley, *The Assassination of Trotsky* (London: Michael Joseph, 1972), p. 159.

Page 208 — The poem's source is given by J. P. Nettl, *Rosa Luxemburg* (London: Oxford University Press, 1966), p. 484, as the January 13, 1919, issue of the German Socialist Party newspaper, *Vorwärts*.

Page 209 — Luxemburg's dissertation was called *Das industrielle Entwicklung Polens* (Leipzig, 1898).

Page 209 — "a utopian mirage": I am quoting Nettl's (p. 49) translation from the minutes of the First Congress of the The Social Democracy of the Kingdom of Poland (published in *Sprawa Robotnicza*, no. 10, April 1894).

Page 210 — "What other fatherland . . .": *Volkswacht* (Freiburg), no. 57, March 9, 1914.

Page 210 — On Parvus, see Z.A.B. Zeman and W.B. Scharlau, *The Merchant of Revolution: The Life of Alexander Israel Helphand (Parvus) 1867–1924* (London: Oxford University Press, 1965).

Page 211 — The Cozma remarks are reported by Jean Hatzfeld, "Retour sur l'épopée des gueules noires de la vallée du Jiul," *Libération*, October 29, 1991, pp. 16–17.

Page 211 — Csurka's anti-Semitic pronouncements appeared in the Hungarian press almost immediately after the collapse of the communist regime in 1989. Some of his remarks about the alleged international conspiracy against Hungary were reported in *The New York Times*, March 19, 1993.

Chapter 10

Page 212 — The opening quote is from Cynthia Ozick, "Notes Toward Finding the Right Question." *On Being a Jewish Feminist: A Reader*, ed. Hannah Heschel (New York: Schocken Books, 1983), p. 125.

Page 213 — Orthodox Jews bar women from all ritual functions in the synagogue, and in public Jewish life restrict them to auxiliary functions such as organizing social events or charity. Traditional Jewish scholars are permitted to live off the labour of their wives, which frees them to study. In Israel some ultra-Orthodox groups have called for taking away women's right to vote. Nevertheless, traditional women often say that they feel fulfilled in the role of home-maker, which includes the supervision of major domestic rituals. It must be said that the eji male does not necessarily treat women with more respect than the Orthodox. In Freud's Vienna, misogyny and Jewish "self-hatred" curiously went hand in hand. Weininger was the most tragic example of what was a widespread phenomenon. See Jacques Le Rider, *Modernité viennoise et crises de l'identité* (Paris: Presses Universitaires de France, 1990), pt. III.

Page 214 — Belle Barth's "gelt and shmuck" aphorism and Sophie Tucker's mink poem that follows are both quoted by Sarah Blacher-Cohen, "The Unkosher Comediennes," an article included in *Jewish Wry*.

Page 215 — Midler's joke about the weight of her breasts is from *Mud Will Be Flung Tonight*, a 1985 record album.

Page 216 — The Balzac quote is from *Splendeurs et misères des courtisans*, as translated and quoted in Charles C. Lehrmann, *The Jewish Element in French Literature* (Rutherford: Fairleigh Dickinson University Press, 1971), p. 166.

Page 216 — For a more extensive discussion of the Jewish whore symbol, see Livia Bitton-Jackson, *Madonna or Courtesan?: The Jewish Woman in Christian Literature* (New York: The Seabury Press, 1982), p. 80.

Page 217 — The "Torpedo" quote is from Honoré de Balzac, *A Harlot High and Low* (New York: Penguin, 1970), pp. 41–42.

Page 218 — The exchange between Abigail and the monk is from Act III, scene 6.

Page 220 — In the 1969 Bantam Books edition of *Portnoy's Complaint*, the passages about picking up the phone and about living in a Jewish joke are on p. 39. The capitalized complaint is on p. 136. The Ming Toy joke is on Page 213.

Page 222 — The quotes are from Heinrich Heine's *Memoiren*, first published in 1884, but written for the most part at the close of the 1830s. *Heines Werke in fünf Bänden*, ed. Helmut Holtzhauer (Berlin and Weimar: Aufbau, 1981), vol. 5.

Page 222 — Heine's ironic comment on his mother's cooking is in his poem, "Germany, A Winter Tale."

Page 223 — I am using JAP jokes here from an article by

Fred Bruning, "The Perils of the Good Life," *Maclean's*, October 5, 1987.
Page 225 — The magazine writer who was told that anyone can be a JAP was Fred Bruning.

Chapter 11
Page 229 — The opening quote for this chapter is from David Biale, *Eros and the Jews: From Biblical Israel to Contemporary America* (New York: Basic Books, 1992), p. 206.
Page 230 — Dylan's testimony was summarized by *Vanity Fair* in its November 1992 issue. The quotes here are from p. 217.
Page 230 — "He didn't get drunk . . .": "Unhappily Ever After," *Newsweek*, August 31, 1992, p. 53.
Page 234 — The von Bredow joke is from Salcia Langmann, *Der jüdische Witz* (Olten und Freiburg in Breisgau: Walter-Verlag), p. 286. A whole chapter of this book is devoted to jokes about Jews in the military.
Page 237 — On Jews in Israel minimizing the Holocaust and not giving enough help to the persecuted, see Tom Segev, *The Seventh Million: The Israelis and the Holocaust* (New York: Hill and Wang, 1993).
Page 237 — The sports agent's remark about bar mitzvahs is reported in a footnote by Alan Dershowitz, *Chutzpah* (Boston: Little, Brown and Company, 1991), p. 100.
Page 240 — Kafka's comment on passing by the brothel is from his diary: Franz Kafka, *Tagebücher, In der Fassung der Handschrift*, ed. Hans-Gerd Koch, Michael Müller, and Malcolm Pasley (Frankfurt a.M.: S. Fischer, 1990), p. 13. This passage was omitted from the first edition of Kafka's diaries, edited by Max Brod.

Page 243 — The quote about the hidden agenda of the Woody Allen style comic is from David Biale, *Eros and the Jews*, p. 207.

Page 245 — On the Jews in television in the early nineties, see Sheli Teitelbaum, "Prime Time Exposure," *The Jerusalem Report*, April 8, 1993.

Page 246 — One of the most reliable sources of statistics on intermarriage among Jews is the census of Canada, which, unlike the U.S. and many European censuses, asks for the respondent's religion and ethnic identification. The 1990 results for Jewish brides and grooms show that 74 per cent of the women married Jews, compared to 71 per cent of the men. There is no guarantee that these results can be generalized to other countries. However, similar statistics on the relative intermarriage rates of Jewish men and women have long been reported from the United States. See the comments on this issue by Louis A. Berman in his *Jews and Intermarriage* (New York: Thomas Yoseloff, 1968), p. 94.

Page 253 — Woody's statement about having had only age-appropriate relationships is from "But She's Not Part Of My Family," an interview with Jack Kroll in *Newsweek*, August 31, 1992, p. 55.

Page 253 — For Milan Kundera's views on the relationship between the author and the work, see his article, "L'ombre castratrice de Saint Garta," in *L'Infini*, autumn 1990.

Page 254 — "The Heart Wants What It Wants": interview by Walter Isaacson, *Time*, August 31, 1992, p. 43.

Chapter 12

Page 262 — The Lévi-Strauss quote is taken from *The Origin of Table Manners (Introduction to a Science of Mythology: 3)*, trans. John and Doreen Weightman (London: Jonathan Cape, 1978), pp. 497 and 499.

Page 262 — Lévi-Strauss's remarks about eating habits in different European nations are on p. 498 of *The Origin of Table Manners*.

Page 271 — The quote on WASP costume is from Joseph Alsop, "The Wasp Ascendancy," *The New York Review of Books*, November 9, 1989, p. 49. Prepublication extract from the memoirs of Joseph Aslop, *I've Seen the Best of It* (New York: W. W. Norton, 1992).

Page 272 — The Sartre passage is from his *Jew and Anti-Semite* (New York: Schocken Books, 1965), p.132.

Page 275 — Berlin's words are from his essay "The Apotheosis of the Romantic Will," reprinted in *The Crooked Timber of Humanity: Chapters in the History of Ideas*, ed. Henry Hardy (London: John Murray, 1990), p. 209. Berlin does not like the term "relativism," because to some it means the belief that there are no absolute values. "Pluralism" would be a better term. But the physicists and anthropologists whom I discuss below, and who used the terms "relativity" and "cultural relativism," respectively, did, like Berlin, believe in some absolute values: that of tolerance above all. I keep the term "relativism" for this reason.

Page 275 — Einstein's aphorism is reported in Theodor Reik, *Jewish Wit*, p. 222.

Page 278 — Regarding Leo Szilard's role in the development of the Bomb and the subsequent fight to limit its destructive potential, see *Toward a Livable World: Leo Szilard and the Crusade for Nuclear Arms Control*, ed. Helen S. Hawkins, G. Allen Greb, and Gertrud Weiss Szilard (Cambridge, Mass.: MIT Press, 1987).

Page 279 — Isidor Rabi had been brought to the United States in his infancy.

Page 280 — See Lord Zuckerman, "Nuclear Wizards," *The New York Review of Books*, March 31, 1988. The article is an overview of books on Rabi, Szilard, and Teller, with valuable insights by Zuckerman himself.

Chapter 13

Page 285 — Chomsky's "butterfly" comment is from an address at the University of Toronto, 1981.

Page 290 — "I do not believe . . .": Robert Faurisson, *Mémoire en défence, contre ceux qui m'accusent de falsifier l'histoire. La question des chambres à gaz* (Paris: La Vieille Taupe, 1980), p. 3.

Page 290 — The petition signed by Chomsky is found in Serge Thion, *Vérité historique ou vérité politique? Le dossier de l'affaire Faurisson. La question des chambres à gaz* (Paris: La Vieille Taupe, n.d.), p. 163.

Page 291 — The participation of Jean-Gabriel Cohn-Bendit is mentioned in *Faurisson, Ich suchte — und fand die Warheit: Die Revisionistische These eines französischen Forschers* (published as a separate issue of *Kritik: Die Stimme des Volkes*, no. 58, Lausanne: Courrier du Continent, 1982), Appendix 1, p. 43. The statement of purpose of the Vieille Taupe publishing house appears at the back of Faurisson's *Mémoire*.

Page 291 — "partisans of American savagery . . ." and the subsequent passage on free speech are found in Faurisson, *Mémoire*, p. xii.

Page 297 — The quote from Abraham Serfaty is from his interview with the Dutch journalist Rinke van den Brink: "Abraham Serfaty, de Marokaanse Mandela," *Vrij Nederland*, December 7, 1991, p. 19.

Page 299 — The Nazis were hesitant as to just what they wanted to do with the Gypsies. In Auschwitz, Gypsies wore the black badge reserved for "anti-social elements." This expressed the Nazi view that the Gypsies' "sin" was primarily their nomadic way of life. The solution was to settle them by force and make them do "useful work." The Gypsy "family camp" in Auschwitz appears to have been built for this purpose. Here Gypsy families were allowed to stay together, and were assigned various forced labour tasks. This policy contrasted with Nazi directives ordering that the Gypsies be treated "just like the Jews," that is, that they be persecuted on racial rather than social grounds — and that they be "liquidated." Gypsies were repeatedly rounded up and murdered *en masse*, resulting in a tragic Gypsy Holocaust. The Gypsy policies of the Nazis are insightfully explored in Michael Zimmermann's *Verfolgt, vertrieben, vernichtet: Die nationalsozialistische Vernichtungspolitik gegen Sinti und Roma* (Essen: Klartext, 1989).

Page 301 — Robert Jay Lifton, *The Nazi Doctors: Medical Killing and the Psychology of Genocide* (New York: Basic Books, 1986).

Page 302 — On the "Society for Ethical Culture," see Leonard B. Glick, "Types Distinct from Our Own: Franz Boas on Jewish Identity and Assimilation," *American Anthropologist*, vol. 84, pp. 555–556, 1982.

Chapter 14

Page 305 — The opening quote is from James B. Stewart, *Den of Thieves* (New York: Simon and Schuster, 1991), p. 227.

Page 306 — My description of events concerning Boesky and the associated financial scandals are based on Stewart's book. He culled his information on the Guterman bar mitzvah from Georgia Dullea, "Coming of Age on the Ocean," *The New York Times*, September 16, 1986.

Page 306 — Stewart refers to Mulheren's arrest on p. 366 of *Den of Thieves*. He bases his report on police evidence introduced in U.S. v. Mulheren. That Mulheren actually wanted to kill Boesky has never been demonstrated.

Page 307 — I heard the joke about the B'nai Brith reward from a Jewish vice-president of a major stock brokerage.

Page 310 — Understandably, most of the literature on the Panama affair is in French. See, for example, Jean-Yves Mollier, *Le Scandale de Panama* (Paris: Fayard, 1991). The Dreyfus Affair, which caused a serious political crisis in France, was the case of the highest ranking French-Jewish officer, Captain Adolph Dreyfus, who was tried repeatedly on charges of spying for Germany. He was eventually acquitted, long after it first became clear that the evidence against him was fabricated by an anti-Semitic fellow-officer.

Page 311 — The quote from Chesterton's autobiography is reproduced and discussed by Michael Coren, *Gilbert: The Man Who Was G.K. Chesterton* (London: Vintage U.K., 1990), ch. viii.

Page 312 — Stewart uses the New Testament passage about the "den of thieves" in the Temple as the epigraph for his book.

Page 313 — The auction of Drexel's offices was described in an Associated Press release. This appeared in *The Globe and Mail* on June 14, 1990.

Page 314 — The quote by Melnitzer about criminals and clubs appeared in *The London Free Press* in a 1991 interview with Patricia McGee (*The Globe and Mail Report on Business*, February 1993.)

Page 315 — The headline about Melnitzer is found in *The Globe and Mail Report on Business*, February 1993, p. 16.

Page 316 — Even within the "Jewish firms," many of the

major players were descendants of long-established American families of German-Jewish origin. Judith Ramsey Ehrlich and Barry J. Rehfeld's *The New Crowd: The Changing of the Jewish Guard on Wall Street* (Boston: Little, Brown, 1989) chronicles the way the financial citadels of these aristocratic financiers were invaded by the children of "ordinary" Ashkenazim with East-European roots.

Page 323 — According to *The New York Times* (March 7, 1992), the alleged Baker remark was referred to by Edward Koch in his weekly column in the March 6, 1992 issue of *The New York Post*. (See also *The Globe and Mail,* March 7, 1992.)

Page 324 — The phrase, "free marketeers with libertarian social attitudes," is from Robert Shepherd's *The Power Brokers: The Tory Party and Its Leaders* (London: Hutchinson, 1991), p. 197.

Page 324 — ff. On the Reichmann story, see e.g. Peter Foster, *Towers of Debt: The Rise and Fall of the Reichmanns* (Toronto: Key Porter, 1993).

Page 325 — Regarding the difficulties of the Bronfman companies, see *The Economist,* February 20, 1993, p. 77.

Page 326 — The quote about the Bronfmans skating to the edge of the prohibition laws is from Peter C. Newman, *The Bronfman Dynasty: Rothschilds of the New World* (Toronto: McClelland and Stewart, 1978), p.17.

Page 329 — Boesky's aphorism about greed is quoted in a *San Francisco Chronicle* article by Kathleen Pender ("The World According to Boesky," May 10, 1986), and also used by Stewart, p. 223.

Chapter 15
Page 333 — The Passover Haggadah Supplement

published by *Tikkun* magazine has appeared for a number of years as an insert in the March/April issue. I am quoting from the 1993 version.

Page 338 — The statistics about the relative number of racist incidents in eastern and western Germany are taken from Bill Schiller, "Germany is torn by refugee crisis," *The Toronto Star*, November 21, 1992, p. A17.

Page 339 — For an interesting discussion of current German anti-Semitism as an after-effect of communism, see the article "Nationalism and Identity in (Former) East Germany," by Marla Stone, which appeared in the November / December 1992 issue of *Tikkun*.

Page 340 — Malaysia's ban of "Schindler's List" was reported in *The Economist*, March 26, 1994, p. 6.

Page 341 — "Socialism of the fools" is a phrase coined by the socialist August Bebel.

Page 342 — Spike Lee's comment on race versus class was quoted in an interview in the October, 1992, issue of *Esquire*.

Page 345 — See Nathan Glazer, *Affirmative Discrimination: Ethnic Inequality and Public Policy* (New York: Basic Books, 1975).

Page 348 — The Dershowitz passage is from his book *Chutzpah* (Boston: Little, Brown and Company, 1991).

Page 348 — "Humboldt's Gift": Robin Williams interviewed in *NOW Magazine* (Toronto), December 17–23, 1992.

Page 351 — Hillel's sayings appear in Chapter 1, Mishnah 14 of the *Pirkei Avoth* or "Ethics of the Fathers."

Epilogue

Page 357 — The reference about Jews choosing rather than being chosen is from Sara Bershtel and Allen Graubard, *Saving Remnants: Feeling Jewish in America* (New York: The Free Press, 1992), p. 300.

NAME INDEX